SLOBBERKNOCKER

SLOBBERKNOCKER

MY LIFE IN WRESTLING

As Told to Scott E. Williams

JIM ROSS

with PAUL O'BRIEN

FOREWORD BY

VINCENT K. McMAHON

AFTERWORD BY

"STONE COLD" STEVE AUSTIN

SPORTS PUBLISHING

Sports Publishing books may be purchased in bulk at special discounts for
sales promotion, corporate gifts, fund-raising, or educational purposes. Special
editions can also be created to specifications. For details, contact the Special Sales
Department, Sports Publishing, 307 West 36th Street, 11th Floor, New York,
NY 10018 or sportspubbooks@skyhorsepublishing.com.

Sports Publishing® is a registered trademark of Skyhorse Publishing, Inc.®, a
Delaware corporation.

Visit our website at www.sportspubbooks.com.

10 9 8 7 6 5 4 3

Library of Congress Cataloging-in-Publication Data is available on file.

Cover design by Brian Peterson
Cover photograph courtesy of Craig Hunter Ross

Print ISBN: 978-1-68358-397-4
Ebook ISBN: 978-1-68358-114-7

Printed in China

To my best friend, biggest fan, and the love of my life . . .
my wife Jan. I miss you dearly.

TABLE OF CONTENTS

We would like to take a moment and offer a special thank you to Scott E. Williams, who passed away suddenly on August 17, 2016. He was forty-six years old.

Scott was instrumental in the foundation of this project, from gathering facts and source material to interviews which appear in this book. There are no words for the appreciation we have for him, his hard work, and his writing—not only on this project, but the numerous wrestling books he wrote during his career.

We lost a good one, and his memory will live on through his family, friends, and stellar work.

Thank you, Scott. We miss you.

FOREWORD BY
VINCENT K. McMAHON

When Jim Ross first came to work for WWE back in 1993, little did I know then that nearly a quarter century later "JR" and I would still share a bond built on mutual passion for the business we love—and even more importantly, an enduring friendship based on respect for each other.

For the better part of two decades, The WWE Universe has embraced JR as "The Voice of WWE." It is JR's voice that painted the pictures, crafted the stories, and created a whole new dimension to all our favorite superstars each and every Monday night. Indeed, JR was our tour guide through an era that changed sports entertainment forever. In fact, JR is still considered by most to be the greatest announcer of all time.

Jim's contributions behind the scenes were equally as impactful. As head of Talent Relations, Jim proved an insightful, creative, and dedicated senior executive, signing a plethora of legendary talent during his tenure who were essential to building WWE into what it is today.

No one appreciates what Jim Ross has done for WWE more than I do. His contributions to our industry are as legendary as his character, and will leave an indelible mark for generations of WWE fans to come.

WRESTLEMANIA XV: 1999

"Courage is being scared to death, but saddling up anyway."

That John Wayne quote stuck with me so much over the years that I even had it printed on my coffee cup at home. "The Duke" always faced down his fears; always won in the end. But as I hid backstage at Philadelphia's First Union Center, *I* didn't much feel like saddling up at all. As a matter of fact, *I* was so terrified of what was about to happen that *I* began puking in the sink in front me.

What am I doing here? I thought to myself between heaves. The biggest professional night of my life and I was alone, in full tuxedo, having a Tony Soprano-like panic attack in an empty shower room. By my time, the main-event was next and I knew I would soon have to leave my hideout and go before the world. Twenty thousand in attendance and millions watching at home was a scenario that I had dreamed about as a boy—and worked hard to achieve as a man—but this night it terrified me.

WrestleMania XV, March 28, 1999, was, at that point, the biggest night in our business. World Wrestling Federation was on fire and its two top stars, "Stone Cold" Steve Austin and The Rock—two of my all-time most memorable signees—had independently lobbied management for me to return and announce their main-event match. Their stratospheric professional rise intersected starkly with my own personal low. While Austin and the Rock were demolishing box-office records and pay-per-view buy-rates, I had been off TV a few months after suffering a devastating family bereavement—and my second bout of Bell's palsy. Because of the resulting facial paralysis, I had been primarily working from home as I wanted as few people as possible to see the way I now looked.

This grand entrance back to pay-per-view was going to be the first time anyone other than close family and friends would see me. I was vulnerable, self-conscious, and sick with worry.

The paralysis affected my speech, and I had no idea if I could still do the job I loved the way that I loved to do it. As much as I wanted to return Austin and Rock's faith in me, I certainly didn't feel ready. Not one little bit. I made my living from telling stories as a commentator—coloring in with words that the audience was seeing in pictures. How could I do that when I had to literally hold one side of my face up to help me enunciate; to simply be understood?

As my time drew closer I couldn't help feeling that this was all a huge mistake. I just wanted to run out of there; make my way home where I knew I could hide or avoid people if I wanted to.

I wanted to find Vince McMahon, the Chairman and owner of the company, so I could tell him that I couldn't do it. But to admit such a thing would be admitting weakness, and the Chairman detested weakness and negativity from anyone around him. McMahon believed in the old law of the jungle: that "only the strong survive," much like my father had instilled in me as a boy.

So I left the shower room and walked the busy corridor with my head down. I tried to block out the sounds and noises coming from the packed arena. I was merely hoping to get through my performance without stinking up the joint. I didn't want to embarrass myself, my family, my company, or the two Superstars who requested my presence on their biggest night. And I didn't want to disappoint Vince.

Everyone was expecting the "Good Ol' JR" that they'd come to know, but I knew that the version of me that was walking to the curtain wasn't what people remembered.

I got to the packed "Gorilla Position"—the waiting area just behind the curtain—and made an effort to keep my head down, blend in, and review my bullet-pointed notes. I made a list on my first day as an announcer and the practice of bullet-pointing had followed me every day since.

I peered up to briefly exchange glances with Austin and the Rock. Both men were already where I was trying to get to: "in the zone." Rock flashed his million dollar smile and Austin was painted with that look of dogged intensity that became his trademark. They weren't talking. Not to me, not to anyone. They were focused and looked confident. I wanted to give them their space, and I certainly did not want them to be able to detect my apprehension of my return to ringside. They had enough on their plate without me adding to it.

People passed with greetings of "Good luck JR" and "Welcome back JR" as I distilled all my nervous thoughts down into one line of comfort: *get through this match and you won't have to endure this stress ever again.*

In that second I had made my mind up that this would be the end of my broadcasting career in WWF. I had a head full of great memories and experiences in the business that I grew up loving. I remembered where I began; how I used my army figures as a kid to "play wrestling"; my time as a driver, a referee, the good nights and bad. I remembered it all—my time in this crazy business. And all I wanted for my last shot was for *them* to like me.

I just wanted the people to like me and to not notice that I was different. That I had changed.

"Ladies and gentlemen," Michael Cole said over the PA system in the arena. "Here to announce the main event . . . JR, Jim Ross."

Ready or not, it was time to saddle up.

My beloved University of Oklahoma fight song, "Boomer Sooner," began playing through the sound system in the arena to usher me out through the curtain. It was now or never. *Please go easy on me*, I thought as I took a deep breath and cracked open the curtain.

I could feel the energy from the crowd, and it immediately raised my confidence a little.

"Don't worry if they boo you," a stage hand said from the darkness.

I stopped immediately. "What? You think they'll boo me?"

"Maybe. This is the city that booed Santa Claus. Have fun out there."

I peeked out through the curtain at the raucous crowd in the arena. "Well, fuck," I whispered to myself as I walked out to face the world.

PART ONE

Before Wrestling
1952–1974

Chapter One

GROWING UP

1952

Right from the start I was defying expectations. I wasn't even supposed to be here—as in, here on this planet. I was born at only five pounds, six ounces, and when they brought me home from the hospital I was small enough to fit in a shoebox.

This was the last period of my life where I was ever considered small . . . except when I skinny dip in cold water.

I was born on January 3, 1952, in Fort Bragg, California. My mom and dad—Elizabeth Ann Sheffield and J. D. Ross—had been high school sweethearts. By my math, they might have been a little too sweetheart-y because they suddenly got married, bolted from their hometown of Westville, Oklahoma, and had me eight months later. In that era, conceiving a child out of wedlock in a small town of about a thousand people could have created issues for my folks, as everyone knew each other's business. As I grew up, if my mother was ever asked about the timeline by someone who was nosy and had done the math, she would say that I was born premature.

Not only was my birth a delicate issue for my folks, it was also a tricky one for my mother's parents, who were very well established in their small

Oklahoma community. They were involved with the bank and also ran the town's dry-goods store—or mercantile as it was known back then. As part of the normal day, various workers would come into the store to buy the sandwiches that my grandmother made. They would stay to tell various tales of their hunting and fishing trips, or their experiences serving our country in combat. Talk could easily turn from fishing and war stories to matters a little more prying, a little more personal—say, like a child being conceived out of matrimony. So to avoid the prying eyes and the listening ears, my folks decided the best thing would be to take their pickup truck—and their delicate situation—and drive 2,000 miles from Westville, Oklahoma, to Fort Bragg, California.

This trip would mark the beginning of a few return trips between my mother's family in Oklahoma and my father's family in California. Fort Bragg was a natural destination, as my dad had family there and knew he could get a job in the logging business.

In our first couple of years there, my parents had another baby boy who unfortunately died during childbirth. Delivering and losing a baby made my mom even more protective of me—and living around my father's father certainly put her protectiveness to the test sometimes.

My grandad, James Dee Ross, gave me my first alcoholic drink—some of his Falstaff beer—when I was three. My mother was livid when she realized that something was a little "off" on my return to the house. James Dee had taken me to his favorite tavern and snuck me some sips of his drink while we were there. When my mom finally realized that I was a little more uncoordinated than usual, she put two and two together and exploded.

Little JR was buzzed and Grandad Ross was in real hot water.

Such was her anger on that day that it became something of legend in our family, told and re-told over the years. I grew up to learn that my grandad's judgment wasn't always the best, and his own drinking created many uncomfortable family situations. As a result, my own father rarely drank, save for the occasional cold beer in the summertime.

My grandad was ambidextrous and could drive nails using two hammers simultaneously if required. He was 6-foot-1, 200 pounds with huge hands and was wiry and strong. A sober, clear-headed James Dee Ross was a hilarious storyteller who had a way with words. An inebriated James Dee Ross, however, was another matter entirely.

I didn't know it then, but alcohol would lead to several embarrassing, dangerous, and downright stupid situations in my own future, too.

My family returned from California to Oklahoma when I was six, but I was only there from first to third grade before we packed to move back out to California. On this occasion, the move was more strategic. It was simply to raise the capital for an opportunity that presented itself. My mother's aunt and uncle offered to sell their 160-acre Oklahoma farm to my parents. California was where my parents could accumulate the money needed for the down payment in the quickest amount of time. All that moving might have been jarring for someone else, but I never had issues making new friends and had a lot of cousins in Northern California to keep me company.

Once my parents had saved enough money for the down payment for our farm, I was mid-way through the fourth grade. We returned to Oklahoma for good and bought the land where my parents grew a massive garden and raised livestock while we resided in a four-room, concrete block house. Now when I say *house*, what I mean is that it was an old dairy barn that had a concrete floor and raw block walls. But luckily my parents hired Oklahoma's finest interior designers to come into the space and make it "fabulous."

That's not true. Actually, my dad spent a few weeks using basic carpentry skills and grandad's help to partition that barn into two bedrooms, a kitchen, and a living room.

And that was our home.

You'll also notice that nowhere in my description did I use the word bathroom. We had an "outhouse," which is *like* a bathroom, only more rural. And less warm. And further away from the house. And a little scarier at night-time in the middle of winter. Ah yes, there's nothing quite like having to get fully dressed on a perishing night just to use the *facilities*. I soon figured that the bush at the back of the house was nearer if only a pee was in order. I'm not saying I have superhuman DNA or anything, but that bush never even wilted, never mind died, in all my years living there. Having said that, if you want to know what fear is, try pointing your delicate bits in the direction of dark shrubbery at one in the morning with only moonlight to guide you.

It's funny, growing up I had a lot of friends who hosted sleepovers, but they never wanted to stay over at my house. No idea why.

I graduated high school in 1970. Westville High was a smaller school, which meant the teachers could help each student more and give individual attention when needed. I never felt like "just a number." I was somebody the teachers knew. I even had a couple of teachers who taught my mother and father a generation earlier. It was a very comforting environment and I involved myself in a lot of school activities. Senior year, I was president of both the student body and the State VP of the Future Farmers of America. The FFA was a national organization which aimed to make its youth membership leaders by giving them tools for career success in the agriculture sector. I was the State FFA Speech Champion in my junior year at Westville High.

As you can imagine, a position like that was just laden with chicks . . . or not. And the thing was, even though I had a huge desire to be a leader, it just wasn't in the agriculture sector. Even though we lived on a farm and my extended family owned a lot of land and worked extensively in agriculture, that wasn't the life I wanted. I didn't like the fact that so many of the factors that determined my success were out of my control. I grew up seeing the frustration in the faces of my dad and grandparents; the heartache of finding a dead animal that had not yet yielded the return on the sizable investments that livestock require. Even though most people I knew who farmed also worked other jobs, many counted on that farm income just to get by. I knew from an early age that I wanted to find myself in a whole other line of work.

Little did I know just what kind of work that would be.

In Oklahoma, a lot of people usually went into the family business, but neither of my parents' career paths appealed to me. My mom had a variety of jobs including a retail sales clerk and a bookkeeper at the farmers' co-op. My dad worked for Adair County on a road crew, making next to nothing. From there, he went on to work for the Oklahoma State Highway Department; he was one of the guys in the yellow trucks who would remedy unsafe road conditions, like salting an icy bridge. He eventually worked his way up to head of the department in our county.

With my parents working so hard, I essentially grew up a latchkey kid. Maybe it would have been enjoyable if I'd had a brother or sister, but the isolation was no fun. There was also no visiting with neighbors, as the closest one was a mile or two away. It was basically me, in the house, on my own, till my parents came home.

Now, being an only child wasn't all bad. The solitude gave me a chance to cultivate my imagination and encouraged me to read more books. My mother taught me at a very young age how to read. Ever since I could remember, both she and her father would read to me, give me books, and generally spark my love of language. So much so that by the time I was five, I was reading the sports pages of the newspaper.

Friends at school would tell me about all the fun things they'd been doing outside of school. The conversation would come around to me.

"What did you do this weekend, Jim?"

"Well, I picked up some rocks. Put 'em back down again."

"Oh."

It was around then that I knew I needed some more hobbies or things to do.

Much more so than the other kids who lived in town, chores were a big part of my non-school time. But the more time I spent working around the farm meant I got to spend more time with my father. My dad, whose birth certificate read, J.D. Ross—as in J(only) D(only) Ross—was a big, strong guy, about 6-foot-3 and 275 pounds. He wore a size 15 ring and a size 14 shoe, and was blond-headed with a slightly red beard. He looked like the classic image of a lumberjack, the Swedish giants who immigrated to California to work the logging camps. He was always a hard worker and took that work ethic to our farm. As we'd move from one chore to the next, he'd use situations or scenarios to teach me how the world worked. Some of those lessons were tough and others seemed small at the time, but a lot of what I learned I still hold dear to this day.

He wasn't one for talking much if it wasn't needed—he was a natural sound bite guy who rarely showed on his face what might have been going on in his head. He was tough, quiet, and sometimes hard to read. I loved just simply fishing in our pond together, not saying much. Not having to. He wanted me to be independent, wise, and trustworthy—like he was. He believed in the bond of a handshake; the strength of a person's word, and those were traits he took time to instill in me.

As I got older, he'd give me more responsibilities as he saw I could handle them. Some I took to like a duck to water, and others he knew he needed to check up on with me.

"Did you get the hog watered?" he asked.

"Yes, sir. I watered Charlie about an hour ago."

He stopped suddenly and looked me right in the eye. "Charlie? You can't be getting attached to these animals."

"I—"

"Because they're there to feed our family for the next few months. That's it. You understand, son?"

I nodded my head.

"You don't need to be giving names to these animals because one day you're going to see me shoot that hog, and it's not good for a boy to be affected like that."

My father could see in my face that I knew exactly what he meant; no need to elaborate further. Because we were on a working farm that functioned to feed and sustain a family, I knew he was right. If we didn't have animals, we didn't eat. They were going to be used as food or sold for money. But not *all* animals on the farm were seen that way.

As cut-and-dry as he was about the role of the hogs on our farm, he was completely different when it came to his pets—especially his bird dog, a short-haired pointer named Lady. She was a great dog who had her own pen and doghouse that always had fresh straw. She ate well and drank fresh water because Dad would breed her with another pedigree dog and make good money from the resulting offspring. Such was the pedigree of the resulting litters; we ended up with a waiting list of people looking to buy one. Working full-time on a road crew was making my dad less than $100 a week. Selling those puppies would net him $25 each, so I knew it was big money for us.

"What age are you now?" he asked.

"Eleven," I answered.

"You're old enough to look after Lady, so," he said.

I couldn't have been more proud that he asked me to look after his prized dog. I saw it as a sign of just how much he trusted me and how much responsibility he thought I could now handle.

My father decided to keep one of Lady's pups to train, as he hoped that the pup would be a chip off the old block. My job eventually expanded to both dogs; I had to make sure Lady and her pup were tended to several times a day. Over the course of a couple of years I brought food and water daily, fresh straw weekly, and the odd treat for both when nobody was looking. They were worked, trained, walked, and looked after. I kept them together for company a lot, but separated them when Lady entered her breeding period.

Well . . . except when I forgot to close Lady's gate.

She was in heat and, unfortunately, the young male dog got into her pen. Dad discovered the male dog in a compromising position with his valued matriarch, and he knew exactly whose mistake it was. Even more unfortunately, their brief union produced a litter. Dad was not going to sell those inbred dogs without telling his buyers about the parentage, because that would have been dishonest. He didn't do business that way and he wasn't going to risk the reputation of his prized dog. He remained strangely silent about the situation, and I never broached the subject with him; I knew that I had screwed up, and I knew the situation had affected him.

Shortly after the puppies were born, my dad called for me. He was standing in Lady's pen with a tow-sack in one hand and a hammer in the other. Inside the tow-sack was the entire litter of inbred puppies.

"Take them to the dump," he said. "Take the pups out and, one by one, destroy all of them." He put the sack in one of my hands and the hammer in the other. I looked over my dad's shoulder and could see my mom standing in the kitchen doorway, crying. My dad was trying not to cry as well. In the sack, the pups were tiny; just a few days old; they hadn't even been weaned yet and their eyes were barely open.

"Go on," my father said.

As I walked from my house, I too broke down.

About a mile south was a patch of uneven land that had been used for years as a sort of dumping ground. As I walked there I thought, *What if I don't do it?*

Maybe there was a fairytale ending—maybe they'd all find homes? But I knew the landscape well enough to know that they were too young and small to defend themselves from predators. Also, if I didn't do what I was told to do, my dad would never trust me again. So I sat at the edge of the waste-ground with my eyes blurry from tears. I couldn't let them go and I couldn't bring them home.

So I did what I was told to do.

When I returned back to the house with the bag empty, I could see my father was waiting for me. He was quiet. Even more so than usual.

"Everything in life has a consequence, son," he said. He couldn't look down because I could see he was trying to hold himself together. I had never heard or seen him like that before. "We have to take care when we have responsibilities," he said before guiding me toward the house. He stayed outside; I watched him from my window and he never really moved from his spot. Just sat there with his head down until it grew dark.

The next morning he was waiting for me. "Wake up, son. We're going to town," he shouted.

For all the hardness that sometimes came from working on a farm, there were also rewards for a boy and his father—especially when we had potatoes to sell in town.

"Here's your share," he said as he put a dollar in my hand. That was my cut of the sale. "There's enough money there for a haircut and a movie."

"A movie?" I asked.

He nodded and smiled when he saw how excited the thought of seeing a movie on the big screen made me.

I said, "On my own?"

"Yeah, why not," he replied.

My first movie on my own. Like a man. The haircut was a quarter, and admission to our local theater was a quarter. That left me a nice piece of change for popcorn and a drink.

"Thank you," I said.

His smile grew wider. I think he was happy to see me excited—not that he could bring himself to say it.

"I'll be across the street," he said. "Come and find me when you're done, son."

I knew Dad sometimes went into the hall opposite the Sunset Theater, where he'd play snooker, dominoes, or pool. I even saw him a couple of times slip over to the bar and have his occasional cold beer with some of his buddies.

I, on the other hand, had a date with whatever double feature was playing at the single-screen cinema. No matter what the movie was, it sure beat the hell out of picking up rocks.

I gladly sat in the theater with the last of my hard-earned dollar sitting on my lap in the form of a soft drink and popcorn.

As time passed in my childhood, my father and I would come into town most every Saturday for a haircut, a movie, and a game of pool for him. I watched some of the all-time greats on that single screen—sometimes with my school buddies, or with a girl as I moved into my teen years.

Growing up outside of a small town, the big screen became a place of escape for me. But as much as I loved watching my idols on the big screen, it was the small screen where I found my true heroes.

Chapter Two

WATCHING WRESTLING

1963

I discovered Oklahoma's wrestling territory TV show largely through my maternal grandparents—the ones that owned the mercantile. I stayed with them many Saturday nights so my parents could socialize with their friends and take a break from their work.

We had three choices for TV in Oklahoma, and pro-wrestling in America was divided into regional offices, with each area promoter effectively running a monopoly business producing their own, locally produced, weekly TV shows.

We'd watch the courthouse drama *Perry Mason*, followed by the western series *Gunsmoke*. Then when the local news came on we'd have a bowl of vanilla ice cream, with Hershey's Chocolate Syrup poured on top. But 10:30 p.m., right after the local news, was the time that I waited for the most: wrestling time.

I was immediately drawn to wrestling because the action usually followed the same rules as the movies I loved so much. Good guy versus bad guy, with the good guy usually finding a way to win in the end. It was easy to get behind the titles because they were always presented as prestigious, and only the very cream of the crop became champions. What made it even more of an obsession of mine was that the issues between the wrestlers were personal, logical, and felt like "a happening." Wrestling combined the two things I loved most in the world: sports and storytelling.

From the moment I first saw it, I was hooked.

When I wasn't watching, it was all I could think about. I'd worry about the well-being of my favorites when they were in trouble, or when the bad guys did something dastardly to get the upper hand I'd wait all week to see them get what they had coming. I would take my army men and make a pretend ring on my bed and spend hours acting out the matches and commentating on the moves.

It didn't take long before my parents quickly took notice of my new fixation and, while they were never fans themselves, they didn't discourage me from being one. In fact, it became a powerful incentive. I was really motivated to do all my chores and do them right because, if I did, one reward at the end of my week was getting to watch that weekly hour of televised wrestling.

But as much as I loved to *watch* wrestling, I was also pulled in by what I *heard* during the events.

Danny Williams handled play-by-play, while Leroy McGuirk was the color analyst. Danny would describe the action as it occurred in the ring while Leroy would explain the backgrounds of the wrestlers and logic behind the moves being used. Danny oozed legitimacy as he was already an established radio and TV announcer and everyone knew Leroy McGuirk had been the world's junior heavyweight champion. Just being associated with wrestling fanned rumors about Leroy and his ever-present sunglasses. Most people accepted that it was because he was blind, but the "wrestling is fake" crowd bet their lives that he wasn't truly blind—as if it were a gimmick of some sort. And that was the thing about wrestling in general: most cynical people wouldn't believe what was actually true, and most fans were willing to accept what wasn't. It was when wrestling managed to land in that magic spot of convincing you what you were watching was indeed the real deal—that's where the money was made.

And that's how wrestling got me as a fan.

I sat down with my grandparents—the ice cream and Hershey's chocolate topping already dealt with—and saw something I had never seen before on TV: *real* blood, *real* anger, *real* outrage.

It was The Kentuckians versus The Assassins. The Kentuckians were two huge country boys—the 6-foot-6 Luke Brown and the 6-foot-10 Grizzly Smith, who was also the father of wrestlers Jake "The Snake" Roberts, Mike "Sam Houston" Smith, and "Rockin" Robin Smith. Their bitter rivals were The Assassins who were masked, devious cheap-shot artists who always looked for an unfair advantage. Joe Hamilton and Tom Renesto were a magnificent "heel" duo. Both teams were set to do battle on TV, and I couldn't wait to see the match unfold. During the melee, Hamilton punched Grizzly Smith over the left eye, busting him open the "hard way." Griz was bleeding like a stuck pig. The match ended in a disqualification and when they came back from commercial, Danny was interviewing The Kentuckians, who were vowing revenge.

I looked to my grandparents and they were as mesmerized by what was happening on TV as I was.

Danny seemed somewhat incredulous about the cut over Grizzly's eye. The camera zoomed in as Danny took his fingers and gently pulled on the gash, which he appeared horrified to learn was all too real.

Now *I* was pissed, too. How could The Assassins get away with something like that? I wanted to take them on myself. The bad guys couldn't just get away with something like that. That's not right. I would pay money to see those guys get theirs.

"I apologize to the management of this station and to the viewing public," said TV announcer Leroy McGuirk. The same Leroy McGuirk who secretly owned the company *and* had signed off on the bloodshed before the show went on air. However, his public persona was horrified. "I assure you that nothing like this will ever happen again and these two teams will be kept apart."

"Until next time," my grandfather muttered.

He obviously knew something I didn't. "What do you mean?" I asked him.

"Give it a week and they'll be telling you where you can buy a ticket to see these men get their revenge."

"But Leroy said it wouldn't happen again."

My grandfather smiled, patted me on the head, and left the room. I looked back at the TV and tried to figure out what was going on.

Chapter Three

GOING TO THE MATCHES

1964

I was watching TV and trying to tune out the sounds of Mom and her friends' "games night" in the room next door. Through the noise of my show and cackling of their laughter I somehow heard my favorite word seep through the wall: *wrestling*.

Even though Mom wasn't a big fan, her friends liked wrestling. Leroy McGuirk's promotion was bringing a show to the high school gym in Stilwell, which was about 15 miles south of Westville.

I put my ear against the partition wall and could hear my mom's friend saying, "Something, something, something, **wrestling**, something, something, **matches**, something, something, **this week**, something, something."

This news was big.

I walked to the door to get a better listening position.

Mom's friend continued, "They're coming to Stilwell, and I'm going to go."

Stilwell? That's only a few miles from here!

I had a shot to get to the matches, but I had to convince my mom to take me.

Besides, how cool would I look if I bumped into some girls from my school there? I'd be cooler than all getup sitting there at a wrestling show with my mom and her friends.

No, wait.

"Please, Mom," I begged when her friends left. I had my whole speech memorized.

"OK," she said, cutting me off. "We can go."

"You mean it?"

That was easy.

I counted down the days, the minutes, and the seconds until show time. I snuck into the local gym and hurried to my seat. I tried to act like I didn't know who the troop of mothers were beside me. I didn't want their presence to take cool points away from the chubby kid with the flat-top haircut and plaid shirt that was tucked into his jeans. I'm sure I managed to pull off the bad-ass exterior I was looking for. Pretty sure.

The venue itself only held a few hundred people and, despite my reservations about my party of moms, it was one of the greatest things I had seen; each match told a story and I was glued to the action.

Seems I wasn't the only one glued to the action. The mothers were pretty transfixed, too—especially to Jerry Kozak. Kozak was a popular wrestler who was a good looking guy with a great physique.

Jerry became a favorite of mine, too, because he gave me my first wrestling autograph. He signed his name and said, "Thank you."

Jerry Kozak thanked *me.*

I thought it was the neatest thing that this macho, muscled guy would be so polite to a nobody like me. In a small gym in Stilwell, Jerry Kozak made some fans for life: me, and the group of eyelash-batting women beside me.

As I walked out, I knew I wanted into this crazy business somehow. I just didn't know how I could find a way in.

Much less with a phone call.

Chapter Four

LEAVING HOME

1969

From the Saturday haircut/movie routine to saving up for a car, my folks helped me place true value on money. I knew it was important, but it didn't bring happiness and it didn't come without earning it. We didn't have much of *anything* even though my mom worked upward of 60 hours a week and my dad worked full-time on the road crew *and* another 40-plus hours a week on the farm. But what we did have was the small things that really mattered.

Like watching ballgames with my dad. As much as I loved my late-night radio commentary or the announcing on my weekly wrestling shows, it was my father who sparked my love for sports analysis.

As I got older, he'd break down the game for me, explain *why* the action we just witnessed had occurred. He'd lay out the difference between one play or another—and why one was more suited than the other given the circumstances. It was over these sporting events that we found our middle ground. Our thing in common.

I wasn't blessed with the ability to work with my hands like my father and grandfather. I didn't have their natural size or ability as a farmer or hunter. I even felt a little guilty about that as I was growing up. But one thing I did have was the ability to talk. Soon my father was asking *me* to break down the games for *him.* I'd enthusiastically "sell" the various key points of the game, piece-by-piece. I learned to be concise, because that's what held his attention. I pulled out interesting facts or tidbits about *why* this game was going to be one for the ages. Or *why* this team was vulnerable this week even though they had a great record. I learned in those hours, before a game with my father, how to tell a story. More importantly, I learned how to pull that story from the center of a sporting event.

I learned how to make him care about the players, the stakes, the personalities involved.

I began to see that my father didn't want the farmer's life for me, just as much as I didn't want it for myself. He seemed torn by wanting his son to go out into the world—and all the new challenges that the big world presented. For a small-town quiet man like my dad, the post-Vietnam landscape was a hard one to fathom; it was for most of the country. People were divided, unsettled. It was a new world full of dissent and danger. I was his only son, his only child, and he thought the only armor against such upheaval and uncertainty was toughness and steel.

"I want you to be able to stand up for yourself without siblings to fall back on," he said. "I want you to be able to take anything out there. Life is hard. I wanted to show you how to cope with that."

Even though my dad never had the chance to attend college—mainly because I had come along unexpectedly—he was a very intelligent man who understood the growing value of higher education as times changed throughout the 1950s and 1960s.

He said, "You know your mom and I will always love you, and we'll do anything for you that we can. But you need to know that we're done here, son. You're your own man now."

I wasn't immediately sure what that meant, but I soon figured out that he was telling me it was time to bait my own hooks; cast my own line and see what I could catch. If I managed to run my fishing boat into a pier my folks would be there for me, but in terms of taking daily care of me as their kid, we were done.

Chapter Five

COLLEGE

1970

Even though I left the farm, I still found myself watching a cow. This cow, however, spent the night dancing sexily on its hind legs in a rundown motel.

I graduated among the top kids in my class at Westville High School in 1970, and had earned a President's Council Leadership scholarship to Oklahoma State.

As much as my dad wanted me to stand on my own two feet, my mom opened a secret account for me with Harold's, a menswear store in Stillwater. She wanted me to fit in with the guys in the fraternities; to be accepted in this new big-city type environment. I don't know what made her think that I wouldn't fit in. You know, naturally.

But her secret account worked as Sigma Chi, an esteemed social fraternity, recruited me out of the gate. They figured between my FFA credentials and high marks in school I could be an asset. Truth was, it was an honor for me to be considered, as Sigma Chi was pretty much the top dog on campus and I was elected president of the fraternity's pledge class.

The OSU campus was a whole new world for a small-town farm boy like me. It was also a culture shock in the sense that, for the first time in my life, I'd met several people who woke up on third base and thought they'd hit a triple. Daddy had gotten them to third and they thought that made them special. It certainly made them *something* all right, but *special* wasn't it.

Frankly, my own mindset left something to be desired. I'd made all A's and B's in high school, but as I exercised my newfound freedom by joining my frat brothers for "nickel beer" night and planning frat-house events, my grades plummeted. I began to see that one or two drinks just weren't enough for me. If it was there to be drunk, I could stand long enough to drink it.

I only lasted one semester at OSU, though, as my grades fell dramatically. I was coming from a county that had 8,000 people tops, to a campus that had 30,000 students and hundreds more on staff. I saw more beautiful women on my first day than I had in my whole life up to that point. When I added to that parties, nickel-beer nights, and fraternity mixers, there were just too many distractions for a wide-eyed country boy to handle. All of that, plus a lack of money, meant I had to re-think my college plan.

As much as I loved OU, I couldn't afford to go there, so Northeastern State University, which was in Tahlequah, about 25 miles from where we lived, made the most sense money wise.

And that's where I'd meet the *dancing cow*.

I settled into Northeastern State quite quickly. On top of my new surroundings, my new studies, and my new fraternity (Phi Lambda Chi), I also joined the college flag football team. We entered to play in the intramural football league. Our team consisted mostly of guys who were, in one way or another, trying to re-live their high school football glory days. Myself included. Our bellies might have been a little rounder and our legs a little slower because of the college overabundance, but we loved football. We were good, too. We always found another gear when we needed to, played hard and made our way through many tough games, and eventually found ourselves in the intramural league post season game, which for us was about a 500-mile round-trip from Northeastern State to Little Rock.

Preparation was key—not for the game, but for the bus to take us to the game. We immediately bought a keg. And some weed. And a few other things that I didn't know about.

We boarded our chartered bus and I knew immediately I wasn't the only wide-eyed farm boy who was trying to hide the fact that he had never been on a big bus like that before. I took my seat—not too close to the front like a sissy and not at the back like a jock. About six rows from the back was where my social standing in life landed me.

Before the engine even started there was rowdiness in the air. The keg was in play and there were some wafts of smoke rising up from various mini-huddles around the bus. I tried my best to not get mixed up too much in anything other than the beer, or "belly wash" as my grandfather called it. I wasn't too sure what all the other stuff going around was, but I was sure of one thing: I didn't want anything to do with it.

The first couple hundred miles were almost civil. People were toasting and making little speeches. New friendships were being formed and bonds were strengthened. I'm not exactly sure when it became a little less civil, but I'd hazard a guess that it was right about the time the mescaline came out.

I'd heard something about hallucinogens, LSD, peyote, but never thought to ask more because I didn't figure we'd ever cross paths. How wrong was I? Very wrong.

"Jim, have you ever tried this?" someone asked.

Sober Jim would run a mile from any drug like that. As a matter of fact, Sober Jim made Drunk Jim promise not to get involved in anything like that. Drunk Jim agreed, of course. Turns out, Drunk Jim is a liar and can't be trusted one bit.

I put out my hand and someone over my shoulder put something in the palm of my hand.

"Don't think, just slam them back and wash them down," I was told.

"No problem," I dutifully said as I threw them into my mouth and rinsed them down by chugging my beer.

I remember a mini cheer and someone saying that I didn't take enough "to do shit."

"Really?" I said as I put my hand out again. "Give me more."

Drunk Jim was invincible. Or a dumbass. One or the other.

Once again my palm was sprinkled, and once again I slammed the seeds back. I didn't even look to see how many this time. Another cheer. My back was heartily slapped and comments were made about how I was going to regret that.

I already did.

Not that anyone on that bus would know that. I just sat, my head against the window, waiting for something really bad to happen as I watched the country blur past as we traveled.

An hour passed, and I'm not one bit ashamed to admit I was delighted to find out that it was a false alarm. The seeds had no effect, thank God. My one and only mescaline trip was a false alarm.

A little while later, we arrived at the Little Rock Motor Lodge, which was even shittier than the name suggested. Eighteen drunk college boys spread over just three, $20 rooms was never going to be a good idea, but it was all we could afford. After the initial stampede for beds, toilets, and more beer, I settled by the window and noticed all the cars parked outside the rooms, the stars in the sky—and a cow dancing outside my window.

What the hell?

I peeked again, and there it was, like a bovine Michael Jackson, just cutting it up outside my window. The more I watched, the more I thought this wasn't *that* unusual.

The rowdy, loud atmosphere faded off, and I wasn't the only one sitting there entranced by a single sight. By now all of the team were sitting silently in the one hotel room. Someone had run across the street and stolen a traffic cone that had an orange rotating light attached. That light was now almost like the center of the universe. The whole room just sat in silence, staring at its orangeness. It soon pulled me in, too. It was mesmerizing. Like a moth to a flame.

There we were, eighteen college boys on tour, crammed into a tiny motel room, tripping on mescaline, smoking a cone as a dancing cow tried desperately to get my attention from an orange light. It was at that point that I felt confident enough to tell myself that there was a pretty good chance I was probably, completely, and utterly stoned out of my head.

I was so far in that I didn't care. I felt warm, comfortable, and totally at ease. So much so that I became captivated by a spot of saliva on the side of my fellow teammate's mouth. It wasn't anything hugely exciting in the course of a normal day, but on this occasion it was nothing short of fascinating. And funny as hell. Just a spot of saliva.

I slid back onto the bed and put my back against the wall as the TV talked away in the background. The light, the cow, the saliva. Hours gone. Just watching. Just sitting in silence and smiling as my mind went through the process of being completely blown.

It was a beautiful night outside and a sticky hot night in the room. That many people huddled in, sucking in the same air as the last guy just blew out. And the AC was barely there. People just left when they wanted to . . . or could.

The sound in the background began to pull me in. It was the familiar sound of flesh on canvas.

Wrestling.

I peeled myself from my bed and took a seat front and center and watched as WCIU out of Chicago came through on the hotel antenna. It was snowy and barely viewable, but to me it was perfect. Pat O'Connor versus Dick the Bruiser in a TV classic in black and white. It made everything else disappear. No cone, no cow, no saliva. Just wrestling. Just perfection. Just where I wanted to be. Ringside. Involved. Sweeping the floors, handing out programs. I didn't care. I just wanted to be there.

Tripping in Arkansas, I had no idea just how close I was to getting in.

Chapter Six

THE CALL

1973

We got destroyed in Little Rock. The next morning, after our mescaline trip, we stood on the field and just got mowed over. For all our ra-ra attitude on the bus on the way down, we were like church mice on the way home. I got a pretty cool looking burst vessel at the top of my arm, though. That earned me some cool points.

We were determined to avenge our loss and become the best, most feared team in the league. And that's how the dean of students came to know us well—but for all the wrong reasons.

If there was a last straw, it was likely the conflict that broke out during an intramural football game between our team and the men of Alpha Phi Alpha, an African American fraternity. They had a really good team but, in the heat of a championship battle, we had issues over each other's tactics. It was, to us, as high-stakes as a game could be. For flag football, there was an awful lot of trash-talking, an awful lot of physical contact, and some late hits by players on both sides.

But the real damage was done off the football field. The fall-out of the game became an uncomfortable issue for the administration, simply because it was a heated issue between an all-white fraternity and an all-black fraternity in a politically charged era.

Particularly when it made the school paper.

The optics of the situation meant that people were going to see racial undertones when there were none. The skirmishes; the competition between our teams were motivated solely by a desire to win the trophy. None of us wanted to back down, none of us wanted the other guys to win. It was passionate, it was hard-hitting, and filled whistle-to-whistle with a desire to win. It was this exact desire that got several of us summoned to Dean Baker's office.

I was such a naïve country boy that at first, I didn't even realize he held *the position* of dean of students—I really thought his first name was "Dean."

Either way, "Dean" quickly let us know that, if we wanted to preserve both Phi Lambda Chi and our own lives as Northeastern students, our best course of action would be to become more civilized and to take on some projects that would rehabilitate our fraternity's image. Something to do with charity. Something to do with fundraising. Something that people could see.

As my fellow fraternity brothers planned fundraising ideas, I began to think a little differently. They were talking about selling candy bars or cookies to make some cash for a local charity. Maybe a pop-up car wash? But I had another idea. One that I wasn't sure I wanted to voice. Unfortunately, my mouth seemed to open before my brain could intervene.

The words I had been chewing on all day suddenly fell out of my mouth, "Or we could try something else?"

"Like what?"

I paused. I knew it was kinda *out there*; a little far-fetched. "How about wrestling?" I murmured.

I waited for the dismissive laughter, but I immediately saw Jerry Donley's eyes light up from across the room. It looked like he'd been thinking the same thing but just didn't want to say it. Jerry and I had become great friends, in part because we were both huge wrestling fans, so I knew if there was anyone who would back me and try to get this done it was him.

"We could put on a wrestling event," I said. "Raise some money that way."

As the others in our group scoffed and faded off to continue talking about the more traditional fundraising efforts, Jerry and I were becoming even more adamant that we had something—a great idea.

We just had to figure out how two kids with no contacts in the business were going to put on a wrestling card with name talent from TV. We had heard the stories about how hard it was to get "inside," that wrestling was a closed shop; a mysterious business. What stroke of genius could we come up with to break into the clandestine inner circle? The wrestling business was notoriously hard to get into unless you had a family member already inside, or you were a star athlete. Both Jerry and I had no family in the business, and we certainly weren't star athletes.

"Think we should just phone them?" Jerry asked.

"OK," I replied.

So we phoned them.

* * *

We were shocked. The call worked. We were invited down to the Monday night event in the Tulsa Assembly Center to meet Leroy and his behemoth partner: known to his family as William F. Watts Jr., but as "Cowboy" Bill Watts to wrestling fans across the country. I didn't even know that Leroy was an owner.

The plan was we were to come down to discuss what we had in mind. But before we could talk business, "The Cowboy" had a little business of his own he needed to attend to: an NWA World Heavyweight Title match against the tough-as-nails Harley Race. And we were comped ringside seats!

I watched from the edge of my seat as the referee was inadvertently knocked out. Bill and Harley took bumps to the outside of the ring, on opposite sides of a corner ring post. Harley managed to get to his feet first and, seeing the referee was still "unconscious," he grabbed Watts and ran his head into the steel post.

As Race gloated, the referee finally came to and slowly made it back to his feet to begin his count. If Watts didn't make it back into the ring before the count of ten, he would lose.

"One . . ." shouted the still groggy ref.

No sign of the Cowboy making it back to his feet. As the ref continued up the number scale, the crowd went nuts. There was no way the dastardly Race could come into Watts's backyard and win by cheating.

"Eight . . ."

Men, women, and children roared Watts's name; willing him to rise up and make it back inside the ring before . . .

"Nine . . ."

And from the far side of the ring: a defiant hand rose up. Then the top of a bloody skull. Watts's eyes were distant, rolling in his head. His face was covered in his own free-flowing blood. He was badly hurt, but not out of the fight.

"T . . ."

Just before the ref could finish calling the last number, the Cowboy threw himself under the bottom rope and just made the count.

I was hoarse. Jerry was hoarse. Watts was in no fit shape to continue, but that didn't stop him from trying to find his feet.

The referee approached him and immediately wanted to stop the match due to Watts's blood loss. The Cowboy, barely conscious, face completely covered in blood, was insisting the match should continue. The official waved off the Cowboy's pleas and called for the bell out of concern that Watts was unable to defend himself.

The official call was a stoppage due to excessive blood loss by the challenger. I would have been as angry as the rest of the crowd if I didn't know that myself and Jerry were about to have a private audience with the valiant challenger and his partner.

It was show time.

Jerry and I lingered near our seats for a while as the crowd filtered out of the arena. I ran over my pitch and tried to put in order all the thoughts I wanted to verbalize. After the building was emptied, Jerry and I tentatively headed back up to the lobby of the arena, where we'd been told the office door was located.

I timidly knocked on the door and, to my surprise, Bill answered. I don't know why I was surprised. After all, I was there to meet him.

He'd had a chance to grab a quick shower, but his head was wrapped in gauze, tape, and bandages right above his eye. He was still sweating as we entered the smoky office. Leroy McGuirk sat in a chair, puffing on his cigar, with the walls around him covered in pictures of him with the Hollywood elite of the day from his time wrestling in the Hollywood territory.

Up close, Watts was even bigger. It was kind of surreal to finally meet in person two people who I had watched for so long on TV.

"Well, I heard you had a rough night out there tonight," Leroy said to Watts.

Bill answered as he sat down behind his big oak desk, "Yeah, Leroy, he got me on that ring post, and it's a pretty good gash; I lost a lot of blood and the referee was worried about me and stopped it."

Leroy shoved his cigar in his mouth, "Well I know that's got to be disappointing for you, but it's better to be safe than sorry. Don't worry—you'll get another shot at it."

Leroy and Watts were putting on a masterful performance for an audience of two and both Jerry and I were eating it up like it was vanilla ice cream with that beloved Hershey's chocolate syrup on top. I kinda thought this was my first experience of "kayfabe," which I'd heard was old wrestling behavior that was designed to keep the secrets of wrestling away from the paying customer.

"What's your marketing plan?" Watts asked.

Jerry bumped my leg, as that was my cue. Watts nodded for me to begin so I cut to the chase.

"I can get us radio air time for free," I said.

"And how are you going to do that?"

"We're making this a public service announcement," I replied.

Watts smiled. He looked to Jerry to see if I was serious. Jerry nodded in affirmation.

I knew I had their attention, so I quickly continued. "Our fraternity is non-profit. We can get the on-air time."

Watts leaned in. "I won't stand for any of my wrestlers getting stabbed, so you provide security. And I also don't want any fights before the show, so we're going to need two separate dressing rooms to keep some of our wrestlers apart."

Leroy chimed in, "Two dressing rooms or no deal."

Watts continued. "We'll provide the card. That's eight men and a referee. I'm not going to say who those men will be, but you'll have a good card. And we'll mention the event on our local TV show."

I tried to cut in. Cowboy wasn't done.

"On top of the security, you provide the venue, the ring, and an announcer—and sell the tickets."

I was trying to get in and simply say, "Okay, sir," but he *still* wasn't done yet.

A red dot of blood was beginning to seep through Watts's white bandage, though he didn't notice. "You can keep the concession money for soft drinks and popcorn, and we get 80 percent of the gate—you get 20 percent. Plus, the first $250 comes off the top to us to pay for the ring usage and transport."

"Deal?" he said.

I could hardly wait to reply.

"Deal," I said.

And with a handshake across a big oak desk, my journey into wrestling was about to begin. But first there was a slightly awkward pause before Cowboy nodded at the door to let us know it was time to go.

As I walked with Jerry in the empty parking lot outside, I realized that we had to pay $250 to the guy who supplied the ring and drove the truck. Of course, that guy was their employee; it was their truck and their ring.

"I know people say wrestling is fake," Jerry said. "But did you see his head?"

"Maybe some of it isn't on the up-and-up, but those title matches are legit," I replied.

Chapter Seven

THE FUNDRAISER

1974

We didn't get Bill on the card for our fundraiser, but we did get the legendary Danny Hodge. Bill was smart—he didn't know how well we would do, but if the show died a natural death . . . well, it must have been Hodge's fault. As far as I was concerned, this was about the best news we could have gotten. We had Danny Hodge. People used the term "living legend" a bit too freely for my taste, but that term perfectly described Danny.

He was a collegiate wrestler from the University of Oklahoma, where he was undefeated in 46 matches and never taken down. He was also a three-time Big Seven Conference champ and won the NCAA championships those same three years.

On top of his wrestling credentials, he was also a Golden Gloves boxer as a heavyweight, finishing his amateur career with 17 wins, no losses, and 12 KOs—all with no formal training.

And as great a competitor as he was, Hodge also did not disappoint as a gate attraction when he moved into professional wrestling. Our show sold out the school's basketball arena, which seated about 2,500 people.

And it was probably one of the safest sporting events in school history because it sure seemed like a third of Oklahoma's law enforcement community was in attendance. We had state police there, plus the Cherokee County sheriff's department, city of Tahlequah police, and members of our Northeastern State University police department. I'm sure that everyone in attendance's safety was the top concern, and the lawmen getting to see a free wrestling show headlined by Danny Hodge was just a happy by-product.

Regardless of the officers' reasons for being there, I knew McGuirk and Watts would be both impressed that the show had such a strong, uniformed presence.

One of the main reasons for the large crowd was the pre-show publicity we were able to obtain leading up to the event. I wrote the copy for the advertisements, voiced over the spots, and then delivered recordings to every radio station within a 60-mile radius of Tahlequah.

Several months later we co-promoted a second fundraiser with the wrestling promotion; this time, Bill booked himself in the main event. We sold out again. Before the show started, Cowboy had one burning question for me.

"I don't understand this. How are you making this work?" he asked.

I told him about the radio spots, among other things, which I had also prepared and distributed for this second show, and he said, "Well, I've got to get ready for my match, but let's talk when the show's over."

It was a different kind of main event because, at our first show, Hodge had put in about 30 minutes of mostly chain wrestling and technical battles of holds. Watts's main event only lasted about ten minutes, but it was a high-impact affair, with the big Cowboy putting his tremendous strength on display with his arsenal of power moves. And no one felt cheated because both shows clocked in at just over two hours.

"Heavyweights didn't need to go that long—except for special occasions," Watts said to me after the match.

We found a place to talk and I went into more detail as to how we'd promoted the event. I talked about radio, as well as how I'd peppered the town in posters and got the newspapers to use publicity shots with enhanced captions for the event information.

He was also impressed with our handling of the event itself. We did a lot of things that just seemed to be common sense, but which the regular local promoters weren't doing. And the radio promotion was something that Bill and Leroy weren't even doing in Tulsa, which was their flagship city! Bill later told me how that Oklahoma promotion ended up being the first to use radio spots, because not even the promotions in the media capitals of America were doing that.

Cowboy was impressed enough with my efforts and ideas that he said to me, "I'll tell you what, kid. You've got something going for you, and you've got a feel for promoting wrestling. When you get out of here, if you decide you want a job, I'll have one waiting for you."

At that point, I was close to graduating; all I had left was one semester of courses, a second semester as a student teacher, and I was done.

Instead, I left school.

In a lot of ways, getting into the wrestling business was a crazy decision. I knew I was starting a job without even knowing exactly where I'd be working, to whom I'd be reporting, how long the job would last, or even what the job entailed. One of the only things I did know about my new career was that there were no benefits—no health coverage, no dental, no retirement plan. I was going to make $125 a week as an independent contractor. Wrestling was one of my passions and, the way I saw it, if it didn't work out, I could always go back to school, finish my degree, and make a living teaching and coaching. However, the reverse might not be true; if I passed on this offer, there might never be another chance for me to enter this very closed-off business.

I was married, and we had very little money. We lived in a very spartan, small rented house literally surviving paycheck to paycheck, and even though I juggled course work with three jobs, making ends meet never got easier.

I figured I'd try my hand in the wrestling business for a while, and then be back at school, possibly as early as the following fall.

I was twenty-two years old.

PART TWO

Mid-South

1974–1985

Chapter Eight

START IN THE BUSINESS

1974

"Hey, kid, is my wife still a fat bastard?"

Helluva question to ask a twenty-two-year-old kid fresh off the farm, especially when the heartbroken wife in question had just walked into the room, unannounced, and heard the query.

Leroy McGuirk was looking straight in his wife's direction but couldn't see her. This answered any doubts I had as to whether the man I saw on my TV wearing the dark glasses was, in fact, blind.

"I said, goddammit, is my wife still a FAT BASTARD OR NOT?!"

I sheepishly looked at Mrs. McGuirk, and the look of embarrassment on her face made me want to apologize for her husband's outburst. I opened my mouth to speak but she got there first. "I'm right here, Leroy," she said.

Silence.

Her pain and humiliation was palpable before she turned and left the room. She hadn't just been shamed in front of her blind, drunk, cigar puffing husband—but also in front of me, her husband's brand-new "assistant."

There was a long, sobering stillness before Leroy slowly pivoted his head to my general direction. His sharp and gruff demeanor had changed. He looked troubled; hugely disappointed.

But in me.

"YOU SHOULD HAVE TOLD ME THE FAT BASTARD WAS STANDING THERE, KID. YOU HEAR ME? DO YOU HEAR ME?"

As I stood there with Leroy continuing to chew me out, I had a feeling that this new job, in this new business, mightn't be like all the other jobs out there.

There was no easy way into the wrestling business. The old timers reminded me again and again just how lucky I was to be in *their* world. To know that nearly everyone I was surrounded by got into the wrestling business by being either an amateur wrestler, an outstanding athlete, or related to or knowing someone already in the business. I ticked none of those boxes; I had no one who would even vouch for me. The chances of being "let in" were minuscule, and yet there I stood, green as gooseshit and scared as hell.

It was like I was trying to break in to a non-violent mafia. And my schooling started immediately. Not only was I allowed into the business, but I was almost immediately placed slap-bang in the center of it because Leroy's lack of sight meant I was his official note-taker at the booking meetings— where all the most delicate of plans where discussed. I found out that Leroy had lost sight in one eye as a child before a car accident blinded his other eye in 1951.

Watts wasn't so sure. "He lost his good eye in a bar fight," he told me.

Bill and Leroy couldn't agree on what happened to Leroy's eye, or anything else for that matter.

Right from the start, I got a double-shot of the Leroy McGuirk/Bill Watts philosophies as they routinely butted heads. Their arguments, though, were a master class for me to witness. I was frequently exposed to two professors who had different theories on how to make money in the wrestling business.

Within a couple of weeks I saw that McGuirk was the figure-head boss who had enough clout to make changes to a card. He was brilliant, when sober, when it came to verbalizing the basics and the psychology of a wrestling match. His theories and base philosophies of good versus evil, building personal issues, keeping a strong value on the territory's titles, and not insulting the audience were amazing lessons to learn. I could see that behind the smoke and liquor breath, Leroy was an extremely smart man.

Watts, however, was the real boss who slowly revealed himself to be a legitimate pro wrestling genius who had great vision for the long term, big picture. I watched him time and again expertly explain that vision to the broadcasters, wrestlers, referees, and TV directors, so that all of the cogs in the wheel were turning fluidly. Bill also had a magnificent eye for talent.

Even though both Leroy and Cowboy oftentimes mixed like oil and water, observing them both began to cement my own theory on where I might carve out a career for myself in the business—if I were to last.

Even though I was a passable athlete, I knew I wasn't ever going to have the physique to be a successful wrestler. The guys I grew up seeing in the magazines, by and large, appeared to be bigger than life in some way or another. Dick the Bruiser, the top star in Indianapolis and one of wrestling's most legendary brawlers, was only 5-foot-9, but he had a 60-inch chest. The world heavyweight champ for most of my formative years was Lou Thesz. Thesz, like his junior-heavyweight counterpart Danny Hodge, was a thoroughbred. He was long and lean, with unbelievable physical conditioning and endurance. "Cowboy" Bill Watts himself was 6-foot-3 and 300 pounds, and one of the strongest men in all of sports. I knew I would never be any of those things, and as enthralled as I was with the business, the idea of in-ring performance just never called to me. So if I wanted to make a go of it, I knew it would have to be behind the scenes.

And that's where I was positioned.

The way Watts described my initial job with Leroy was: "You're going to pick up Mr. McGuirk in the morning and bring him to the office, run errands for whatever he needs, help him out around the office, and then take him home."

I quickly learned what Leroy *needed* first, before anything else, was his daily El Producto Presidente cigars and a pint of whiskey.

"And every other Tuesday, you'll be responsible for getting him to Shreveport for TV," Watts continued.

On those TV days, I was to make sure that Leroy's coat was buttoned and fly was zipped; that he was wearing the right shirt with the right pants—basically making sure he was presentable for the TV cameras where he would then color commentate the matches.

Tulsa to Shreveport was about 330 miles each way, which translated into several hours in Leroy's Cadillac. I always enjoyed those journeys because up to that point I had only ever seen a few Cadillacs from afar, much less sat in one.

En route to Shreveport, the level of conversation depended largely on Leroy's mood—and how much whiskey he'd polished off. Some days he'd had enough that he'd doze off pretty quickly, which made for a peaceful ride. Other days he'd be angry at one of the boys, one of their wives, or one of his office "stooges." Leroy was frequently surrounded by these sycophants; guys who would tell him whatever they thought he wanted to hear just to keep themselves in plum positions within the promotion.

Sometimes Leroy was mad at Bill, and I'd get to hear about it the whole way to Shreveport. For five hours. Five miserable hours. Most often, it was because Bill had booked a card and Leroy, half drunk and with an earful of whispers from the sycophants, would change it. Bill would then change it back.

Booking decisions, "stooge" rage, or inebriated rants were one thing from Leroy, but this day, as we left Tulsa, he took his Cadillac rancor to an entirely new level.

"Did I tell you what we're going to do when we get to Shreveport tonight?" he asked me.

Before I could answer, Leroy opened the leather satchel that usually only housed his whiskey and cigars. Except this time I could see the smokes and alcohol weren't lying in the bag alone—they were accompanied by a .44 Magnum revolver, the *Dirty Harry* version.

When I saw the gun I momentarily forgot his question, my answer, where we were going, and most everything else. He placed the revolver on the dashboard and calmly lit a cigar. "What we're going to do in Shreveport tonight is kill Ted DiBiase," he said.

"Yeah?" I said, my heart thumping in my chest.

"Yeah," he replied, cool as ice.

I peeked over and saw Leroy was indeed in the killing mood.

"Why are we going to do that?" I asked.

Leroy seemed surprised at my response. "Haven't you heard he's dating my daughter?"

DiBiase was a newcomer, the step-son of veteran wrestler "Iron" Mike DiBiase and son of Helen Hild. The youngster was defying Leroy's number-one in-house rule: No wrestler was to date his lovely young daughter.

No matter the circumstances, or that Ted and his daughter were of a similar age, Leroy wanted his offspring completely separated from the business he immersed himself in.

"Let's go," he said.

I put my hand on the key in the ignition but couldn't bring myself to turn it. "How are you going to kill him?" I asked.

I mightn't have been a genius, but even I could figure out how limited a blind assassin might be. *And also,* that same blind assassin kept using the phrase *we.* As in *"we* are going to kill Ted DiBiase tonight."

Leroy, nursing his bottle of whiskey, laid out the master plan. "*We* check into the Alamo Plaza as usual when we get to Shreveport," he said. "You get me to my room, sit me in a chair facing the front door. Leave the door cracked open a little." I nodded, even though he couldn't see me. He continued, "Then you point my gun hand, point it in the right direction, and tell DiBiase that I want to see him. You tell him it's because I have a great idea for him."

The way Leroy mapped it out, DiBiase would knock on Leroy's door and when he'd announce himself in his distinctively deep voice, Leroy would start shooting. He'd unload the .44 chamber and hope the law of averages would put a bullet into the rookie who dared woo his daughter.

"You understand?" Leroy asked.

"Got it," I replied.

I tried to console myself a little with the fact that Ted would at least meet his maker in the nice Alamo Plaza, as there were two in Shreveport, sitting side by side. One was a nice hotel where Leroy was going to commit murder, at $25 a night, and the other was where I was staying, a $10 a night, no-frills dump.

As we silently continued our drive to Shreveport, I kept glancing at the revolver rattling freely on the dashboard. Leroy was drinking more and more and fogging up the car with his cigars. I was typically a very careful and attentive driver, but couldn't help but notice the barrel of the gun slowly vibrating its way around to me.

The slow roulette of the business end of the Magnum inching around to my direction kept me from being fully focused on the road—or my boss.

Leroy always wore Jaymar Sansabelt slacks, double-knit polyester pants with an elastic waistband and a size bigger than he needed for comfort. This meant there was a lot of extra material to the pants.

Usually, I would tell him when his cigar ash was getting long enough for him to flick into his old coffee can, but I was so fixated on the gun pointing at me *and* my impending accompaniment in a murder that I didn't realize that the ash from Leroy's cigar was getting longer with each mile we drove. Inevitably the hot, long ash fell squarely into Leroy's double-knit slacks, where it smoldered, unnoticed by us both, until it burned right through the polyester, settling neatly onto his old man crotch.

"What the fuck?!" Leroy screamed as he leaped suddenly from his seat. His unexpected shriek startled me into thinking the gun had gone off and I swerved the big Cadillac and nearly lost control as Leroy, in his pain and panic, wailed away on me and roared for me to do something. The car weaved all over the two-lane road as the untethered Magnum slid from one end of the dashboard to the other as my boss rapidly slapped his own crotch like a drum solo.

I slid the car to a stop, hopped out, ran around to the passenger's side, and opened Leroy's door. The other cars on the road were hurtling past dangerously close as I got down on my knees to help my shrieking boss.

"Do something," he roared. "For the love of God . . ."

I could see exactly where the smoke was coming from, and I wasn't totally happy about going in after it.

"My balls, Jim. They're burning!"

I began to lightly blow at first, like they were birthday candles. It made no difference.

"Did you just try to blow out. . . ?"

"No," I lied.

Leroy, sick of waiting for action, thrust his pelvic bone into the air and it was in that moment that I prayed a state trooper wouldn't pull over to see what was going on. Here I was, young and green on the side of the road, with my Oklahoman face in the testicle region of a blind, older gentleman who was totally agitated, confused, and inebriated.

But I knew what I had to do. I did what any decent human would do in that situation: I slapped my boss repeatedly in the balls.

"Is it working?" I shouted. I don't know why. He was blind, not deaf. I picked up the pace and widened out my hand to cover a larger area. I was into it now, totally onboard with the nut touching. Leroy was thrusting and I was slapping. Between us both, we managed to snuff out the source of the scorching without any permanent scar tissue. There was silence between us. A knowing.

I got back in the car, composed myself, and took the opportunity to place Leroy's wild-and-free Magnum back into his leather satchel.

I said, "Everything OK down th—"

"Yep," he said.

It was the kind of "yep" that meant "shut up and drive." So I did.

I motored for another few, quiet miles before I stopped at a service station to look for a phone. The "burning crotch" situation may have been dealt with, but the "DiBiase" situation was still very much on the table.

I didn't know what to do, so I used the public phone booth and called the office, collect.

Bill had established that the code name for collect calls to the office was "Gene Kiniski"—a former NWA Heavyweight Champion. Watts told me if the office got a collect call with that name attached, they knew that it was a serious call that needed addressing.

This also helped the office save money, as ringing "Gene Kiniski" back was cheaper than taking the charge of a collect call. The office would tell the operator, "There's no one here who can authorize taking a collect call, but if you'll give us the number we'll have someone call back." Another few dollars saved.

I called, gave the Kiniski name, and waited for the operator to tell me they would call back. Even though Cowboy was wrestling on TV the next evening, he was still in the office because he was going to fly his plane to Shreveport, which meant he'd get there in a fraction of the time it took us to drive there.

The service station payphone rang after a couple of minutes with Bill on the line.

"Well, your partner and I are on our way to Shreveport, to kill Ted DiBiase," I said.

"What?" he replied.

"Yep. Leroy's drunk, he's got a .44 Magnum, and he's worked out how to kill Ted—and make me an accomplice."

Bill started laughing. I didn't think it was funny at all, but Bill was just howling.

What a team of hitmen we were: a sightless, drunken senior citizen with smoldering slacks and his greenhorn assistant who had just spent the last two minutes punching Mr. McGuirk in the balls.

Finally, after a few seconds, Bill settled down enough to say, "OK, let me think. All right, Jim, he's got to be close to passing out from the whiskey, so just get him to the hotel and get him into bed. I'll be down there about the time you guys get there, and I'll take him off your hands."

My call to Bill confirmed to him that I was indeed doing what I was mostly hired to do: babysit Leroy McGuirk. I didn't even realize that was basically my job at the beginning but, more importantly, neither did Leroy.

Chapter Nine

REFEREEING

1974

Bill pegged the cost of my services to the company at a hefty price tag of $125 a week. As time passed, he could see I had a good grasp of the basics and took notice of how nothing they said in their meetings ever got out through me. "I can rely on your discretion," he said, "which was in dangerously short supply in the wrestling business."

Leo Voss, a referee who'd been a journeyman wrestler in the 1940s and 1950s, took me under his wing because he could see that integrity in me, too. Leo spent around five years at the beginning of his career as a wrestler, but the following thirty years as a referee, booker, and valued member of the office. His career was cut short when he got hit in the head by a glass bottle by a fan in Louisiana. In less than a month, cataracts were forming on his eyes and Leo's vision and mobility began to rapidly decline.

But he stayed around the office, with not much to do. I, for one, was happy that such experience and wisdom was on tap.

"If Leroy or Bill find that you've told anyone anything from those meetings, they will fire you," Leo warned me. "You know that all the Boys know you're in these meetings; they're going to do anything they can—they'll ply you with liquor, they'll try to get you laid, they'll buy your meals—whatever they think it will take, to entice you to reveal booking secrets. And also know that most of them are con men, lousy, no-good bastards, so you don't want to tell them nothin'! Don't try to make up a story, just tell them you don't know anything about what they're asking, or you're not allowed to say anything."

Leo's advice was very good because, before long, it seemed like half the wrestlers in the company had attempted to ingratiate themselves with me so that I would spill the state secrets to them. They wanted any little nugget of booking information that they would then use to manipulate themselves into better positions.

I never said a word.

Leo himself tried to get information from me, and if he saw for a second that I was to crack, he would say, "You can't trust me either, kid."

Keeping Cowboy's confidence was the foundation to make sure I survived within the promotion. Bill in particular could see I wasn't in the company to politic my way into being a manager or wrestler. I was genuinely happy to do whatever the company needed me to do.

The only way Cowboy could convince Leroy to lay out the "exorbitant" sum to pay me was by assuring him that I would be working *three* jobs for the one paycheck.

As always, by hiring me, Bill was moving his chess pieces around the board a couple moves at a time. I wouldn't just be Leroy's assistant; I would also help out in the office all week during the day, and then at night I would work as a referee.

The officials were all fine referees, but they all were getting older and Bill wanted a referee with a little more mobility; one who could get more mixed up in the physicality when needed.

He was selling wrestling matches as if they were a "shoot" or legitimate contests. This called for physically capable looking officials in order to convince the audience that you could keep up with the pace of the contest, and not make bad calls caused by being caught out of position. In reality, the true skill was to place yourself out of position without it looking like you meant to, so the "heel" or bad guy wrestler could cheat without penalty. This would drive the audience nuts as the dastardly deed would go unpunished.

Even though he wanted changes, Bill didn't rush me into the ring. I only started refereeing a few months after they hired me. He ensured I was being indoctrinated properly by first enrolling me in the "COWBOY" BILL WATTS SCHOOL OF PROMOTIONAL PSYCHOLOGY. Our campus was whatever rental car we were using as we went from market to market through Louisiana. Bill had me drive while he spent mile after mile talking with me, educating me, and getting me ready for my upcoming role as referee.

"Approach every match with the same decorum and seriousness that you use in those football games you officiate," he said. "The wrestlers aren't going to treat you any differently than those players. They're not going to abuse you *and* they're not going to make a mockery of you, because you represent the integrity of this organization."

This approach also meant the wrestlers had to be alert. If a heel was too lazy to hide an illegal hold such as a choke, I would order him to break the hold—even if that conflicted with what the heel was planning. The great heels were the ones who could maneuver me into a position where I honestly couldn't lay eyes on their rule-breaking acts.

"Our interest lies in the fans hating our bad guys, so they finally pay to see our heroes beat them," Watts continued. "And they set themselves out as bad guys, at times, by doing chickenshit moves. And what gets a crowd hotter than someone cheating? When they don't get caught cheating!" And they lie or deny when asked.

Watts always wanted to maintain credibility with our fans and get across our key points as effectively as possible, in every aspect of the promotion.

* * *

My first match as referee was a young Mike George versus Memphis veteran Henry "Treach" Phillips. Before the match, one of Bill's office guys said to me, "Hey, kid, you know you're doing a ten-minute Broadway?"

Clueless, I said, "OK."

I thought it was some sort of reference to New York, as if something was going to happen in the match that would lend itself to a big stage show, but I wasn't sure so I sought out Leo Voss again—who had a world of experience.

"What's a 'Broadway' mean?" I asked him.

Leo was more than happy to answer. As a matter of fact, I think he was as happy to have me around as I was having him around. I was the eager young kid looking to learn, and he was the old soldier who loved passing on his considerable knowledge.

"A Broadway is when a match goes to a time limit draw," Leo answered. Bill overheard our conversation and asked Leo to get me ready. "Take the kid and explain how this works," Bill said.

To everyone else who was smart to the business and had their own work to do, having an old referee hang around the office was a bit of a nuisance. To me, it was another opportunity to learn everything I could—in this instance, about refereeing.

"Referee like it's a shoot, like a real contest," Leo said. "Watch for rule violations and make sure you're in position to see both shoulders during a pin attempt. If you see an illegal move or hold, admonish the heel before starting your five count to force the break. If the heel doesn't stop whatever illegal activity he is doing before you reach the count of five: disqualify him. If he's stupid enough to get caught and defy your count, stop the contest; let Bill deal with him when he gets to the back after the match. Remember, see what to call and call what you see, like real life."

My first match went okay. I was out of position in places and nervous as hell. I knew I had a lot more to learn. I went from Leo to Bill to anyone else I could ask for more advice. I wanted to learn more and more about the nuances of the business. I would ask the old timers, the wrestlers, and even some legends as well.

"Show me how you count."

Harley Race and Dory Funk Jr. were in the midst of their pre-match warmups. Dory was off in a corner, doing pushups, and Harley was sitting on a bench, smoking a Marlboro.

Race and Funk were to go to a one-hour "Broadway," and this time I didn't need to ask what it meant.

"Show me *how* you count," Harley said again.

I got down on my knees and slapped my hand to the floor three times with even intervals of about a second each.

Harley took a drag and asked, "And you count that way every time?"

"Yes, sir."

He seemed pleased by my answer. "Just make sure you count at the same cadence, every time."

"Yes, sir. Anything else?"

"Yes. If you see me cheat, make me break," Harley said. "If you don't see it, then don't let the audience officiate for you. Remember, they're going to see me cheat because my goal is only to keep *you* from seeing me—not them."

The beauty of that was, when I finally did catch him—and I was under no illusion that I only caught him when he was ready for me to catch him—he'd mumble, "Come on, now give it to me. Give it to me."

I'd start pointing my finger at him and gesturing dramatically, and Harley sold it like he was both furious with me and afraid of the sanctions I could bring down on him. In the story we were telling, if Harley pushed me too far and I disqualified him then he would lose the match and the winner's end of the purse. Here he was, maybe the best wrestler in the world, and one of the greatest of all time, and he was selling for a twenty-something green-as-grass kid because he respected the business and the value of the referee in the match process.

Harley knew how to use the position of referee to accentuate the match; to give it more flavor. Others, who were not so generous, tried to use the referee to *take* from the match.

Jerry "The Duke" Miller was a veteran villain out of Moline, Illinois. He was a skilled in-ring talent, but was an old school, carny sort of wrestler who was always looking for the shortcut in life. He was known in the business as a "carpenter." Someone with the skill to "build" another wrestler into a main-event player.

He was also a little bit of a "freak" with the ladies, as he carried a wide assortment of vibrators and dildos with him in his wrestling bag. These "toys" were so important to the Duke that they had their own bag *within* his gear bag. A sovereign state of sex toys, if you will. He was also a hairdresser. Not a barber, but a stylist. Jerry knew most everything there was to know about conditioners and coloring. He was quite possibly the first man in all of wrestling to have a mullet. He was Mr. Ground Zero of the "business in the front, party in the back" haircut—and when he wanted to wrestle, he was actually very good. But when he didn't, he was savvy enough to take the shortcuts that made others look bad—i.e. me.

I was working my count just like Leo taught me and the Duke was walking around outside the ring. I knew this was nothing unusual, as skilled heels used as much of the twenty count as they could for the crowd. It was their job to use that time to stall and mouth off to the fans. It was my job to count. So that's just what I did, with conviction and authority. As I made my way into the teens, I could see that Jerry wasn't getting any closer to the ring.

"18 . . . 19 . . . eh . . . 19 . . . um . . . 19?"

He was nowhere near getting back into the ring to break my count and continue the match to its *planned* finish.

The Duke knew exactly what he was doing. Just like Leo Voss had told me, just like Bill Watts had drilled into me: a referee stands and falls on his ability to command a match. His authority is the key to heels cheating and good guys persevering. By Jerry staying outside, and me not counting him out, *I* looked at fault. *I* looked weak.

All I could think to do was stall myself; look around the ring like something else had distracted me. Lucky for me the other person in the match knew exactly what to do. Danny Hodge—a legit amateur wrestling legend and childhood hero of mine—was about to give me some much needed assistance.

Hodge could see the "heat" from the crowd was going to the wrong guy: it was going to me, the ref. Danny was a legit shooter; a total badass who knew the wrestling business inside and out. He didn't need to see any more of

Jerry's antics to know that the audience was getting the wrong kind of pissed. It was taught that in wrestling you wanted the crowd to be angry enough at the bad guy to want to buy tickets to see him get his ass kicked the next time. Referees don't sell tickets and Danny wasn't going to work a multiple week program in the ring with me—thank God—so the audience turning on me wasn't going to sell one single ticket for Danny's next encounter with Jerry.

The Duke was now potentially taking money from Danny Hodge's future payoffs . . . and that wasn't going to happen.

"Stand aside, Tiger," Hodge said as he passed through the ropes. He caught up to Jerry and manhandled him back into the ring. The Duke tried to put up some resistance, but I quickly learned when Hodge wanted a man to acquiesce there wasn't much that man could do *but* acquiesce. I had personally seen Hodge break pliers and turn whole apples into pulp with his legendary grip strength, so I could only imagine what he could do to a man's bones and muscle tissue.

Jerry begged off for real, but Hodge wanted to make sure there would be no further nonsense. Danny took him to the canvas and applied a legitimate double wrist lock to subdue any remaining resistance from Jerry.

"I quit," he shouted. "Danny, I quit."

When Danny didn't let up, Jerry turned to me, "I quit, referee! Call the match!"

I looked for my cue from Danny who simply instructed me to ignore the Duke's call because that wasn't the planned finish either.

After squeezing all the friskiness out of his opponent, Danny whispered, "Let's go home," which was wrestling speak for ending the match.

Jerry nodded furiously in agreement. "Yes, go home. Go home."

And that's just what we did. Danny released his hold and Jerry moved into position to finish the match. He miraculously remembered just where he had to be, and just what the finish of the match was.

Hodge won.

"Don't ever jack around on my watch again," Danny said to Jerry back in the locker room.

The Duke nodded. Hodge wasn't loud or aggressive, because he never needed to be. He was all matter-of-fact. All business.

"Don't ever do anything that could mess with my money again either," Danny continued.

Jerry nodded again.

Danny put his hand on my shoulder and said in Jerry's direction, "And don't ever let me see you middling the referee again either. There's no money in that."

Danny put out his hand to seal their "understanding" with a handshake. He took Jerry at his word and didn't need, or want, the rest of the locker room to hear about it.

"You're right, I'm sorry." And with that, Jerry "The Duke" Miller made the mistake of shaking Danny's hand.

Miller got the point, the nuances, the gist, the flavor, the story, the picture, and the exclamation point.

I handed the Duke his bag of sex toys and he left, gingerly, for the next town while massaging his aching hand.

In that moment I saw in Danny Hodge just how I wanted to navigate this crazy business I found myself in. My handshake mightn't have the same power attached to it, but I wanted it to mean something.

Chapter Ten

STILL LEARNING

1975

I was about a year into my "summer job" in the wrestling business and, having bedded down my position in the company somewhat, I began to look for more ways to make a few extra dollars. At $125 a week, the incentive was there to look into other money-making opportunities in other areas of the business. I began hauling the ring. I then agreed to haul the ring *and* set it up for an extra $50 a night. I quickly moved from hauling the ring to hauling the Boys. There was a standing deal with the veteran wrestlers in which they would pay young guys two cents a mile to drive them to and from the shows. A full tank of gas was about $5, a hotel room was about $8, and a seasoned wrestler knew the location of every $2.99 "all you can eat" buffet in town. By the end of the week, I could rack up an extra $30 per wrestler just running the 1,500 miles per week that constituted the low end of the territory. That was a pretty good little bonus for being a wheelman.

Apart from the money, every car trip was a potential learning experience as the conversation would always drift into the wrestling business. Of course, being surrounded by some of the best in the business, wrestling wasn't all I learned about as I drove. I learned how to carry myself around champions and conmen. I learned about life. And most importantly, for my survival, I learned how to roll the world's best joints while steering a car with my knees.

I knew if I wanted to make myself indispensable to the veterans, I had to drive well and roll even better. They saw nothing wrong with me driving with no hands—but they never wanted me stoned while driving them, so I always got passed over. Not that it ever really mattered, as I got a contact high more often than not.

Rolling joints added another string to my bow. Another reason to keep me around. And I rolled enough bones to get pretty damn great at it.

Of course, hauling such a collection of persons in my car meant that it damn near needed fumigating after a few days of travel. We didn't run shows on Sundays, but I still didn't get my biblically prescribed day of rest. Sunday was my day to clean out the car and try to make it smell like new again— instead of a sewage treatment plant. Between the farts, the food wrappers, the marijuana smoke, and the spilt booze it smelt like the unscrubbed armpit of a long dead farm animal.

My car saw quite a difference between the smoky, raucous nights with the wrestlers, and the calm Sunday mornings with my family. I was very much aware that I was a farm boy living both sides of one life.

Despite his lingering dislike for me, and people in general, Treach Phillips was one of my frequent passengers. His antipathy toward me didn't stop Treach from jumping in my car at the end of a show. He always insisted we stop and get beer . . . and I don't mean every now and then. I mean, he needed a six-pack after every single show. Not that drinking between towns was unusual—it's just that others *asked*. Treach *demanded*. He also refused to pay me for the trip most times. He'd tell me that he was Leroy's guy and that Leroy said he didn't need to pay. No matter the length of the journey, he seemed comfortable sitting in the awkwardness between us, drinking, scowling, and smoking his cheap cigars.

The more he traveled with me, the greater the tension grew between us.

"Pull over," he said as we left another town.

We were in the middle of nowhere.

"Where?" I asked.

"Don't care. I need something to drink."

Treach crushed his empty beer container and dropped it on the floor of my car. I couldn't take it anymore.

"Something to drink?" I asked.

He never even looked up at me to answer. "Now."

So I did hurry—to the nearest Dairy Queen.

"What are we doing here?"

"Well, Treach," I said, "you said you wanted something to drink."

He looked at me all confused. "Beer Goddammit. Wrestlers drink beer," he growled. "Wrestlers don't drink milkshakes!"

"That's funny," I said, "because Danny Hodge drinks a milkshake just about every trip we go on."

Treach opened his mouth to speak, but knew better than to say anything bad about Hodge. Even though I was a greenhorn and couldn't really call him on his bullshit, he wouldn't dare talk smack about Danny.

"Chocolate shake?" I asked as I got out of the car.

As I walked away I could hear him cursing me. I finished out the last 50 miles of that trip slurping as long, and as loud as I could on my 'shake while I watched Treach seethe in the backseat.

That was the last time he rode with me. Guess I won the competition overall.

* * *

I started to get more selective about who I would drive around with. Danny Hodge and Jim "Skandor Akbar" Wheba—who were my absolute favorite passengers. Behind the scenes, they were great friends—and driving them around was always fun. Danny didn't smoke and hardly ever drank, aside from the very occasional Mai Tai or some other fruit drink as Danny's only vice was that he had a big sweet tooth. Akbar would occasionally smoke a cigar but, like Danny, he didn't need to stop and get beer after a show as he wasn't a big drinker.

As much as I enjoyed and respected Akbar, it was Hodge who was my wrestling hero.

I could still remember watching him wrestle on my TV during the summer of 1964, when the unthinkable happened: Hodge lost the world junior heavyweight championship to the villainous Hiro Matsuda. When I met him years later, of course, the "villainous" Matsuda turned out to be one of the nicest men in the business—but I was devastated as a kid when he beat Hodge, the Oklahoman hero.

Danny was so admired and respected where I came from, that he was always known as "Champ"—even when he wasn't holding a title.

I was going to show my hero that I was as good at my job as he was at his. I was going to take him from town to town, set up the ring, *and* referee all his matches—and he wouldn't have to worry about a thing.

After a few months of that schedule I began to feel like I might have overthought my position. Sleep, as it happens, *is* important to the human condition. And I wasn't getting much.

"You've got to keep your eyes open," Hodge told me as we each downed our post-match milkshake. "People in this business like to cheat, even when there's no reason. And I'm talking inside *and* outside of the ring."

I listened; I nodded, but he knew I didn't really know what he meant yet. I was only a couple of years in the business, but Danny had a soft spot for me and knew it was better for me to learn that important lesson from him rather than from someone else. He finished his 'shake and signaled for us to hit the road again. "You want me to drive, Tiger?" he asked.

He could see my eyes were heavy after another long day working in the office, then hauling and setting up the ring for the show, refereeing the matches, tearing down the ring, and driving to the next town.

"No, Danny. It's fine," I said. "I do this all the time."

I knew by the way he looked at me that he wasn't sure. I was determined, but five minutes into the drive and my eyes were already closing. Danny could see it, and I knew he could see it, but damn it if I was going to look like less of a man in front of the Champ.

"You okay?" he asked again—a little more concerned this time.

"Yes sir," I answered way too loudly, and way too enthusiastically.

Hodge chimed in again. "Tiger, you need to get some sleep. You've had a long day and I can drive for a while."

As much as I wanted to, I couldn't resist the offer of sleep any longer. *Every day* was a long day for someone in my low-level position, so the thought of a quick snooze between towns was a hard proposal to turn down.

We pulled over and swapped places. "Sorry," I said.

"Don't worry about it."

I lay my seat back a little and finally giving my eyes permission to close was damn near heavenly. I quickly fell asleep feeling an overwhelming sense of contentment.

And then awoke again with an overwhelming sense of terror. "Danny!?" I shouted as I saw Hodge was sleeping now too and the car was veering onto the gravel track off the road. "Danny!" I yelled again.

This time my words bored through his sleep.

"What? What?" he said, and jumped to attention. Danny immediately slammed on the brakes and slid to a stop along the gravel.

I may or may not have peed myself a little.

Silence.

He slapped himself in the face and shook his head—annoyed with himself for nodding off. I didn't want to say anything because he looked like he was giving himself a hard enough time for nearly killing us. I also didn't want to open my mouth because I was sure there was a lady-like scream still caught in my throat. Without opening his mouth or looking at me, he started the car and slowly got us back on the road.

All I could do was watch from the corner of my eye for another few miles just to make sure everything was all right. It wasn't, I could see him slipping toward sleep again.

"Dammit, Danny, just pull over! I'll drive!" I said.

There was a second of silence before he answered, "Are you sure, Tiger?"

It was written all over his face that he hated letting something beat him—even sleep.

"I got it," I said.

From that night, I never let Danny drive again.

Both Hodge and Akbar were veterans, and if driving other wrestlers around was a learning experience, driving Hodge and Akbar was like going to an Ivy League university. They both were very thrifty and taught me how to save money, especially on the road. They taught me where to eat, when to eat, and even *how* to eat. They knew where to stay and how to make the most out of every dollar they had to spend.

When we had to stay at a motel during a long road trip, they let me room with them. We'd be in a two bedroom and I would take a pillow, both bedspreads, and make a make-shift bed on the floor—some of the grimiest, dirtiest floors in America.

All they requested in return for my free lodging was that I become their remote control and errand boy. When they were bored or done with a TV show they'd shout, "Kid?" and I'd switch the channel. When they were hungry and wanted something brought to the room, they'd call, "Kid?" and I'd go fetch whatever they wanted. They were always polite, decent, and respectful of me when they really didn't have to be.

They also taught me the small things, like filling up the car with self-service gasoline instead of paying premium prices for full service. I stopped many times and filled up my own tank while the Champ was checking the oil and everything else under the hood. As we drove away, Danny did the math to let me how much money I saved by doing the work myself.

Hodge was a star and that meant the friend of a star, me, also got preferential treatment. I'd get a free piece of pie for dessert or a "care package" of food to take with us when we were leaving a restaurant. Getting an extra piece of chicken or a sandwich was a lifesaver after the matches because without that I generally would not eat after a show due to lack of funds.

Danny even took me to the homes of fans that he had known for years while working the basic same "route" in the territory, where the lady of the house would prepare a feast akin to a holiday meal—*plus* we always left with a paper bag full of leftovers.

Both Ak and Danny knew every trick in the book to help a young kid who had never traveled or stayed in hotels survive on little earnings.

"You should always value a dollar, Tiger. Be respectful, never be late, and have a travel strategy when you're on the road," Danny told me. "And make sure you cultivate relationships with restaurateurs who manage the hotels that we visit."

He also taught me how to wash my referee shirt and pants in the sink at the hotel, and then roll the shirt or pants up in a towel and twist them until they were dry.

"And free is the buzzword," he said over and over again.

We rarely passed a food stand on the side of the road that was giving away anything free without stopping. Little did the fans know that the personalities they saw on TV every week had so little disposable income they were simply trying to get to the next meal, cheap hotel room, or tank of gas.

But I had a plan of my own on how to make a few extra bucks.

"Tiger here wants to play poker with the Boys," Danny said to Akbar as I drove.

Akbar just shook his head.

"I'll be all right," I answered. "I know what I'm doing."

But of course, Danny and Ak knew that a rookie could never win against the table of guys I was involved with. As a matter of fact, the *worst* thing I could do was win. Especially against the guy they knew I was playing against: Bruiser Bob Sweetan—a skilled, Canadian villain who liked to be referred to as "Mr. Piledriver" because of his love for that same maneuver. Mr. Sweetan was not a nice person.

A couple of months later, Danny was away in Japan and I was struggling to find new passengers, so I did what many boneheads do and tried to make some extra money from cards. Truth was, my seat at the table was little about money and more about being accepted as one of the Boys. An equal.

Because he knew Danny wasn't around, Sweetan cheated and relieved me of two days' worth of payoffs—all with a smile on his face. And in life, as in the ring, he wasn't above a little sleight-of-hand to win his contest. Both he and I knew what had gone down. Sweetan also knew that as a neon green rookie I was expected to keep my mouth shut and move quietly onto the next town. Which I did. But Bruiser Bob wasn't happy with that. When I was left with no money to buy food, I quickly learned my lesson and stopped playing poker. But Bruiser Bob wasn't happy with that either. The very next night he "accidentally" busted my nose with a "stray" elbow as I refereed his match. The night after that, he blackened my eye with another "accidental" strike.

I knew what was happening, and I was happy to again put my head down and move on to the next town. I also knew the worst thing in the world would be to complain. I took my licks, and knew it was all about "no-selling" them—not letting Sweetan see he got to me.

I got in the car with Akbar that night and when he saw my black eye and busted nose, he said he'd drive, which I appreciated. I was feeling a little sorry for myself and the chance to get some sleep before the next town was a welcome one. So I stuffed my nostrils with a tissue, curled up on the passenger seat, and let General Skandor Akbar take the wheel.

And it was great. For fifteen minutes.

"Ak!" I shouted as I woke suddenly.

The car had left the road and the sound of the gravel hitting the underside of the car made a familiar, terrifying sound. Akbar was driving, slapping himself in the face and shaking his head.

It was déjà vu. Akbar could see I wasn't amused.

"What? Dan already use this rib on you?" Ak asked with a smile on his face.

"Huh?" I said, still half asleep with tissue up my nose.

"Nothing," he replied.

"Wait a minute . . ." The reality began to dawn on me.

"Danny nearly killed us, too. The very same way."

"Imagine that," Ak said.

"He pretended to kill us?" I asked.

Akbar began to laugh. "He'd do anything not to drive at night. Sounds like it worked."

Turns out Champ actually *did* have trouble seeing in the dark and staying awake while he drove. Also turns out that Danny was told about what Sweetan did to me. Also, also, turns out that Bruiser was turned inside-out in a match with Danny when Champ got back from Japan. Champ hated bullies, and I never did play cards again. Or let Danny or Ak drive.

Lessons learned.

Chapter Eleven

BEHIND THE MIC

1975

It broke my heart, but I moved back to my hometown, population of 800, as wrestling wasn't a steady way to make a living. Driving, hauling rings, changing channels, working in the office, refereeing, and looking after Leroy were all fine for someone who was single with no responsibilities. But that just wasn't me. I had a wife and a child on the way.

Even doing all that I was doing in the business, it was hard for me to see where exactly I fit into the bigger wrestling picture.

Until one Wednesday at a Shreveport TV taping. That was the day I finally found something in the business that I knew I could spend my life doing.

And it happened because of a mix-up.

"You think you can handle this?" Bill asked me.

We were alone in the corner of the small TV studio.

I knew he wasn't looking for a "maybe" or an "I'll try my best." He was looking for a firm answer, yes or no. I didn't even need to think about it.

"Absolutely," I said.

Bill took out some money and gave it to me. I was wearing a short-sleeved shirt and slacks—not suitable of TV.

"Go and buy yourself some TV clothes," he said.

His words cemented the fact that I was about to get my break on TV. Bill handing me the money to get properly suited meant "show time" was fast approaching. No build-up, no fuss, no training, no time to prepare. The lack of communication between KTBS and the office led to neither telling the other that their regular TV announcer, Reeser Bowden, was going to be on vacation for that taping. They had no other announcer so Bill had no other choice but to try something, and someone new. Me.

I rushed across to Dillard's department store and bought a blue blazer, a light blue shirt, and a red tie—because that was what I saw TV weathermen wearing. The entire ensemble cost about $50 because I was buying off the rack—the "sale" rack.

As I hurried back, I ran over the format in my head. It was a one-hour show with five commercial breaks and six matches—all squash bouts. The studio audience was always approximately seventy-five people, who were essentially the same faces that came to the same tapings and sat in the same seats.

"You ready?" Watts asked as I re-entered the building at pace. Bill didn't wait for my reply. "You want to know the number one rule to making money in the wrestling business?" he said.

I began to answer but he again cut me off. "The money is in the *vertical* depth of the roster. Unless it's in the *horizontal* depth. *Horizontal* depth is where your show features a lot of tag teams, or guys who always have to work together. That can make money, too. But, if you stack that one single match with everything you have, and the fans aren't interested, they're not going to pay to see your show. So there's no money there. Unless you have a hot team or faction. Then you make money. You understand, Jimbo?"

I was barely following, but Bill wasn't waiting for questions or follow-ups. "But *vertical* depth in your roster means that you have a show with five or six different potential attractions. That's where the money is, because you can present a singles main event with two top guys, but if a fan isn't crazy about seeing that match there are four other things on the card that might compel them to buy a ticket. You understand now?"

This time Bill waited for me to reply. I had no idea what he was saying.

"The money is in the vertical depth?" I said. "Except for when it's not. Then it is sometimes. But not all the time. Especially when you have a great team or a few single attractions."

"Sometimes," he replied. "All that *horizontal* and *vertical* depth ideas are just general guidelines. I've lived through periods where multiple tag-team feuds were the main attractions; the only absolute rule of making money in pro wrestling is this: if it's drawing money, it's a good idea!"

I was totally lost. Maybe that's what he wanted. There was something in his eye that told me he was trying to overload me; give me too much to think about, to see how I'd react under pressure.

"Jimbo," he said. "You look like you don't know whether to scratch your watch or wind your ass."

"Huh?"

He patted me hard on the shoulder one time and said, "You lead, Jimbo. Create opportunities for Leroy to contribute. Make sure to get our upcoming dates plugged."

Bill left as I changed into my newly acquired attire and got my own thoughts together. Despite his verbal peppering, I knew the basic points Watts needed me to get across because I'd always paid attention to our shows; I understood who was feuding with whom and what was at stake. Most of the matches were "enhancement" matches, what some folks called "squash" matches, because they each featured a star against a guy who, for whatever reason, was not equipped to be terribly competitive. In any promotion at that time, it was the announcer's job to believably play up the athletic ability and credentials of the "enhancement" wrestlers so that when the stars beat them, those stars had actually accomplished something.

It also fell to the announcer to play up the star in the ring, as well as the man with whom he was presently feuding and what their issues were. In the Oklahoma territory, however, the announcers had an extra task. They had to present all this information, while focusing on what was occurring in the ring, in an explicit enough fashion that Leroy McGuirk, the show's blind color commentator, could visualize it well enough to "tag in" every now and then to add something.

Our money was made purely off of ticket sales to non-televised live events, so Star Number One would "squash" a wrestler, then Star Number Two would do likewise, and then we'd have localized interviews about how you could buy a ticket to see the two stars square off.

I walked into the studio in my new suit and Bill approached.

"You ready?" he asked one more time.

I nodded. And meant it. I *was* ready.

"Can I have my change," he asked.

"What?"

"That suit didn't cost you a hundred bucks."

He was right; I rustled through my old trouser pockets and handed him the balance of his investment.

"Receipt, Jimbo?"

He could see I was getting a little impatient as I went again into my old trouser pockets. I wanted time to get my head in the game.

He said, "Here's the real lesson of the day. Nickels make dimes. Dimes make quarters. Quarters make dollars. And dollars make?"

I didn't want to answer.

"Dollars make what, Jimbo?"

I just wanted to get out of there and onto the studio floor. "More dollars?"

"No, dollars make me damned happy."

Cowboy smiled and left me to it.

* * *

I pulled out my metal folding chair and sat in front of the mic stand at the announcer's desk. It was an ordinary piece of furniture, but to me it was like sitting behind the wheel of your very first car. There was a romance to it. I could hear the sounds of all the great announcers from my childhood in my ear.

As a boy, I loved *listening* to the games by myself at night. I had a single earpiece which connected me to my transistor radio, which in turn connected me to an entirely new world of sports. Because of how early we had to get up to do chores on the farm before school, my bedtime at ten years old was 8 p.m. I'd go to bed with that ear-plug between my ear and the pillow, so if my parents poked their heads in the door they wouldn't be able to see that I was tuned into a baseball or football game. I'd listen to the Cardinals play on KMOX, the Saint Louis AM radio station whose signal carried all the way to Westville. Listening to such broadcast greats as Jack Buck and Harry Caray, it was like the entire culture of sports washed over me. Those guys made me understand the concept of radio as the "theater of the mind." They could paint a picture of what was going on, as vivid as any image—televised or live—could be. I felt like I was at Busch Memorial Stadium, and I thought that was a true art form.

I contrasted the style of the commentators on the radio versus the guys on TV. I started to notice that the TV announcers did not talk quite as constantly. They knew their audience was watching the games they were calling so they could lay out and wait for a big play to make their big call.

I looked at my bullet-point notes in front of me and tried to find my big call. I knew I wouldn't find it on the page, but I was *looking* for it because I was afraid I wouldn't be able *feel* it.

I glanced at the stationary camera operator who would give me my cues. He was ready. I was, too. Leroy was already in position: quiet, composed, and ready to go to work. I couldn't help but look down to make sure his crotch was smokeless—you know, for old time's sake.

"Beverages on the floor, out of sight," someone said as they passed behind me.

"You ready?" another voice asked.

Maybe they all saw a nervousness in me that I didn't feel. But I was too naïve to be anxious. Sometimes ignorance truly is bliss.

I dipped my head and closed my eyes and tried to summon up the voice of the greatest commentator I ever heard: Gordon Solie.

Since I joined the company, I watched the tape of Solie's call of Hiro Matsuda beating Danny Hodge at least sixty times in its entirety. Leo Voss sat beside me on every viewing. He told me to listen to how Solie approached the in-ring action with a subtle flair for the dramatic; never taking things to an eyeball-rolling level. It was Gordon's authenticity that made him the most trusted voice in wrestling. He spoke in eloquent terms about holds and particularly body parts. So much so that in college I took Kinesiology just so I could sound like him. Solie had a strategy that made many fans forget that what they were watching was staged, and that might be the greatest compliment that a pro wrestling broadcaster could receive.

I began to practice my opening to myself at the desk.

"Hello, ladies and gentlemen and welcome . . ."

Watts, now standing behind me, interrupted. "If I wanted Gordon Solie, I would have hired Gordon Solie."

"What?"

"Be yourself," he said.

Leroy sniggered at Watts's critique. Cowboy leaned down closer so only I could hear him. "You can learn a great deal from Solie's storytelling. But you need to find your own voice. Approach this like a sport, don't insult the people, and put the talent over."

"OK."

"OK?" Cowboy asked.

"OK," I said.

Leroy turned to me and said, "You ready?"

He didn't wait for me to answer before the countdown began to show time. All these great commentators in my head. All the great plays I'd heard. All the times the greats would "lay out" and let the pictures do the talking. All the emotional calls and vivid pictures they painted. The gravity of their voices; the command of their craft. And in a small KTBS studio in Shreveport, Louisiana, I was about to take my first step in joining them.

And I felt absolutely ready.

"3 . . . 2 . . . 1 . . ."

* * *

"You did good, kid," Leroy said quietly, as the audience filed out after the taping was over.

I was still buzzing; filled with adrenaline. I felt I had done well, and tried to tick all the boxes that Cowboy told me to tick. Neither the camera guys nor the crew were giving me any feedback one way or the other. They were focused on getting home, or to the next town.

"Not bad, kid. Not bad. You've got a lot of work to do," Watts said as he approached.

"Thank . . ."

"Now, get changed," he said. "You're refereeing the matches in Baton Rouge tonight."

Not only was my "weatherman" suit bought on sale, but it was also on loan. And it was now time to take it off and get back to my real job.

Although Bill's praise was faint, I was happy to hear his words. "Got a lot of work to do" meant I was going to get a chance to do it again.

Maybe I found my way out of $125 a week. Maybe I found my calling.

Chapter Twelve

NOT BEHIND THE MIC

1976

Now, finding one's calling and finding an opportunity to continue that calling are two completely different things. I wanted my wrestling journey to fall into place from that moment; that the wrestling gods would smile down upon my round Oklahoman head and I would call matches forever. It just didn't happen like that. There was only a limited amount of spots available and I was still the "new guy" compared to the others. I felt I'd done a good job—but I was only standing in. I soon learned that my real value wasn't in my ability to call matches, but my ability to be an all-rounder. Doing more, and doing it well, meant my value to the company rose. But I was still struggling to make a living from it.

Mid-South, however, was rolling along just fine because Bill loved to keep an iron fist on all parts of the business. He wasn't afraid to put his foot down when he needed—especially with the wrestlers he fought so hard to protect. Most of the Boys would take Cowboy's famous fines with their mouths shut, but some wouldn't.

Like Dick Murdoch.

Now, Dickie struck me as a loud, obnoxious Texas Longhorn who liked to drink a lot of beer and eat a lot of mayonnaise on his broccoli. But we soon developed a natural chemistry. We both enjoyed our spirited debates on the OU-UT rivalry; I think each of us was surprised to find someone on the other side of that chasm who could match our own knowledge of players, stats, and other useless trivia.

Murdoch was just fun to be around—maybe sometimes a little too fun. We started traveling together on occasion; he liked to drive, which didn't bother me, but he also liked to drink and drive, which did. When he was in the car it was country music on the radio—and *only* country music.

He hated guys who smoked pot or did other types of drugs, even though he secretly, occasionally enjoyed speed, which was how he could drive all night while drinking beer after beer and still remain alert.

"Hey, Jim. You hear about my check?" he asked me one night as we drove to the next town.

"No, Dickie. I haven't heard anything."

"Well," he said, "Watts did it to me again, but I'm gonna get even. He's not gonna get away with it this time."

I was starting to have flashbacks to Leroy wanting to kill Ted DiBiase when Dickie said, "Well?"

"Well what?" I asked.

"Don't you wanna know what I'm gonna do?" he said.

"Not really."

"Look at that," he said, ignoring the road and throwing me his check.

I opened the envelope, removed the paycheck, and saw Murdoch's pay for the shows he worked, and then a space for a draw—or an advance payment—and finally a space for fines.

Dickie had a hell of a week with $6k earned, however, he'd been late to almost every town and he'd clowned around in at least a couple of that week's main event matches.

"You know how much he fined me?" Dickie asked.

"How much?" I asked.

"Everything, except one fucking dollar."

I looked again and, sure enough, the check to Dickie said $1. Seeing Murdoch seethe was actually kinda funny, but I knew if I laughed he'd probably kill me for real.

"He wants to teach me about being professional," he said. "So here's what I'm gonna do."

I was bracing for the worst because I was in an awkward situation. I worked for Bill but liked Dickie a lot.

"You know how meticulous Bill is," he said. "He accounts for every dollar and every cent; he never misses a detail. So what I'm gonna do is, I'm never gonna cash this check."

Dickie looked at me with the biggest shit-eating grin I had ever seen in my life. But I didn't get it.

He continued. "For the rest of his life the son of a bitch will never be able to balance his checkbook. Eventually it'll drive him crazy, and he might end up killing himself or something good like that." Murdoch's blue eyes sparkled as he flashed a smile of victory.

He took that check to his bar in west Texas, "Dick's Dive," and had it framed and posted on the wall.

I learned as I watched him that Dickie had few equals as a wrestler—when he was motivated. He was 6-foot-5 and 275 pounds, and never lifted weights. He was just a naturally brilliant performer. He had it in him to be as good as anyone I ever saw and prided himself on making the other guy look good.

And in a completely different way, that's what I wanted to do when I got the chance, too. I wanted to make the guys in the ring look better, perhaps, than they actually were.

Going into the events, I was calling the matches in my head. Microphone or no microphone, I was imagining what I would say about the wrestlers to the audience at home. Night after night, I was coming up with new ways of explaining *who* these wrestlers were and *why* you should care. I imagined my dad in front of me and I would explain to him what the stakes were—just like our days at home.

Over and over: phrasing, cadence, tone, lift, drama. I'd bring the "viewer" in and reel them back out again. I'd envisage elevating my voice to complement the story in a match and then fade out again when the unfolding story called for it.

I noticed that many of the wrestlers who came through required a lot of selling from the announcers, and then there were some guys who needed hardly any—like Stan Hansen and his fellow West Texas University alum Frank Goodish, aka Bruiser Brody.

Both men had reputations for being difficult for some promoters to work with, but I liked Hansen and Goodish right from the start. They were tough, ex-football players who were just naturals in the ring. Watts's only gripe with them was that both men wanted to stay together as a tag team while Bill saw a lot more money in them as singles attractions. They were so opposed to that plan that they eventually gave notice. The irony was that in their last weeks with us, Bill split them anyway, and they both flourished. I called every match, and every move, without being anywhere near a microphone. Murdoch, Brody, Hansen, Hodge, Sweetan, or whoever. I wanted to be good enough, when the time came, to call all their matches, and elevate all their moves.

As Hansen and Brody packed their bags for another territory, they weren't the only duo who split up under Cowboy's watch.

Chapter Thirteen

TRYING TO STAY
IN WRESTLING

1979

Bill Watts and Leroy McGuirk were never a match made in heaven. Leroy was stuck in the old school way of doing things while Watts was looking to the future of the business. Leroy was surrounded by old-timers hanging around the office trying to hold onto any kind of payday while Watts was on the road working the main events and trying to grow the business.

Bill would book the shows only to find out that Leroy had changed them, based on the "advice" Leroy was getting back at the office. Things were obviously getting ropey between both men and it was a situation that I didn't want to find myself in the middle of. So I kept my head down as much as I could and did my job—or jobs. But like most things that turn sour at the top, it has a way of turning everything underneath the same way, too.

Because I was a "Watts guy," I was about to find out just how sour.

Watts and McGuirk finally reached the point that they just couldn't stand each other any longer, so they split the territory. Leroy took the northern half: Oklahoma plus a few towns in Arkansas, northern Texas, and Southern Missouri, while Bill took Louisiana and Mississippi—the states that would form the core of "Mid-South Wrestling."

Much to everyone's surprise I stayed in Oklahoma, Leroy's turf, because I had complex family issues unfolding there. I had just been through a divorce, which I knew was my doing, and I wanted to be closer to my daughter.

I was still infatuated with the wrestling business but was also realistic about where it was going with the two bosses at war. Without Bill to keep a lid on the prevailing shenanigans, Leroy's office quickly devolved into a political cesspool with all the old stooges tattling on each other trying to curry favor. The more "power" the stooges gained, the more I could feel myself getting squeezed out. "Watts's boy" was not "loyal to the cause." What cause exactly I didn't know, as most of the paranoia going around was stirred up from nothing but whispers and alcohol.

I was still seeing to my duties and doing my best to be a good employee, but I couldn't help but feel that I was made to fulfill tasks that Leroy's syco- phants wanted to go awry for me.

They'd send me to the airport to pick up "higher maintaince" wrestlers without smartening me up to their real names. So I'd found myself standing at arrivals looking for Dick the Bruiser, Indiana's top wrestling star, without even knowing what to call him.

"Hello, Mr. Bruiser, my name is Jim Ross and Leroy McGuirk sent me to pick you up," I said as I approached him at the gate.

Dick, with an unlit cigar clamped down between his teeth, looked me up and down before answering. "How'd you know it was me, kid?"

The airport wasn't exactly full of 5-foot-10, 280 pound men with flat-top haircuts and massive traps, so I had an idea this might be my guy. "Well, sir," I said, "I've seen your picture in the magazines and I'm a huge fan. Even before I got into the business you were always one of my favorites."

"One of?" he asked. "*One of* your favorites?"

"Shit . . ."

Bruiser smiled a little and we walked to the car together.

"Dick Afflis," he muttered.

"What's that, sir?" I asked.

"My name is Dick Afflis."

"Mine is Jim Ross."

"I know, you told me."

"Shit."

"It's okay, kid."

Dick and I became "best buddies"—at least for that trip.

But I knew I needed to add another string to my bow to keep the axe from falling, and the only thing wrestling bosses loved more than getting their asses kissed was getting their pockets lined. So I found a way to make myself even more useful: I would run my own one-off shows, known as "spot" shows, and bring Leroy in as a partner. It was like free money to him because he didn't have to do anything for his slice of the pie.

I figured it was a good time to be in the spot-show business because with Bill taking half of the area, Leroy needed new towns to run in order to keep things going five or six nights a week. I put together a brochure that explained what wrestling could draw and how the shows worked, and I sent copies to nearly every local, non-profit organization in Oklahoma and Arkansas, from chambers of commerce to Kiwanis clubs to the Jaycees.

If a group decided to do it, I'd get with Leroy and we'd work out everything from the date to the building we'd book. Leroy would come up with a line-up of matches based on who was available on that date, and I'd compose the TV plugs and make sure they were running in the appropriate markets.

I had a feeling this could do well because it was a rare chance for folks in smaller towns to see the stars from TV. Our cards would usually be the first wrestling events the smaller towns had in months or years, and in a lot of cases the first ones ever held in those localities.

It was my plan to leave nobody disappointed, from the sponsors to the popcorn vendors. Even in the Fayetteville, Arkansas, rodeo arena where they didn't have concession-stand vendors set up, I went to Wal-Mart and bought cases of canned sodas, baloney, and bread, and we had one of the ring crew guys' wives selling baloney sandwiches and Cokes to hungry fans.

I also went back to what brought to me to the dance in the first place—linking up with non-profit groups. They would get the free advertising and radio spots and in return we'd give them 20 percent of gross and they kept the money from food and beverages . . . after they paid us $250 for the ring, of course. Leroy and I would get 80 percent of the gate, of which we paid the talent about 35 percent cash before they left the venue, and then Leroy and I would split the remaining monies 50/50.

I borrowed a buddy's pickup truck to haul around the ring. I had a small crew in my hometown that helped me set up for shows, putting up the ring and arranging the audience's seats. I also reffed matches, managed the money and booked the matches' finishes. The office stooges hated my shows, which were making good money and being well advertised. Most of the wrestlers preferred working my shows, too, as I made sure to have complimentary catering, hot water, and free towels for them when they came in. The Boys loved the little bit of pampering and TLC that came with working on my shows.

One of my most successful stretches came when I promoted a series of shows featuring the McGuire twins, Billy and Benny. The brothers were best known as the Guinness record holders for heaviest twins, at 600-plus pounds apiece. They became semi-famous when a picture of their gargantuan forms on mopeds began to appear in the newspapers. I knew from time to time, they also worked as wrestlers, coming in as "special attractions," because they were far from skilled in-ring performers. But that picture of them on the mopeds was one that every newspaper within 100 miles of one of our shows was willing to publish, and the image made the twins enough of a curiosity that they could draw a crowd.

Having that image was a major plus, because I was running on a shoe-string budget.

The McGuires' opponents were Siegfried Stanke and Bob Sweetan. Stanke was portraying an "evil German" stereotype, which had been a powerful role for a heel in the early 1950s and 1960s. In real life, this sneering, "Nazi" villain was native Texan Bill Lehman, a good guy All-American foot-ball player at Texas Lutheran.

How Bill tolerated his partner I'll never know, because Bob Sweetan, as I knew well by now, was one of the most cantankerous human beings I had ever encountered. Since our card games, him taking liberties with me in the ring, *and* his resulting run in with Hodge, Sweetan had gotten even more miserable in the few years since I'd last seen him. I don't know whether I was happy or not to find out that his bullying wasn't just limited to me. Not by any stretch. Sweetan also took advantage of job guys, wrestlers just passing through, or locals—the guys who were least likely to say anything that could make waves for a top heel.

He also took liberties with the McGuire twins. He took advantage of their lack of experience in the ring and just beat the shit out of them. I knew by now that wrestling was a tough, physical sport, but if you're going in with the intent of hurting your opponent, you're in the wrong field.

I was the referee and saw first-hand just how brutal the shots were. I tried to intervene, but Sweetan was not exactly of a mind to heed my feeble warnings. So he took his time at making himself look like the baddest guy around and when it came time to finish, he would tag in his partner, Stanke, to get pinned after a splash by one of the huge twins. Lehman didn't mind doing the job, both because he knew we wouldn't be back in the same little town for a while and because he was a professional. Sweetan, on the other hand, was a piece of feces.

He operated how he wanted because he knew he enjoyed the protection of Grizzly Smith, Leroy's right hand man. Griz and Sweetan were friendly, as they had a few things in common—including an interest in *very* young females. Leroy had even told me that he had to stop running Texarkana as part of a deal to allegedly get Griz out of a charge involving a young girl there. And since part of Grizzly's job was to make the house shows and report back to the office, he was always in close enough contact with minors for something bad to happen. Parents would drop their kids off at the shows and, because we hit the same towns weekly, it was easy for young ladies to figure out what restaurants the guys visited and what hotels they occupied. In that environment someone with a perversion could easily become a predator.

I learned a lot from Leroy and Watts, but I'll never understand why they were willing to keep Griz on. I understood why he had appeal as a wrestler;

there weren't a lot of 6-foot-10 guys around, much less ones who understood ring psychology—and Griz knew the business. But there had to come a point where the rewards of a good gate were outweighed by a person's proclivities.

I wanted to ask, "Leroy, you've still got this man on payroll after all this? Why do you keep using him?"

But I didn't. I didn't feel like it was my place.

I still remember the first time I became acutely aware of Sweetan's part in it, and that memory still makes me nauseous. We were waiting to do some interviews at the local station after a show at Fort Smith, Arkansas, one night and one of the sponsors was there with his wife and little girl, who was maybe twelve, to meet the wrestlers.

Sweetan muttered to me, "I could make her purr like a kitten."

I leaned toward Sweetan, mortified that the sponsor might overhear this discussion, and said quietly, "Well, that might not make her husband too happy."

He said with a smile, "I'm not talking about the mother."

Sweetan liked to take advantage every chance he got. Even if it was with a pair of 600-pound brothers.

"You guys coming out," I asked very softly, so that no one else in the locker room could hear.

The twins had been in the showers an awful long time and I was on the other side of the door wondering if they were okay. I had just gotten off the phone with Leroy and told him the situation. His words to me were: "Do whatever you have to do to make sure those boys fulfill their bookings with us."

He meant it. And I knew he meant it. The more time I spent outside the door, the more it started to become obvious to the Boys that a situation was arising. A situation I didn't want getting back to Leroy's stooges.

"Billy, Benny? You guys doing okay in there?" I whispered through the door again.

Still no answer.

As large as they were, they were also soft-hearted guys who didn't like real-world conflict. They were big for sure, but not tough in the slightest.

Sweetan had gone so hard on them that both men were crying in the ring as the match played out. When they came backstage they said nothing and headed for the shower. I knew this was a bad situation.

Now, even though Billy and Benny weren't the greatest in-ring grapplers in the world, they were an attraction and the main event of the shows I had lined up. Without them my gates would flop and not only would I not have any money for Leroy, I wouldn't be able to pay the other wrestlers what they were used to either.

I could see everyone in the locker room was watching and listening, even though they pretended they weren't. I needed some time alone with the brothers to see what we were going to do. So I did the only thing I could think to do in that situation: I opened the door and went into the shower.

It was three husky gentlemen, sandwiched into a small hot, steaming shower room.

"Eh, hey guys," I said, trying to avoid the splash of running water as it hit the tiled floor.

Judging by their non-reaction to my appearance, I guessed both guys didn't seem to mind my joining them on this particular evening.

"You guys doing okay?" I asked, as I tried not to see things that a man can't un-see.

Too late. I saw it. Well, both "its" to be precise.

Neither brother answered me but I could see they were bruised up pretty good, and frightened, too.

"That guy is an asshole," I said about Sweetan. "I promise you here and now that you won't ever have to step in the ring with him again. You guys are who everyone is coming to see. You guys are our stars."

That statement seemed to work a little as Benny nodded slightly.

"And how about I throw in a little extra money for your meals, too," I added, "as a good will gesture for the work you guys are putting in?"

Billy looked to his brother, and they came to an understanding without having to say anything.

I was thinking: *please don't drop the damned soap.*

"What do you say?" I asked. "You want to finish up here and we go out for something to eat?"

A little nod from the brothers. They weren't happy, but they were coming around.

"Ok then," I said as I turned to leave.

"Jim," Billy said as serious as can be. "Will you wash our backs?"

"Excuse me?"

Billy explained, "We usually help each other out, but Benny's arm isn't doing so good."

"Will you?" Benny asked.

"Your backs?" I said.

"Yeah."

"Wash them?"

"Yeah."

"Eh . . ."

And did I? With the office "watching" and my upcoming shows on the line? You bet your ass I did.

My first experience of talent-relations had me standing fully clothed in the shower with two naked, 600-pound men who were sobbing as I soaped up a sponge, ready to wash them down.

I knew at that moment that I'd be in the wrestling business forever.

Chapter Fourteen

OUT OF THE BUSINESS

1979

Two weeks later, I was out of the wrestling business.

McGuirk's stooges got to me—or got to McGuirk. They convinced the old man that I was too loyal to Watts and that I wasn't a team player, so they lengthened my loops and kept my pay at $25–$40 a day. The longer Cowboy was gone, the longer my trips became. If there was a backroad long-ass journey to be made, then I was the one who was making it. Griz, who had McGuirk's ear more than anyone, made it his mission to starve and frustrate me out of the business.

And eventually it worked.

Life on the road was never-ending, and I looked as if I had aged significantly before my parents' very eyes. The miles, staying in flea-bag motels, eating unhealthy fast food was putting years on my body. I was also deep into bad personal habits such as drinking most nights while driving, and experimenting with various drugs to better "fit in" with the Boys. That drug culture, mixed with the lies and drinking, was destructive to say the least. And it was sure doing a number on me and my personal relationships.

At times I was having a lot of fun, too much fun, as I lived a life of irresponsibility filled with foolish acts. Being away from home and earning virtually no money was almost like being a prisoner to the business that I loved, even though I had forgotten why I loved it. I knew that if I continued to be "one of the boys"—without Hodge and Akbar to mentor me—the end result was going to be a disaster.

I had a young family who, even though I wasn't living with, I still needed to look after. I had bills that were waiting to be paid, and responsibilities above and beyond myself. I decided that I could no longer travel as much as I did, work as hard and as long as I did, for as little as I did. I had already made enough really bad decisions, which led to both mental and physically abusive behaviors.

I was trapped and I had to escape, or lose everything.

A few years before, back home in Westville, the President of Peoples Bank, Mr. Earl Squires, approved a loan for me to come home and buy my grandparents' mercantile store—but only if I was going to be a full-time owner who was on-site daily. That particular stipulation was going to be easier to fulfill seeing as my wrestling days looked numbered. My parents and friends were happy that I was "settling down," as none of them really understood my fascination with pro wrestling or the lifestyle that came with it. For my dad, returning home was like I had finally come to my senses. He was happy to see me get planted in one place and get on with a "normal" life.

I wasn't as happy. Or happy at all.

Once I was home, I buried myself in local charity work, little league baseball, and other civic activities. I officiated high school and college sports which allowed me to "escape" the department store and get back on the athletic field. I even presided over high school state championship games, but nothing could hold my attention for long. Truth was my heart was broken. I was trying to do all the right things for all involved, but me. I was restless and missed life on the road. I was obsessed with wrestling and just couldn't shake it; couldn't kill it off. Occasionally I'd cover for Cowboy when his regular commentator was off or I'd help run some spot shows with McGuirk, but I had little more than a toe in the water so to speak, and that was even more frustrating. I had spent that last few years with my eye on a business I wasn't truly in, and neglected a marriage I was. Now that I was "settled" I was going to try marriage again.

To say that I could have handled things better with my relationships would be an Andre the Giant–sized understatement. Even though the women in my life changed, the issues within myself had not, so marriage number two started as rocky as the first one ended.

"Son, you just might not be the marrying kind," my dad said to me one night as we sat otherwise silently. It was hard to disagree.

For a couple of years I fumbled around, clearly searching for something that I couldn't find making mistake after mistake along the way. Added to my terrible run of events was the foreclosure of my store. Wal-Mart had become my competitor and there was no way, no how I was winning that particular battle.

I stood one last time at the back of the store where my fellow townspeople had come for decades to tell their stories and eat their homemade sandwiches. I turned off the lights and locked the door and thought of how many times I visited my grandparents there as a kid. I walked to my car with my head bowed. I was ashamed and beaten down. I couldn't possibly think how I could feel much worse about myself, and what my life had become.

Until I filed for bankruptcy.

It was then that I found out that my mom had secretly mortgaged her own home to secure my loan for Mr. Squires. Discovering what she did made my failure all the more heartbreaking. I didn't think I deserved a mother like that. Not then. Not when I had messed up so bad in my personal life and fell flat so hard in my business life. But she loved me. Maybe a little too much.

When I asked her why she'd do such a thing for me she said, "I wanted to do my part, and I don't give a damn about the money. I want you home. And I want you to stay home."

She could see what having my eye on the road was doing to me. My mom knew me better than anyone, and all 90 pounds of her was going to do everything she could to keep her boy, even if he was now a twenty-seven-year-old man, away from the dangers she saw in the wrestling business.

"Jimmy," she said with her eyes full of tears, "I can't stand to see you like this."

I could see she was hung on the notion of me being home and staying home. She saw what being on the road did to me. How it affected me. The short temper, the edginess, the withdrawals I was going through to get myself back in the business. I had come from nowhere to find myself in a job and a business that only a tiny percentage of a tiny percentage got to see—and now I was back home, population 800, and I felt like the circus was leaving town without me.

Maybe staying put was for the best. I had no real other choice anyway. Wrestling wasn't calling and I couldn't figure out how to get back in. I was lost.

Chapter Fifteen

GETTING BACK IN

1982

"Jimmy?" the familiar voice said over the phone. "I need you to put together some ads for me."

It was Cowboy, and I could tell by his voice he was in a real good mood. So he should have been. Things were looking up for Watts in the wrestling business.

The Houston territory had just joined the Mid-South territory out of necessity for Houston promoter Paul Boesch, as his roster wasn't particularly deep and the star names he did have were getting old. Historically, Boesch had run Houston as basically a one-city region which pulled in wrestlers from all over the country. But months after aligning himself with Joe Blanchard's Southwest promotion, which was based in nearby San Antonio, Texas, Boesch was having issues getting talent for his Houston events. Meanwhile, Mid-South with Cowboy Bill Watts at the helm boasted a crew of young, talented wrestlers like Jim Duggan, Jerry Stubbs as the masked Mr. Olympia, and Ted DiBiase. Boesch needed to partner up to survive, and Watts got to add a big money town to promote in. Win/win—for Watts, at least.

"I've got something big cooking and I need to get the word out," Cowboy said.

I was sitting in my new job at the Tulsa radio station KTFX. It was 8 a.m., my show had just ended, but my radio workday was just getting underway. Not only was I an on-air talent, but I also sold advertising at the station.

"Help get the word out?" I asked. I was thrilled to hear from him. Cowboy and I hadn't kept in touch all that much since I left the business.

"Yeah. I'm coming your way," Watts replied.

He could hear the confusion in my voice.

"I've bought Leroy out. The Oklahoma territory is mine now."

"Leroy is gone?" I asked.

"Yep. I'm coming back to Oklahoma," he said.

Wrestling was coming back into my life, but I had another offer on the table. The senior managers who'd brought me aboard KTFX had both moved over to a new station, K-95 FM (KWEN) and wanted me to be their first hire—as a salesman.

Maybe I could marry my new radio offer with my first love: professional wrestling, I thought.

"Can you help me out?" Cowboy asked.

So rather than pick between Cowboy's ads and my new job offer, I brought Watts's business with me when I decided to move to K-95 FM.

* * *

With McGuirk's Tri-State a thing of the past, Bill was looking for someone in the Tulsa market to help him get Mid-South Wrestling established in the minds of fans—and that meant advertising. Before long I was helping him craft and place ads throughout Oklahoma and I was starting to feel alive again. I really didn't understand just how much I missed the wrestling business until it tip-toed back into my life again.

Watts knew he had the talent and the booking skills to continue expanding. Watching his show from the sidelines, it wasn't hard to see that Cowboy was right.

A gentleman by the name of Sylvester Ritter, who was storming up the ranks, was not necessarily the most polished performer in the ring, but his incredible charisma was making him, as the Junkyard Dog, one of the hottest heroes in wrestling.

With JYD, Cowboy had a special person with incredible strength and a rare presence that Watts, and his booker, Buck Robley, planned everything else around. They wanted to continue to create the best possible issues for JYD to overcome; issues that would resonate on a human level with the fans. A couple of years before, they got JYD to the top of the business when The Fabulous Freebirds—Michael Hayes, Terry Gordy, and Buddy Roberts— "blinded" JYD using hair-removal cream that "accidentally" got into his eyes.

To the fans, the villainous 'Birds had deliberately blinded their hero, but Hayes—an awesome talker—swore it was an accident; that they had been trying to remove his hair but JYD moved causing the cream to go into his eyes. The Freebirds's denials left the Mid-South "brass" unable to prove their intent, which meant the dastardly threesome wouldn't be "sanctioned." JYD's only justice would come when his friends took on The Freebirds in bouts that drew thousands of fans, hoping to see JYD's friends exact revenge on his behalf. Of course, no one was able to avenge him, so months later Dog himself came back for a match with Freebird mouthpiece Michael Hayes. JYD, still blind, got a dog-collar bout in which both men wore leather collars that were connected by a length of chain. JYD couldn't see Hayes, so he needed a way of getting a hold of him.

That match headlined at the New Orleans Superdome, drawing more than 30,000—Mid-South's biggest crowd ever. I grew to learn that number was close, but maybe not perfectly accurate, as wrestling was known for trumpeting crowd figures that were always embellished to some degree. Watts knew the old rule of wrestling and promotion in general: say it enough times and it moves from fantasy to fact. The old promoters all did it; Fritz Von Erich did it in Texas, Verne Gagne did it in Chicago, and Watts did it at the Superdome shows.

Figuring out how best to meet Bill's advertising needs also coincided with a realization I'd made about several of my other radio ad clients. If I ran my own ad agency, I could create and broker my own ad packages to bring to the media outlets myself. This would save my clients 15 percent or more based on what they were paying for local ads in each market, and I would also come out *way* ahead, financially.

It took me a couple of years to pull everything together, but I got my own company on its feet and I was finally doing better. Feeling better. Getting to enjoy my "normal" life. My second marriage was somewhat more stable, because I was somewhat more settled, too. We had a new child, a new house and a fresh start. I ended up with about a dozen clients, one of which was Mid-South Wrestling.

"What did you think of the show last week?" Cowboy asked over a quick coffee.

I was now renting office space from Bill in his building and it wasn't unusual for us to meet up to go over new ad ideas, or for him to deliver a check for work completed.

"I liked it," I said. "I would . . ."

"How would you like to come work for me, Jim?" he asked before I could finish my sentence.

I was stunned, but my body filled head-to-toe with a rush of adrenaline just at the mere thought of it. I wanted more than anything to get back to the business I loved. To get back to ringside, to get back on the road that aged me.

Before I could answer, Watts continued, "Things are getting bigger and I want you to come onboard as the director of marketing for Mid-South Sports."

"Yes," I said immediately.

"Yes?" he asked, a little surprised at the speed in which I replied.

"Yes," I repeated.

I knew it wasn't the job I wanted. I knew it was an offer that I could "sell" to all the people who wanted me to just settle down, my wife included. I was back *in* the wrestling business, but not back *in* the wrestling business. I'm the marketing guy. I'm back *in*, but not back *in*.

But I *was* back in.

Chapter Sixteen

BACK IN MID-SOUTH

1984

It felt good to be home.

TV tapings were in the Irish-MacNeill Boys' Club in Shreveport, Louisiana, with Reeser Bowden as ring announcer and Boyd Pierce as host of the TV show. I knew I'd have to wait for my opportunity to get back in as part of the show. It might take months, but I was willing to wait years.

"You still interested in broadcasting, Jim?" Cowboy asked straight off the bat.

"What?"

"You heard me."

Yes, yes I did hear him. Loud and clear. "You bet your ass I'm still interested," I replied.

"We'll start you back as a ring announcer. You have experience there. Then we see how you go," he said as he walked off.

I looked around the studio. The ring, the cameras. It was small, dark, but felt like home to me. I knew what other people wanted me to be. People I loved. But I also knew what *I* wanted to be. Or, more importantly, *where* I wanted to be—and that was in the wrestling business.

Within weeks, Watts was looking for more ways to utilize me at televised events. My advertising and promotion of his events was going well and he told me he wanted another set of eyes and ears on his product; basically that he valued my opinion. His words gave me confidence, especially as I was just making my return to the business.

The weeks built into months and time blurred as I submerged back down the rabbit's hole.

Within a year, Cowboy had another quiet conversation with me as I walked into the studio and he was on his way out.

"You heading somewhere?" I asked, as it was unusual to see Cowboy leave when the day was only starting.

"I want to try something new on the promos, Jimmy," he said. "I want you to be the interviewer. You're already doing all the publicity so you know what we need to put out there."

I was thrilled, but a bit shocked. These local promos were the lifeblood of the company. They were our best, most direct route to the fans at home, who we were trying to convince to buy our live event tickets. And those ticket sales were the only revenue stream we had as a company. If no one came to see the shows then no one in the company got paid.

"Whatever you need me to do," I replied. "You can show me what you want . . ."

"I'm not going to be involved," he interrupted. "You're in charge."

I paused. "Me?"

"Yeah, you," he replied as he tried to leave.

"Just me?"

"Yeah. Just you."

I stopped talking as some of the wrestlers walked past us into the building.

"What's the matter?" he asked.

"Won't other people mind if I start telling them what to do?" I whispered.

"Hopefully," he laughed. "Shake things up a bit."

And with that he was gone.

I had only been assisting with the promos for a few months and doing some on-air work since I returned. I worked faster than Reesor, which saved Cowboy money, which meant he liked me doing the job more. As my value grew to Bill, my relationship with one of his other main lieutenants was getting worse. Grizzly Smith had become one of Bill's backstage agents, shortly after Bill split off from Leroy. We never really got along and that situation only got worse when the Cowboy started entrusting me with greater responsibility. Griz started seeing me—the guy he drove out of Leroy's company—as a threat to his position in Bill's inner circle.

Getting the nod from Cowboy to "be in charge" of the promo tapings wasn't going to do anything to change that.

I walked into the studio and all the wrestlers were there. Junkyard Dog, sensing my nervousness, shouted, "Where's the Hat, Jim?!" referring to Watts, who always wore his big western hat outside his home to maintain that "Cowboy" persona. He lived his gimmick.

My voice broke a little as I replied to Dog, "I'm running the interviews today."

There was a little chuckle from the wrestlers. Grizzly couldn't resist joining in. "Yeah, Jim's running the interviews today," he said in a mocking, sarcastic tone. "This ought to be good."

It was 10 a.m. and I walked past a studio full of tired, hungover, road-worn wrestlers who knew these promo spots would take most of the day. We weren't there to record one or two, we had to record dozens based on what towns and cities were on our loop.

"We ready?" the cameraman asked.

I knew all eyes were on me. Even though these interviews were hugely important, they needed to be conducted as quickly and professionally as possible. Studio time was paid by the hour.

Each feud shared a three-minute interview slot that was usually captured in one take. Although, sometimes there were issues that stopped that speed and slickness from happening. Some of those issues I could see coming from a mile away, while others weren't so obvious.

I stood in front of the cheap cardboard backdrop with a single camera pointed at me. I was going to start by interviewing Ricky Morton and Robert Gibson of The Rock 'n' Roll Express.

"Jim?" the cameraman asked. "We ready to shoot?"

I nodded as I checked my notes. Show time. All the Boys were watching. "We do New Orleans first and take it from there," I replied.

I could see The Rock 'n' Roll Express moving closer, just off camera, getting ready to join me when the time was right. I wasn't really sure about their interview style yet, as they were pretty new to the company—having just come in via a recent trade with the Memphis territory. As a matter of fact, a lot of people in the room had.

A few months prior, the live gates were going down a bit, and it was apparent to Watts that we needed some new faces. He reached out to Jerry Jarrett from the Memphis territory and negotiated a trade deal to benefit both companies.

The Memphis owners were invited by Watts to come to a couple of our shows to have a look around. The idea was that both Mid-South and Memphis would trade talents to freshen up their respective rosters and ignite fresh, new feuds to catch the fans' attention.

As part of the negotiation process, Bill even went so far as to ask one of the Memphis owners to sit in with me to call a match.

As a fan who regularly read the wrestling magazines, I was well aware of "The King of Memphis." We had many mutual friends, so when I finally met Jerry Lawler in person it felt like we already knew each other. Jerry had hundreds of hours of TV experience under his belt, so we meshed immediately and seemed to suit each other's style perfectly. He was easy to work with, glib, and knew what to say—and more importantly, knew what *not* to say. During the match, I tried more than once to catch King's eye but he seemed to be more interested in surveying the women in the audience. He was scouting our territory and the amount of women at the show was an indicator if the babyfaces were "over" and "doing their job" for the female fans.

When they'd seen enough, Lawler and his partner, Jerry Jarrett, both successful bookers, had a few pieces of advice. First, they said that in most cases, Bill's heels should be the babyfaces and vice versa. It was an interesting point because we did have a lot of dynamic, athletic youngsters in villainous roles, while many of our protagonists were older, bulky brawlers. Part of the problem with that setup was that in those days the babyfaces' duties frequently included "servicing" the female fans to keep them coming back and buying tickets. As the announcer, part of my job was to get across how much of a ladies' man a young hero was.

They ended up making a talent trade to help the overstocked Jarrett clean out some of his mid-card and to help Mid-South get younger, new talents. The deal was simple: Memphis could have anyone, except the Junkyard Dog, and Watts could have anyone but Lawler, manager Jimmy Hart, or The Fabulous Ones: Stan Lane and Steve Keirn, who were the top tag team in Memphis.

We agreed to send Rick Rude, who was just a rookie, Larry "Hacksaw" Higgins, and Jim "The Anvil" Neidhart.

Watts went to Memphis to scout their talent, and he returned with a list of names that would rejuvenate Mid-South, making 1984 its most profitable year. We received The Rock 'n' Roll Express and their eventual rivals, The Midnight Express: Bobby Eaton and Dennis Condrey, with manager Jim Cornette.

And it was through watching Cornette getting an ass chewing from Watts that I learned one of the most valuable lessons about interviewing.

Watts created The Midnight Express by taking Eaton, who was a middle-of-the-road babyface, and teaming him up with Condrey, who was a heel at about the same level as Eaton. Cornette, who had only been in the business for a little more than a year, was Memphis's secondary manager of bad guys behind perennial instigator Jimmy Hart. Cornette's gimmick was that of a rich mama's boy; a spoiled brat whose mother was spending her wealth on wrestlers for her obnoxious son to manage. When he came in to do his first interviews on behalf of the team, I introduced Cornette with tremendous fanfare. I described him as the manager of one of the most skilled, controversial, sought-after teams in the world.

Cornette blistered me with one-liners, one after another. He'd seen that work for Jerry Lawler in Memphis where announcer Lance Russell was such a beloved institution that making fun of him was enough to garner angst for a villain. Cornette made fun of my hair, my suit, my accent, and my home state. I never said a word, largely because there wasn't a second for me to say anything. It was an impressive display of verbal chops; Cornette barely seemed to take a breath.

When the barrage was over, I had a brief opportunity to end the spot with, "And The Midnight Express will debut this Saturday night, in the Municipal Auditorium!"

We ended the spot and Watts had some choice words for us, many of which began with the letter "F."

"The last thing in my lifetime I want to see is you and my announcer wrestle a match," Bill told Cornette. "Since I have no plans to book that for as long as I live, your clever diatribe didn't sell me one damned ticket! So, we're going to do this again, and this time, I want you to mention the name of the town, your opponents, and tell me a little about your team! Jim Ross gave you a hell of an introduction; he put your guys over, even though you're heels, because as a representative of Mid-South, he's got no dog in the hunt! You need to focus on the guys who *do*, and those are your opponents!"

Cornette impressed me by not getting overwhelmed, by not taking the ass-chewing personally, and, most of all, by showing that he truly got it. He took the Cowboy's instruction and delivered an excellent promo a few seconds later, when we did our second take.

When it was over, Watts walked back over and told Cornette, "Now, *that* was exactly what we need! If you can continue to improve on that and stay on that track, we're going to make a lot of money together!"

And Cornette did stay on that track. He recognized what a big break Watts had given him: a chance to be a villainous manager, on a main-event level; he was living his dream.

And I learned a great lesson on who to focus on when interviewing. A lesson I was about to put to work as I stood in front of the camera on my own and waited for The Rock 'n' Roll Express to join me.

The cameraman counted us down, "3 . . . 2 . . ."

"I'm standing by with The Rock 'n' Roll Express," I said as Ricky Morton and Robert Gibson stepped into shot on cue. "Who return to New Orleans this Thursday to face Jim Cornette's Midnight Express . . ."

I could tell that both men were tired, and a little cranky. Wednesdays were a real grind, with half the guys coming in from the previous night's show in Little Rock, more than 200 miles away, and the other half coming from a spot show in Louisiana. "Well," Ricky began, "we . . ."

I had heard that Robert Gibson was also known as "Hoot" Gibson. I figured this nickname wasn't anything to do with trumpet playing abilities, but it did involve a "skill." Simply put, "Hoot" would pride himself on lacing his and Ricky's long car journeys with the most vile, smelly farts known to modern man. These were the kind of "hoots" that were so disgustingly potent that they could actually make you angry from having to experience them.

And as Ricky was also Robert's travel partner, they would drive hours to get to TV, in a car filled with Robert's farts, to have a match, wait for their chance to promo over and over, just to get back in the car to make another town, where Robert could again crop-dust Ricky the whole way.

"Fans are clamoring to see this epic confrontation, gentlemen," I said as I cut back in. Ricky was now looking distracted and a little lost. I continued, ". . . and Ricky, I know that Robert's good friend 'Junior' is especially concerned about the potential career-ending scenario that you two face this coming week."

Robert's "good friend" Junior was actually his penis. That's what he called it, so I thought referencing it might lighten the mood a little.

"I just want to get this done," Ricky said, obviously wanting another go at the promo.

"OK," I said.

We reset. The room was looking at us. Waiting for us to get it done. Time was ticking and a lot of large, tired men were waiting their turn.

I raised my mic again. "Fans are clamoring to see this epic confrontation, gentlemen. And Ricky, I know that Robert's good friend 'Junior' is especially concerned about the . . ."

Ricky interrupted me. "No I don't want . . . I just want to do it straight."

"OK, sorry," I said. "No more Junior."

Ricky suddenly stared at his partner. Robert smiled a little as it looked like Ricky was about to kill him.

I tried again. "Fans are clamoring to see this epic confrontation, gentlemen, that could end up being a potential career-ending scenario for you in New Orleans this coming week."

As I looked across both their faces, Ricky was now filled with rage as Robert was a picture of pure joy.

"Gentlemen," I said, trying to get them both to focus on the job at hand.

"Aw, Jesus," Ricky said as he stormed out of shot. "You fucking asshole. This is bullshit. I'm done. I'm gone. I'm outta here."

"What just happened?" I asked Robert, who was still standing beside me in the shot.

"Give it a second," he replied.

I replayed my opening line back in my head in fear that I might have said something to piss off one member of the most popular tag team in the company.

"Ricky," I shouted. "Wait . . ."

And before I could finish my sentence, I got why Ricky was so pissed and Robert was so proud. When I say I "got" why Robert was so proud, I mean I "got" it straight in the eye. Yes, the eye. That bastard had conjured up a fart so toxic that it burned my eyes a little *before* it violated my nostrils. Robert's smile broke into a chuckle when he saw how much distress I was in.

"You need to get yourself checked out or something," I said, as I, too, stepped out of shot.

In truth I was a little panicked, as a few months prior I had heard about the Bull Bullinski "incident." Bull flashed his "opponent" off-camera during an interview and Cowboy, who saw it, fired Bull on the spot. No debate, no conversation.

"What happened?" the cameraman whispered to me.

"Gibson poisoned us both. You didn't get that?" I replied.

"Not yet," he said.

"You will. You think Bill saw?"

"He's not here," the cameraman said.

I smiled. "You really believe that?"

Watts was watching from the control room. I knew he was. There was no way he was leaving me there alone on my first outing.

"Jesus Christ," the cameraman finally said as he pulled his T-shirt over his nose.

"Told ya," I said as I looked around to see if my boss was approaching me yet.

But it wasn't my boss that was about to get hot.

"No wonder the houses are so small if this is the way we're doing business," said a deep voice from the back of the room.

"Hacksaw" Jim Duggan was waiting to cut his promos, and wasn't happy about the waiting around.

Ernie Ladd retorted, "If you were over we could draw the people into them arenas."

Now I've got a situation where two ex-NFL players, two alpha males who had probably never backed down in a confrontation in their lives, were getting ready to go nose to nose. If Cowboy was watching from the control room, I was praying for him to come out and save me.

"You wanna step outside?" Duggan asked Ernie from the other side of the room.

Ernie rose up from his seat, all 6-foot-9 of him, and began to slowly walk toward Hacksaw. "Jim, why don't you go out, for a ride?" I said as I walked into the path of both tough guys. "Go on, clear your head and we'll knock your stuff out later."

The "why don't you go for a ride" line was something I saw Cowboy use a ton of times when guys would get pissed and unproductive. The wrestler would get in their car and before they hit the end of the road, clouds of smoke would be escaping from the open windows. Miraculously, the wrestler in question would come back perfectly chilled.

Duggan left. Ernie sat down. I wanted to go to a dark room and change my shorts. Ernie understood Duggan's frustration, though; Duggan was going out and having bloody brawls every night and working as snug and as violently as he could. After seven straight nights of cutting his own forehead, Duggan's head was tender, his body was sore, and oftentimes his money wouldn't be as much as he'd like it to be. By the fourth or fifth night on the road he could get the blood flowing without even using a blade, because by that point his thumbnail, or a stiff shot from an opponent, was sufficient to make him bleed.

"OK, are we all ready now?" I asked as I walked back to the camera. Robert Gibson was still there and I could see Ricky walking back toward us.

"Let's do this," I mumbled to the cameraman.

Ricky stopped mid-stride, Robert smiled, and the cameraman covered his face again.

"Goddamit, Robert!" Ricky shouted as he turned and walked away once more.

Chapter Seventeen

AT THE TOP TABLE

1984

People measured their rising worth in the wrestling business differently. Some of the Boys knew the company was backing them when they got higher on the card, while others knew when their payoffs grew. I knew my stock was rising when I got to eat dessert with "The Big Cat" Ernie Ladd.

One of the office rituals after the promos was that Bill would sit with the booker to finalize our TV lineup and what was happening in the upcoming feuds. It was a small, closed club of two.

Usually.

"You coming, Jim?" Watts said to me after promos.

"Me?" I asked.

"Yeah," Ernie said, as he waited by the door. "We're going to sit you under the learning tree."

I felt like running toward the boss and the booker, but I knew I had to keep my cool. Grateful, but not excited. Poised, but not cold on the invitation.

The small, closed club of two was open for one more: me.

Not only was I back inside the wrestling world—I was learning more, taking on more, and giving more than I had done before. I had been to booking meetings previously, but mostly as a note taker for Leroy. This time I was invited to *be* at the booking meeting. Give my opinion, listen, learn, and understand what really made this business tick. The reasons *why* a certain person or a certain match was the right way to go. But before the booking came the eating. And both Cowboy and Ernie loved to eat—buffet style.

Now, normal portions of food weren't of interest to Ernie Ladd. As he walked to the buffet line I could see him lick his lips right around the roast beef on display. The bored server behind the counter didn't even look up before robotically asking: "What can I get you?"

It was show time for Ernie; time for a little charm to get a little extra. "Now you know you're feeding Ernie Ladd, young lady," he said to the sixty-five-year-old server. She looked up to see the huge, handsome man in front of her. "I'm not like your little, scrawny husband at home," he continued. "So how about a little more for the Big Cat? Cause you know," he whispered as he leaned over to her, "I'm 6-foot-9, 320 pounds, and my feets cover the grounds I walks on."

The server lady coyly laughed, "Well you know what else they say about a man with big feet?"

"He has big shoes?" Bill dryly answered, cutting into the middle of the flirtations.

Ernie beamed his movie star smile back at her and walked away with twice the serving of any other person in the place.

It was my turn next. "I'm Jim Ross," I said to the same lady. "And I'm . . ." she immediately cut me off: "Don't care," she said as she walked away. I stood in shock as I struggled to see what the difference was. Apart from not having Ernie's looks, charm, charisma, stature, or presence, we were practically the same person.

I rapidly left the counter, hoping no one else heard our interaction, and stopped at the dessert station on my way to the table.

Cowboy and the Big Cat buzz-sawed their way through their food as I cleared a small space for my apple cobbler ala mode. Both big men. Both had big appetites.

"You're turning into the Junk Food Dog," Ernie said to me. "You need some real nourishment in your body."

I knew he was right, but apple cobbler was my comfort food. It reminded me of home, and my mama, who was "The Cobbler Queen."

"You won't get far in this bidness eating ice cream," Ernie said. "Real men eat lots of protein."

I could see Cowboy trying not to laugh as he filled his mouth with meat and gravy.

"You ever fear a grown man who talked out the side of his neck while eating ice cream?" Ernie asked. "No, me either."

When the Big Cat spoke, I still wasn't sure whether I should listen, reply, or take notes. Before I chose either option Ernie had moved on, and was now waving to the server lady over my shoulder. He scooped some of my dessert onto his fork and ate it. "That's good," he said with a smile. "You should have some."

And have some I did. If it was good enough for Ernie, it was good enough for me.

Thing was, Big Cat was even more of a legendary figure to me because I knew who he was before either of us got into wrestling. He had played for the Houston Oilers and Kansas City Chiefs, but his greatest football days may have been as a San Diego Charger, where he'd led his team to four American Football League Championships.

As a kid I had several of his football cards, so I was in awe of him when we first met. Because of his background, Ernie understood top-level athletes as few others did, and that meant he fit right in with Bill's serious, sports-based approach.

Apart from all the wisdom and logic Ernie taught me about the wrestling business, he also taught me about life as an African American, something I never got to hear too much of in my hometown. When I was a child in Oklahoma, it was illegal for African Americans to live anywhere they wanted in the county—not because of the beliefs of the people who lived there at that time, but because of one of those old segregation laws. I grew up with a law in my county that literally said it was illegal for a black man to see the sunset while standing in Adair County.

Maybe it was due in part to my mother's Native American ancestry, but I was not raised in a racist household. Some of the Caucasians viewed Native Americans as another race, just as they viewed African Americans. My parents raised me to see that kind of prejudice as embarrassing but, because of the homogenous nature of Adair County's demographics, I grew up not understanding the plight of African American people—especially in the tumultuous 1960s. Giving all people civil rights and equal treatment just seemed like a no-brainer to me.

As a kid, I always made a point of listening to Dr. Martin Luther King Jr., when one of his speeches was being broadcast. The day after I'd look in the papers for snippets of his words, or full transcripts if I could get them. The young wordsmith in me considered those speeches a treat—as much for his presentation and the poetry of his language as for his message of equality. He compelled me to think about other people's lives, other people's experiences, and he did it in my preferred way: with spoken elegance and impact.

In his own way, Ernie was also a trailblazer. He was the first major African American wrestling villain in the 1960s, when most promoters were scared that such a thing would lead to race riots in the arenas. Even by the time I came to wrestling, each territory had no more than one or two black wrestlers in featured positions—and never as the main man. Except in Mid-South, where Watts used both a black booker in Ernie and a black top star in JYD.

Watching Ernie's work had already taught me tremendous lessons about getting across a point in a promo, just as he, the person, taught me about what it meant to live with the prejudice he had confronted his whole life. "It's not enough for people to hear the noise; they must also take in the message," he told me. "We make 'em feel something. Good or bad."

And I sat there listening to two of the best ever, laying out the territory and polishing their finer points. When he was done both booking and eating,

Ernie rubbed his belly and stood up from the table. "You taking me home?" he asked Bill.

Cowboy shook his head a little in disbelief. "Drive yourself home," Watts replied.

"C'mon," Ernie said as he turned and walked out of the cafeteria a few steps ahead of us.

"Why does he want you to take him home?" I asked Bill as we followed behind.

"Watch," Bill replied.

When we got down into the parking lot, Ernie stood beside his navy-blue Lincoln Continental with the driver's door open. Bill had given Ernie the car for a job well done.

"The Hat is driving," Ernie said, using his nickname for Bill. "Junk Food can sit shotgun and I'll take the back seat. Sound good?"

Bill laughed and did just as he was told.

"What's happening?" I whispered before we got to the car. Bill didn't have time to explain before we were all seated just as Ernie wanted.

"Now," said the Big Cat as Bill started the car, "take me to the hotel, mister driver."

I learned as we drove that Ernie got a big kick out of having "a big, white driver" take him around town as people looked on. Bill got just as much fun out of it as his big, black "brother" in the back seat.

I had no idea on that drive that Ernie was winding down his time as a booker. He was burnt out on the business and ready to transition to his beloved ministry work.

But not before he got the Hat to drive him, for the small town to see.

* * *

When Ernie left the business, we got our next booker from Memphis: "Superstar" Bill Dundee. It was a huge boost for us. Watts brought him in strictly to book the shows—but wouldn't let him wrestle. Watts's concern was that the 5-foot-7

Aussie would book himself to conquer Watts's tough giants. Bill just didn't see it as realistic, and if it wasn't "real" then Bill didn't want it on his TV show.

Dundee continued to badger Watts.

"You can wrestle," Watts said.

"I can?"

"I'm sick of listening to you."

"I knew you'd see sense."

"But the second I see you trying to make yourself the center piece," Watts said. "I'm pulling you out of there."

"Deal," Dundee replied.

"Deal," Watts said with a handshake.

Within a month Dundee tried to put himself in featured roles and Bill pulled him back out again.

But as a booker, Dundee helped concoct some incredible stories and feuds. He pushed for smaller, higher-paced wrestler to get more prominent positions. The Rock 'n' Roll Express, The Fantastics, Terry Taylor, Dennis Condrey, and Bobby Eaton with manager Jim Cornette all began to rise to the top of the cards and pull the audience with them. It was a noticeable shift away from the huge, football player–types that had become a staple of the territory.

Apart from bookers, Cowboy was also shaking things up with his announcers, too. One week, Boyd Pierce would become the ring announcer and I would handle play-by-play as Bill's son Joel served as color commentator. We'd take the between-show breaks and then settle in for the second show of the taping, only now I was ring announcer, while Boyd and Bill called the matches for the TV audience. Despite his youth, Joel knew what the boss wanted, because Joel had grown up under his roof. Joel put together the amazing videos for his father's shows.

Besides my increasingly frequent TV announcing duties, I continued to be a bigger part of the booking meetings. My theory on how to contribute to the creative direction was pretty simple. If I saw Bill writing something on yellow legal pad he always brought with him, it would behoove me to do the same, because Bill wasn't going to waste energy by writing down a meaningless point.

One day, when I saw him simply write the letters "J-Y-D" in his pad, I knew something was up. The Junk Food Dog was getting more and more entrenched in the company, but the real Junk Yard Dog had already made a deal to leave.

Chapter Eighteen

CHANGES FROM NEW YORK

1984

I was spending more and more time in the bubble of the wrestling business. My parents were getting divorced and my own marriage began to wobble again. The business began to re-establish itself as my obsession—my reason for getting up in the morning and going to bed late at night. I was learning, hustling, and moving up in the company. But I was putting my family, my daughter, into second place because of the long hours and the chaotic lifestyle.

I worked in front of the camera and behind it, I was making sales, promoting events; Mid-South was my life. And as I was burying myself in deeper, the company's top star had tunneled himself a way out.

Without saying a word to anyone, Junk Yard Dog signed with WWF. No notice, no nothing. Wrong on all fronts.

Even before Vince McMahon began his national push, the New York territory had always been the goal for most pro wrestlers. WWF shows were in the most densely populated areas in the country, which meant the crowds were bigger, which meant the payoffs were better than virtually any other territory. No one could fault a person for moving on to better money. But in the wrestling business, there was a way to move on. A way to do it right.

As we sat and wrote TV, Watts veered from angry to reflective to dejected. "You don't do that," he said. "You don't just walk out on the territory that made you a star, without giving notice. Without making a star out of someone else on your way out."

We had all the other segments written, but Bill wanted to leave some space in the show to talk to the folks at home. As the red light came on at the taping, I had no idea what was going to be said, but I knew it wasn't going to be flattering to JYD.

As I introduced the show to the audience at home, Bill sat beside me at the desk with a headset on, and a little slip of paper in his hand. He raised the subject of JYD and said, ". . . Junk Yard Dog was a great superstar for a lot of time. And I think a lot of the pressure that Butch Reed put onto him maybe, finally, affected him. The only thing I disagree with here is he made a lot of obligations and let the fans down here. He's been under the gun for five years here and Butch Reed is an awesome individual and apparently it kinda made him crack or do something and he's sought greener pastures so to speak. We don't know, this is all summation and speculation, but certainly he's not here and he didn't show up at the matches he was booked against Butch Reed. And of course Reed and Landell are going to take a lot of credit for that."

We then cut to Boyd Pierce, who was in the ring with one of the toughest men alive: "Doctor Death" Steve Williams. I watched Cowboy try to pretend that his feelings weren't hurt.

"Mid-South is known as the toughest competitive wrestling area in the world today," Cowboy continued on commentary. "By all the wrestlers themselves, they acknowledge that area is the finest, is the toughest. 'Hacksaw' Butch Reed seems to have surpassed, with the tremendous pressure he's put on, probably the greatest athlete I've seen in a long time in wrestling. For all JYD's personal problems to apparently cause him to not want to answer the challenge, continuous pressure by Hacksaw Reed."

I chimed in on the action in the ring. "Doctor Death has that big tree-like arm wrapped around the neck of Mike Jackson."

Throughout the show, Cowboy continued his severe burial. His biggest star had left with no notice—Bill had to "spin" the situation back to his advantage as much as he could. Traditionally, if a territory's star left he helped make the next star on his way out. Bill was livid that JYD would leave in a way that showed no respect for the Boys, the territory that had made him a star, or for the business in general. No matter what Bill thought of another promoter, he would never have wanted a guy coming into Mid-South to skip out on the place he was leaving.

But I knew, as I watched him, that what hurt Cowboy the most was that Dog broke a bond that he and Bill had. Sylvester Ritter, the person, was special to the big Cowboy—and when he left, Bill felt like he had lost a family member. A family member who had just simply walked out and left him high and dry.

I found out that in wrestling true friendships weren't all that easy to come by. I also found out when Cowboy came off camera that his mind immediately veered to the business end of the situation.

"We're not going to get the last match out of the Dog, so we can't build a new star that way," Bill said. "Who else we got coming up? We got to keep our territory fresh, come up with something new."

Watts wasn't going to lie down and let his ticket sales take a hit. He knew in wrestling, that if you're coasting you're dying. The biggest enemy to any wrestler, booker, and company in general was the dreaded comfort zone.

Wrestling was all about the *next new thing*.

And the next new thing *was* coming—but it was coming from New York.

* * *

"'WrestleMania?' What the hell is a 'WrestleMania?'" I heard Watts's secretary Georgianna Scay proclaim. Paul Bosech had called and told Watts that New York was planning something big. Something that could succeed hugely—or pull down the new, young promoter who was attempting it.

108

Despite the skepticism and cynicism from those around him, Cowboy knew it was going to be good for everyone if this idea hit. I knew it was good for our business, too, as I was the person responsible for selling the Mid-South TV show in new syndicated markets. Up until then, station managers didn't have that much product knowledge—wrestling was wrestling to them. But once WrestleMania came along, those station managers could see that wrestling was cool, getting a lot of mainstream exposure, and nudging its way back into the public psyche again.

Watts put me on the road even more to sell our show to stations around the region.

"I might be interested in wrestling again, but of all the shows out there, why should I buy yours?" the station manager of WWL asked me. I knew the question well, and I also knew how to answer it. "Would you mind," I said, handing over a document from my briefcase. I had the numbers of their own rating service—Nielsen and Arbitron—ready to go. "As you can see, our shows do really well in other established markets," I said.

I could tell by his face as he read the numbers that he was surprised at the ratings and shares we were earning. These were legitimate numbers using their own terminology and service to measure a viewership that turned heads.

After a few months I was doing so well that I couldn't keep up. I had to talk to Cowboy about getting a little help to sell. The World Wrestling Federation was helping all ships rise on its ambitious wave. And as much as I liked selling, and making some decent money, my eyes were drawn to New York for different reasons.

I wanted in some day, too.

Chapter Nineteen

THE GREATEST

1985

The fastest, most precise punches I have ever witnessed were kissing the side of my face. "I ain't afraid of no snake. He better not get in my face for his own sake," said the man who was throwing them.

I was put on assignment to shadow the three-time world heavyweight champion in his home in LA for a few days. Muhammad Ali was coming to Mid-South and he was practicing his "working" punches on my generous, round face. "Boom, boom," Ali said as he threw perfect right after perfect right. It was day three and I had gotten so used to his sudden bursts of punches that I was no longer fearful for my life.

"I'm going to throw a right," Ali said, as he did just that. "And then I'm going to throw a left." Ali did just that. "And then I'm going to eat this sammich," Ali said as he suddenly sat down and finished his lunch. "You want to see some magic?" he asked as he wiped his mouth. His energy was boundless. "Watch this," he said, as he reached into his pocket. He took out a coin and chomped down onto it, "biting" the coin in half. "You see that?" he asked.

In fact, I *had* seen it. By him. The day before. And the day before that.

"And watch," Ali said, as he blew on the coin and it "magic-ed" back together again.

"Oh my," I said, trying to muster up the same level of wonderment as I had the first few times. "How do you do that?"

"It's a miracle," he replied. "I bring miracles with me everywhere I go."

He wasn't wrong. I could have watched the same tricks over and over for a month. It wasn't the trick, it wasn't the "miracle." It was the delivery. It was the presence. It was the childlike joy he got from it. Ali knew something that was intrinsic to the wrestling business: it wasn't *what* you were selling, it was *how* you sold it.

That same principle wasn't working back in Mid-South for Cowboy, who was trying to replace his top star. Even though Watts had replaced JYD with a similarly jacked, African American man, the Snowman wasn't JYD. Not in the charisma department, nor the box office department. So Cowboy was bringing in Ali as a special attraction for the big Dome show to finally try and "make" the Snowman a star in the fans' eyes. Watts knew his new pick needed a lot of "rub," so he hired Ali and his "spiritual advisor," Bundini Brown, to help corner the Snowman. Across the ring would be despicable Jake "The Snake" Roberts with the huge Barbarian in his corner. It was all to build to a spot where Barbarian's interference necessitated Ali's involvement to level out the playing field.

Behind the scenes, Jake, who was the real life son of Grizzly Smith, was not entirely thrilled with Ali's role in the match. He wanted to make sure Ali knew how to throw "working" punches—the kind a wrestler would throw in a match—so as not to do actual damage. That was why Ali was peppering me with bunches of fluttering working punches in LA. Bill had asked me and his son, Joel, to fly out to the Champ's house and capture some vignettes with Ali for the upcoming TV shows.

"I wanna show you something," the Champ said as he walked down his massive hallway. I immediately followed; anything Ali thought interesting enough to show me, I was going to look at. I watched him walk and noticed, even though he was only retired four years, that he was a little more unsteady; a little slower than I remembered from his boxing days.

We ended up in the huge attic of his house where I spotted title belts and gifts from world leaders and celebrities flowing out of the boxes they were informally packed in.

"Look at all this stuff," he said with a smile. One of the boxes had the corner of a gold garment hanging out. "You like that?" he asked as he saw my eyes drawn to the gold. I wasn't even sure what it was. "Does your mama like Elvis?" Ali asked as he hurried to the box and pulled out a gold jumpsuit.

"Absolutely, she does," I replied.

"Why don't you take that home to her," he said as he handed it to me. "Because I'm sure she would love it."

"What is it?" I asked, as I held it at arm's length to get a better look.

The Champ replied, "That's a jumpsuit that Elvis gave me in his dressing room after one of his Las Vegas Hilton shows. It's never even been cleaned so his sweat is still on it."

"Champ, I can't take this," I said as I tried to hand it back. "It just wouldn't be right."

"You can have it," he said.

"No, really, I couldn't."

"Alright," he said, as he dug through another box. "But it's there if you change your mind."

Having something belonging to Elvis wasn't a big deal to the Champ. Nor was being generous. He just wanted to show a stranger from Oklahoma some cool things from down through the years. His belts, his robes, photographs, magazines. There were all just lying there.

That evening, with the Champ's permission, I used his home phone to call my mom collect in Oklahoma. She was totally in agreement that I shouldn't be rude enough to take such a precious gift from the Champ. Truth is, I also wanted to call home so that I could obtain Ali's home phone number, which would show up on Mom's phone bill at the end of the month. I didn't want to share the number with another living soul—nor would I ever call it. But I did certainly want to have bragging rights to my friends back home in Oklahoma that I had the personal phone number of the Greatest.

We spent our week shooting vignettes and promos, practicing the working punch and talking about everything. Ali would begin a thought and twenty minutes later I would be even more engaged than I was at the beginning. He had a way of crafting a position, a story, a life lesson, and wrapping it around the most entertaining delivery. I knew I was blessed to be in Ali's presence. And wrestling put me there.

I learned a lot. I met an idol, spent time in his home, took his "punches," watched his magic tricks—but most of all listened.

* * *

"Goodbye, my Oklahoman friend," he said to me as I was leaving on the final day. We had the footage we needed and our job at the Champ's house was done.

"Yeah," I said, not really wanting to leave.

"Wanna see a magic trick?" he asked.

I dropped my bags and followed him back into his house. Champ didn't have to ask twice. He seemed happy to have the company, and I was happy to spend some more time with him.

Elvis Presley's gold jumpsuit remained in the possession of Muhammad Ali, but the Champ and I would reconvene several weeks later in New Orleans at the Hyatt Regency across from the Super Dome. We shared a two-bedroom suite with a common living area for three days and nights while doing media and PR for the Dome show. Bill even managed to get him a one-day gig back in Oklahoma, at a rich oilman's son's birthday party, for a cool $25k. Cowboy flew Ali to the birthday bash on his private plane.

As Ali and I walked down Bourbon Street together, he was like the Pied Piper as patrons and entertainers alike filed out of the colorful Nola establishments and followed us up and down the historic section of the city. I watched as Ali talked to person after person about our big Dome show. He rhymed and laughed and charmed. One by one, group by group, they were buying tickets to see the Champ "skin that snake."

The crowds got so intense around us that our only way out was a ride back to the Hyatt in a police vehicle. It was only when I got inside the hotel that I realized the Champ had invited back a group of people so he could regale stories, show them magic tricks, and talk until the early hours.

When the Big Cowboy arrived in Nola the next morning, he took one look at me and said, "What in the hell have you been doing? You look like death!"

I had no issue telling my boss that I simply was trying to keep up with Muhammad Ali, and it was proving to take a lot more stamina than I had as a mere mortal. Ali had the most amazing motor of anyone I have ever met or been around in my lifetime.

We had hours of chats about women—lots of women—racism, our country's future, Frazier, Foremen, promoters, how he and his camp made extra money in an era when boxing stars—especially black boxing stars—still did not make what they deserved or earned. We talked extensively about food and the wonderful meals that our mothers prepared for us growing up, Ali in Louisville and me in Oklahoma, and how we loved going to Dooky Chase's restaurant in Nola.

I also found out first-hand how big a fan of pro wrestling Ali was— especially the promo skills of Gorgeous George and Freddie Blassie. "I heard them wrestlers talk," he said. "And I saw the people listen. Now really listen. Some of the crowd wanted to kill them, some of them wanted to cheer them, but all of them paid to see them."

Gorgeous George and Freddie Blassie shaped the amazing verbal stylings that Muhammad developed over his unduplicated career.

But the Champ's mouth didn't stop Jake from worrying about his fists.

On the day of the Dome show, we were in the locker room and Bill decided to show Ali how to throw a working punch.

"He's worried you're going to clip him for real," Bill said about Jake.

Jake stood up and replied, "Who wants to take one of those punches? Would you?" he asked.

As the Cowboy demonstrated on Jake, Ali winked at me, and I knew Bill and Jake were getting the same routine Ali had given me at poolside back in California.

"So you do what again?" Ali asked, pretending not to know.

"You just—" Bill said as he threw another punch. "Just—" He threw another one. Jake was not enjoying this tutoring session.

Finally, Ali nodded and said, "I think I got it. I should be OK by the time we get out there." The Champ smiled at me as he left. It looked like he enjoyed watching Jake panic.

"Look, if he hurts you, I'll take care of you," Bill said to Jake. Wrestlers had no workers comp and generally paid their own medical and dental bills. So I understood Jake being leery.

"I don't know how his working punch is going to look," Bill proclaimed. "But however it goes, you're gonna have to sell the hell out of it."

I don't think it was the pain of getting hit that was aggravating Jake. It was the fact that if he was to get legit knocked out he would be worthless in the territory, as it would be hard to come back the next week as a threat to the good guys.

But when the time came, Ali, of course, threw beautiful working punches. They looked great, and he didn't hurt Jake one bit. Jake, however, decided that he needed to protect Jake, so he didn't sell the punches as the knockout blows Bill Watts wanted them to be. By contrast, young and up-and-coming John Nord, the Barbarian, a 6-foot-8 monster out of Minnesota, bounced around like a ping-pong ball for the Champ.

But nothing could get the Snowman to the level Bill wanted him at—not even the Ali connection, not the multiple 10-second wins he got on TV and house shows over established stars.

But on that night in the Dome, the Greatest had the crowd on their feet one more time as he peppered Jake "The Snake" Roberts and the Barbarian with rapid-fire, smooth as silk working punches that he perfected on my Oklahoman face.

Chapter Twenty

GOING NATIONAL

1985

"If my value to this company is locked in where it is now, then I'm going to have to look elsewhere to make some money," I said to Cowboy. I knew I was being paid at least $25,000 less than the booker, but I was responsible for promotion of the live events, TV syndication, TV promos, and ad packages, plus being an on-air talent and part of the booking meetings myself. I wasn't posturing or trying to leverage anything—only my track record. When Bill had previously given me a raise I was thrilled, but I didn't have nearly the level of responsibility or workload that I had when I sat in front of him this time.

"How about I bump you up $25,000?" he said. Just like that. I was hoping for a raise, but I didn't expect to get parity with the booker. "Deal," I quickly replied. I'd hoped my raise in money would go some way to making things a little better at home. Bill put out his hand and I shook it accordingly. A six-figure salary was extraordinary money for someone in the "office." I knew it, and I was adamant that I would work even harder to earn it. I saw the bump in money as an even bigger sign of faith in the work I was doing. I was determined to repay that faith, and then some, by upping my game *and* my workload.

Thing was, I had no more to give. I just didn't know it.

Wrestling already had my every waking moment. I was both obsessed and worn down by it; it had a constant need for attention. Realistically, I had no more time or effort to give over to the business but, by God, I was going to try. Less sleep, more hustle, less time for my kids, more wrestling. My dangerous pattern not improving whatsoever.

Little did I know that deals were being made to elevate Mid-South from a touring, mostly regional promotion to a national brand.

The opportunity came when, a year before, WWF programming appeared without warning or announcement on Ted Turner's Superstation. Vince McMahon was expanding, and saw the national exposure that Georgia Championship Wrestling was getting with WTBS. McMahon wanted to buy the GCW timeslot so he would own all the nationally-televised professional wrestling TV shows in the United States. Turner turned down McMahon's offer without hesitation. Ted never liked Vince, and the feeling seemed to be mutual.

If Vince couldn't get on the air through Turner's TV station, he saw an opportunity to get on the air via Georgia Championship Wrestling itself. GCW was owned by four men: Ole Anderson, Jack and Gerry Brisco, and Jim Barnett. The Briscos and Barnett agreed to sell their share of the company to McMahon. WWF found its path onto WTBS—and on the Saturday night time slot Vince originally wanted—due to McMahon becoming the majority owner of GCW.

Out of nowhere, fans who were accustomed to seeing predominantly NWA wrestling, dating back to 1951, were "treated" to WWF pre-taped matches from across the nation. Gordon Solie, the voice of Georgia wrestling for over a decade, was suddenly gone and no mention was made of him. Viewer response, especially throughout the South, wasn't pretty, and TBS was flooded with calls complaining about the new wrestling programming. Turner, too, was irate with McMahon's maneuvering *and* his programming, as it just contained match clips and canned interviews that did little to engage the viewer.

At first, Turner contracted Columbus/Macon promoter Fred Ward, his son-in-law Ralph Freed, and Ole Anderson to produce a Saturday morning show to counter the WWF's presence. *Championship Wrestling from Georgia* brought wrestling back into the TBS studio. But with the 9:35 a.m. time slot, the shows were airing at 6:35 a.m. on the West Coast. The ratings were not good, and the talent roster gradually began to decline.

Turner needed to look elsewhere.

He had always liked Bill since Watts's days of booking the Georgia territory, so Ted asked Cowboy about putting Mid-South programming on his network, too.

"Turner doesn't want Vince on his station," Bill told me. "He needs a few weeks to get McMahon off there, but in the meantime he wants us to make our mark."

"National?" I asked.

Bill smiled and nodded. "This is a huge opportunity for us. Could be life changing."

Watts always felt that he could compete with WWF if he had the right opportunity. And this was the opportunity. The contract was for thirteen weeks with the hope that if the ratings were good, and with Vince gone, Turner was going to hand over the Saturday 6:05–8:05 slot to Watts to produce a studio show in Atlanta. New talent was coming in and we were ready for the big time. There were changes everywhere.

Especially with me.

My workaholic nature began to adversely affect my personal relationships in a harsh way—especially when it came to being a father. Crown Royal and a little marijuana enabled me to self-medicate enough to stay on the road. Being impaired also helped me live with myself; the person I was becoming. I was running around in a loop of work, travel, work, and more work.

On top of commentating on TV and being part of the booking meetings off TV, I was also responsible for helping run up to fourteen live events a week which I had to create radio spot buys for. I wrote all the ads, while also recording all TV spots for our local stations. When the promotion and coordination of the live events was done, I had to switch gears to provide daily updates and pitches on the growth and additions to our syndicated TV networks outside our home area. I also taped the local market TV inserts every Wednesday, which meant a full day of preparation on the Tuesday before. I looked after wrestling before I looked after my family or myself. I made sure that TV had everything it needed. I made sure the Boys were set. I made sure ads were sold, venues were booked, my homework was done for commentary, and the promos were shot, sorted, and delivered to the right stations. I looked after hundreds of details a week—except the things I should have been looking after. When it came to my kids, I made sure I met my financial responsibilities, but little else.

* * *

Wrestling was always calling. And its call could be cruel sometimes. Our show on TBS, *Mid-South Wrestling*, not only debuted as the number one program on Superstation, but was the number one program on all of cable—including all of WWF's shows on the USA Network. The first rating of 5.7 for the month of March was a full point ahead of McMahon's *Tuesday Night Titans* on USA. For the three months that *Mid-South Wrestling* aired on TBS, it was the top-rated program of any kind on cable television.

It was also cancelled.

"Turner met Jim Crockett at the yacht club," Watts said. "Crockett offered to get Vince off TBS—if Turner gave him exclusive rights to wrestling on the station."

Vince McMahon, sensing the backlash to his show on TBS, and seeing Watts rising as a national competitor, sold his coveted TV slot to Carolinas/Virginia promoter Jim Crockett for a million dollars. Turner was having a hard time moving Vince off his station because of a clause in the contract that stated *McMahon* had the right to sell the contract to another promoter if his show was canceled or forced off the Superstation. Vince sold the remaining weeks of the TBS contract to Jim Crockett Jr.—with a clause that Crockett's show would be the exclusive wrestling broadcast on TBS.

So Vince was gone from TBS, but so was Watts.

Cowboy had nine weeks remaining on his TBS deal, where both Crockett and Cowboy were on station. In our final month, *Mid-South Wrestling* averaged a 5.5 rating for the May sweeps. Crockett's *World Championship Wrestling* averaged a 4.8.

Even on the way out, Mid-South was the ratings leader.

As quickly as the dream slot on TBS came, it went.

Again, Cowboy wanted to talk to the folks at home. "This is our last show," he said down the camera. "We've enjoyed becoming reacquainted with so many of you in the Atlanta area and the people we've heard from across the nation. The Crockett organization is going to produce the exclusive wrestling programs for WTBS. They're a fine organization and I encourage all of you to be as loyal to them as you have been to us these last thirteen weeks."

I secretly hoped for Watts and Crockett to team up, because both men together could have taken the number one spot in wrestling. But it wasn't to be.

After the last show was over, I walked to Cowboy's office and took a seat in silence.

"Turner didn't keep his word," Bill said as he sat at his desk in disbelief. "He screwed me." I could see the Cowboy was hurting. We were both burned out by the wrestling business—but neither of us were willing to admit it.

"What's the plan?" I asked.

"We go national," Watts replied.

"But . . ."

"We change, we evolve, we go national," Bill said. "You with me?"

As tired and as beat up as I was, I didn't even have to think about it. I put out my hand for him to shake, just like he put out his hand for me to shake when I asked for a raise. I knew that the tiny amount of time I had for my family was about to get even less.

Even though Verne Gagne's American Wrestling Association had a tenous claim to "being national" with an ESPN contract, with Watts throwing his Cowboy hat into the ring it really meant that there were going to be three legitimate national wrestling companies in the US: Watts, Crockett, and McMahon.

"If we're going to compete with these guys, we need to change our name," Cowboy said. "Something less regional."

"You got anything in mind?" I asked.

"I certainly do," he replied.

I needn't have asked. Of course he did.

PART THREE

UWF

1986–1987

Chapter Twenty-One

THE EXPANSION

1986

"I'm going to put you with Michael, so we get more of a Ying and a Yang," Cowboy said. At that time, Jesse Ventura was catching fire as a heel commentator on WWF TV alongside Vince McMahon. "Michael is going to bring out the heel perspective that the audience mightn't want to hear, but is true."

I nodded along. Whatever the plan was, I was all-in as usual. The "Michael" Cowboy was talking about was Michael P.S. Hayes—one third of the notorious Fabulous Freebirds. Watts never usually considered using an active talent on commentary, but he knew how good Michael was at catching people's attention with his mouth. And, quite frankly, The Freebirds were a better in-ring team with Buddy and Terry—with Michael's forte really being on mic.

"You ready to rock?" Hayes asked me in his gravel toned voice as we waited to go on air. I was indeed "ready to rock."

"You take the nuts and bolts of this deal," he said, "and I'll do what I was put here to do."

"Put on this Earth to do, or at this desk to do?" I asked.

"Both, Jim," he replied as the show began. "Both."

Our newly named Universal Wrestling Federation was being syndicated nationally and receiving a reputation as the best wrestling show in the country. Watts's plan to rival WWF was simple in its execution: "We put on a great, by Gawd, wrestling show," he said.

Now that I could understand.

We had the roster to do it, too. "Dr. Death" Steve Williams, One Man Gang, "Hot Stuff" Eddie Gilbert, along with the beautiful Missy Hyatt, "Hacksaw" Jim Duggan, Bill Irwin, The Fantastics, Ted DiBiase, Chris Adams, Terry Taylor, Rick Steiner, The Fabulous Freebirds, and Sting, among others.

We continued to run shows in our strongholds like Oklahoma, Texas, Louisiana, and Mississippi, but also traveled out around, including out West, in correlation with Watts's national expansion. At one time we actually used the Southwest Airlines routing map to build our expansion.

Looking at Michael, I could tell he liked the gig. He was smart enough to know that the more hats he wore, the more valuable he was to anyone who wanted to hire him. He had a creative mind which the company could see right away. He was personable and entertaining, but sometimes a pain in the ass—especially with booking ideas. But if he was supposed to be at a booking meeting and he missed it, Bill didn't wait on him. The meeting started and ended on Cowboy's time. But Michael was a Freebird in and out of the ring. It wasn't his "character," it was his mentality—his way of thinking. That's why he, Buddy, and Terry were so good: they weren't playing the roles of renegade Southern rockers—they were exactly that.

Michael's mix of unpredictability meshed well with my sports-like approach. I was a regular at the booking and TV meetings now and knew precisely the direction that Bill wanted us to go in; the way he wanted his roster spoken about. Cowboy had definite ideas as to how to describe a heel and to describe a babyface. Adjectives. Descriptors.

"Babyfaces are not stupid," he'd say over and over again. "There are no redeeming social qualities in a heel. I don't want to hear that the heel's a family man. I don't want people to like the son of a bitch in any shape or fashion."

There was 42 minutes of content, and Cowboy wanted every segment to have meaning. He hated throw-away minutes; everything had to have significance in some shape, form, or fashion.

"You know Watts stiffed me on the Superdome payoff," Michael whispered to me across the table just before show time.

I did know. Everyone knew. Not that Watts did or didn't underpay him, but that Michael sure felt like Watts did.

Hayes's heel approach would push the right buttons in me, because just like he *was* a Freebird, I was always me out there, too. I'd take it personally for that 42 minutes because I wanted to come across to viewers that I was damn sure pissed off, or concerned, or fearful for a wrestler's safety or welfare, his livelihood. And I wanted to sound real because to me it *was* real; it had been drilled into my mind that you called everything like it was a real sporting event. That's how I learned. That's how I was programmed. Michael, being an old-school guy, had the same mindset. On TV, the bad guys were dirty, no-good antagonistic bastards..

Just like how I felt off camera.

I was starting to feel down; like I was heading into a dark place. I knew I should have said it to someone, but that wasn't the way men were taught to deal with their thoughts. I swore to myself that after the store failed that I would never, ever find myself in that position of failure again. I would never let my folks down, my family down again. I would work all hours, day and night, to make sure that I wasn't a write-off two times in my life. But that drive and obsession dragged me into a ditch. Instead of talking to a professional to get some help, I went to see a bartender. I was drinking, smoking, working, sleeping a little, and repeating the process over and over again. I believed 100 percent in what we were doing. I saw Watts work even harder than me. I saw the crowd reactions and the ratings coming in. We were doing monster numbers on our TV show. It was working. All the work was coming back to us in the form of happy TV programmers and more interested syndication opportunities. We were now on 120 local channels across the USA and growing nationally.

All of this was happening. All of what I thought would make me happy was coming to together. But none of it made me feel better. None of it was helping to drag me back out of the dark spot I found myself in. All the work did was gave me a little time to forget just how badly I thought of myself in my own head.

As I looked across at Cowboy Bill Watts, I could see fleeting signs that he might have been going through the same.

Chapter Twenty-Two

THE DECLINE AND SALE

1987

The oil industry collapsed, taking down our core cities with it. Bill was counting on those towns to carry the UWF while he built the new markets with our nationwide expansion. Around the heartland of what was called Mid-South Wrestling, there was a real recession going on. Businesses were closing, people were losing their houses. Even Southern Nazarene University and Oklahoma City University almost went under. Expanding nationally was the right idea—at the wrong time in the economy. Buying wrestling tickets just wasn't at the front of people's thoughts. They were more worried about how they were going to pay their bills and buy groceries.

Cowboy was worried about the same thing.

It's not like he forgot how to book, or forgot the fundamentals that kept the company strong. Our TV ratings were stronger than an acre of garlic, right to the end. The UWF didn't lose even *one* station because of ratings. People still had the emotional investment in the brand, but they could fill the void by watching it on TV. The shows were packaged with the Memphis, World Class, and AWA promotions, along with Joe Pedicino's *Pro Wrestling This Week* show, in national syndication with advertisers such as Selsun Blue and Aspercreme buying the package. However, Bill couldn't hold out financially any longer. He began to lose top stars such as "Hacksaw" Jim Duggan and Ted DiBiase to WWF, as word was coming back that Watts's former top star, JYD, had his own action figure that pulled in $150,000 annually—or so we were told.

"Bill," I said, "I've got an idea."

Cowboy was listening. He was burnt out and ready to hear other suggestions.

"Why don't you sell?" I said. "I could ask Crockett if he was interested in buying."

I didn't know if Watts was going to hug me or kill me for even bringing the suggestion up.

"Two million," he said.

"Excuse me?" I mean, I heard him but was taken by surprise at just how quickly and easily he essentially said yes to selling his company.

"You get us two million and I'm out."

* * *

I was making more money than I ever had in my life, but I was living at the Quality Inn in Glenpool, Oklahoma, now estranged from my second wife. I was pretty much just existing as a human being, but as a "wrestling guy" I knew this was the biggest day of my career. Cowboy asked me to handle some business; to see if there was a way for his company and Crockett's to do some joint ventures. But really that was only to get me in the door. I was going to sell the company.

Crockett was gearing up for his biggest run at McMahon and, on paper, Crockett seemed to have a better shot at competing with WWF than Watts did. Cowboy went deep into debt organizing his national television syndication affiliates; he over-leveraged by signing wrestlers to exclusive contracts and was losing up to $50,000 a week. More importantly, his passion for the business was leaving him rapidly.

I knew what my play was. I could see what was coming over the horizon and knew how best to shift gears to not only survive the oncoming realities, but make sure everyone benefitted.

I came in as a gopher, taking notes and buying cigars and whiskey for Leroy—now I found myself on a private jet, just me and the pilot, as I made my way to MillionAir hangar in Atlanta. While in the air I thought of Bill the day before. Cowboy looked tired, almost melancholy. His words were of a man who was still willing to fight, but I knew him long enough to know that his heart was no longer in it.

When I landed in Atlanta, Crockett and his right-hand man, Rob Garner, were waiting for me in a conference room at the terminal. There was no food ordered, no drinks had; it was just straight business. Neither Crockett nor Watts was setting the world on fire with their promotions, and I spent twenty minutes talking to Crockett and Garner about how both companies should come together if they wanted to continue to challenge Vince. In truth, I was trying to read the room and see just how big Crockett's appetite was for continuing to compete with McMahon.

"Cause you know," I said, as the meeting was coming to a close. "If you weren't willing to team up, then Watts might think of selling."

I could see on both men's faces that this news was of huge curiosity to them. Not solely because *they* might have been interested in buying, but that they knew *McMahon* would be.

"Now, the way I see it," I continued, "is that if you were to buy Watts out, you could have yourself a Super Bowl—except you'd own both teams." Crockett's face wasn't telling me much. I didn't know if he was interested or not, but I was "in" now, so decided to keep going. "You keep your show on TBS and you put UWF on there, too. Have your NWA guys win an equal amount and your UWF guys win an equal amount until you cash in once a year with *Supershow*, pitting one league against the other."

"How much?" Crockett replied.

"I expect McMahon will have interest, but we're coming to you first," I said, ignoring his question.

"How much?" Crockett asked again.

Bill's two million price tag was on the tip of my tongue.

"Four million," I said.

Crockett nodded. My personal split was going to be 5 percent of the overall sale price. I brought up the number to give me some room to negotiate.

I could see Crockett wanted UWF, he wanted to double his efforts to compete with Vince, and Watts had 120 individual TV contracts that would hugely help in that regard.

My percentage of a deal would give me room to plan my own next move. I wanted to go home, but I had nothing to go home to.

"Tell Bill to call me," Crockett said as he and Garner left the room.

After they left, I waited a respectable amount of time to make sure both men were gone before calling Bill from a payphone. This time I had a calling card and didn't have to call collect as Gene Kiniski.

This was twice what he asked for—and just as importantly to a stubborn, prideful man like Cowboy, this was a "respectable" way out of the wrestling business. He wouldn't be seen as beaten; he would be seen as someone who sold his company at a price he couldn't walk away from.

"Bill," I said as Cowboy answered the phone.

And in the middle of an airport terminal in Atlanta, I told the man who brought me into the business that I just "sold" the company which started my career.

PART FOUR

Crockett

1987–1988

Chapter Twenty-Three

CROCKETT

1987

Watts finalized the details of selling his company.

Jim Crockett Jr. would buy the Universal Wrestling Federation in a deal that promised both companies would be run like two separate leagues under the same organization. Both "brands" would be kept separate, with distinct rosters and championships. I decided to keep going in the business, too, but my role would now be of "just" an announcer. Crockett already had people to run his promotion, advertising, and live event divisions. And he had the larger-than-life Dusty Rhodes booking his shows.

He assumed the office space that Watts had decided on in Dallas for his national expansion, and Garner, JJ Dillion, Dusty, and others followed Jimmy to buy homes and live that Dallas lifestyle. I packed up my dark blue two-door Lincoln Continental and drove myself, and everything I owned, to Dallas as well. For the first time in my professional wrestling career, I was going to be solely an on-air talent, and I could feel the pressure of trying to be all things to all people slowly lift from my shoulders.

As I walked around the new dressing room, I could see that it was more-or-less the same as all the dressing rooms I'd seen before. There was smoke and ribbing, people telling stories, others catching up on sleep. There were card games and jostling, hangovers and ball-breaking. Professional wrestling, behind the curtain, was like a sophomore locker room for oversized men; some with oversized egos.

And I felt totally at home.

Whatever was coming my way, I felt I had the skill and experience to handle it. Live TV, on-air interviews, press, booking, commentary, advertising, syndication ideas, and contacts; I felt more than adequate handling them all. My thirteen years in the business so far were wide-ranging and diverse, and in my new company I was never as happy to have such a broad range of experience under my brand new brown leather belt.

I could see I wasn't starting over totally new, as there were some familiar faces working for Crockett that had passed through Mid-South more than once. When I first saw Marty Lunde a few years earlier, he was working as a preliminary wrestler in Mid-South. I knew right away he was going to be good—and way better than "good" if he could find the right persona to bring in front of the TV cameras. Even as a rookie, he never looked bad or lost in the ring. He also carried himself as an old-school guy, which doesn't just mean he knew how to work in and out of a hammerlock—although he certainly did know that. What impressed me was that he also knew the value of his job; that he was there to learn, not to be late, or lay on his ass. If Marty was ever told to fix something, he never had to be told twice. He got it right then and there. He had the personality of a gentleman outside the ring, but the look of a classic heel inside of it. Becoming Arn Anderson worked perfectly for him. Marty was now a part of, and surrounded by, the hottest wrestlers in the company. I saw the Four Horsemen as I walked on by, and I could tell immediately that these guys were as tight off-screen as they were on it. They loved every single facet of the "rockstar" lifestyle—none more than their bleached blond heavyweight champion, Ric Flair.

Flair had come to work for Watts several times, even though Watts operated outside the National Wrestling Alliance, the body of promoters that sanctioned all of the NWA World Heavyweight Champion's matches. Watts convinced the powers that be that having him book Flair from time-to-time lessened the NWA's likelihood of an anti-trust lawsuit. After all, how could they be a monopoly if Watts was promoting their champion?

When the Champ came to town, it was my job to tag along and make sure "The Nature Boy" got everything he needed. That, more often than not, meant bar time. Serious bar time. I was a willing accomplice in many long nights and near-scrapes when Flair was in town. He was a machine who had a non-stop engine for drinking, womanizing, traveling, over-spending, and wrestling.

As I walked by, "The Naitch" and I shared a smile and a knowing nod. He had already put out the good word about me and what I could do for the Boys on commentary.

"Jim," Crockett said, as he approached me from his office. "You're going to be play-by-play and Bob here is going to be color."

"Bob" was Bob Caudle, a long-time wrestling announcer for the Crocketts who also had held several other TV jobs, including weatherman, kids show host, and late-night news anchor. Bob Caudle was the true voice of Mid-Atlantic wrestling for the Crockett family.

An impeccably dressed man who wore thick glasses, Bob shook my hand and smiled kindly. Crockett continued, "Jim, you'll start each segment and Bob will join in where a little color is appropriate."

We both nodded in agreement and Crockett left us to see to other matters. I was concerned how Bob might see me coming in and taking over the play-by-play end of things. What Crockett wanted was for Bob to stand aside and let me take the lead; a position that Bob had held with Crockett for years.

"Bob," I said. "I don't have any agendas about wanting to lead off the segments."

"Oh, Jim, it's OK," he replied. "That's what they want. It's no problem at all." What a class act, which, at times, can be a rarity in this business.

I don't know if Bob knew a German suplex from a gutwrench suplex, but that wasn't his forte. He was a storyteller who understood human nature, human emotion, and good-versus-evil. And he knew how to fit right in with his broadcast partner and represent a fan's perspective without becoming a one-dimensional, milquetoast "good guy" cheerleader. As I got to know Bob, it quickly became clear that in a business that's always had a prominent underbelly, Bob stood head and shoulders above 99 percent of everyone I had met in wrestling thus far. I watched how he interacted with others and took mental notes. Even though I had been in the business for well over a decade at this point, I never stopped watching and learning.

Bob and I were placed on the B-shows for Crockett, with the lead team of Tony Schiavone and David Crockett announcing for the *Worldwide Wrestling* show that aired first on the local markets. It was my goal from the second I entered that first day, in Richmond Coliseum, that I would eventually make the lead announce team on TBS. The Superstation was a national star-maker and, in my world, it was that national stage where the best announcers plied their trade.

"Jim," Crockett said as he whizzed past again, "we're going out for some drinks tonight, if you're interested."

I didn't have to be asked twice. I was a newly single guy, in a new job, in a new city.

"Who's tagging along?" I asked.

"Me, you, and Dusty," he replied.

"Yes, sir," I said.

Me, the boss, and the booker. I knew this was a great opportunity to show them both just how professional, trustworthy, and mature I was.

* * *

About six hours later, Dusty Rhodes and I were drunkenly standing in Jim Crockett's driveway ready to do battle. Crockett was watching closely as "The American Dream" and I squared off; our breath smelled of liquor and our steps toward each other were more than a little wobbly. This was the time and place for two specimens like myself and Dusty Rhodes to prove who the better man was. And we were going to do it using a time-honored, American tradition.

"You sure you want this, bay-bay?" Dusty asked through his familiar lisp.

"You bet your ass I do," I replied.

"Alright, man. You asked for it."

My first night on the job and I found myself in the driveway of my new boss at 2 a.m., about to challenge the booker of the company to a game of HORSE.

"You both agree to the rules?" Crockett asked. He was about the same level of hammered as we were.

"It's pretty straightforward, Jimmy," Dusty replied as he bounced the basketball with intent. "Hundred bucks says I whoop Jim Ross's Oklahoma ass."

I reached for my money like John Wayne reaching for his gun. Except I was pretty drunk and couldn't remember where my wallet was. Dusty pointed to the floor.

"Thank you," I said as I stooped to reclaim my wallet. How it got there, I have no idea. "A hundred?" I asked.

"A hundred is what I heard," Crockett replied. His wife was at the top window of their house, anxiously looking down on three drunk fools making noise in her driveway.

"Watch this guy," Dusty said to Crockett about me. "These Okies are born cheaters." Dream bounced the ball in my direction. My hands were too drunk to protect my face, and it took me a minute to realize I had just been hit in the nose with it.

"Oh, Spalding, right in the kisser," Crockett said as he and Dusty creased over with laughter.

I was having a hard time focusing on Crockett's house, never mind the basketball hoop attached to it. In normal circumstances I would have been competitive in a high stakes game like HORSE, but on this night my motor functions were a little impaired. The only thing that gave me hope was watching Dusty struggle just as much as I was. For all his trash talking and court psychology, Dream was as shit-faced as me. It was like if the NBA only recruited chubby, Caucasian players and this was Game 7.

Both Dusty and I took roughly a thousand shots each before we finally made the five, H-O-R-S-E, count. We were out there so long that neither of us even noticed Crockett going to bed and turning off the lights on his driveway. Dusty and I were Texas vs. Oklahoma, mano-a-mano, "stocky" commentator versus "stocky" wrestler. We were impaired, having fun, talking trash—and full of hope.

Between the failed shots and heavy laughs, we talked wrestling, the future. We knew how lucky we were to be on the verge of something new and exciting. The hundred-dollar bill passed hands a few times over the course of the night, but what stayed put was the sense that we understood each other.

"Vince ain't going to give up that easy," Dusty said as we finally walked away from Crockett's house. He had the basketball under his arm and my hundred bucks in his pocket.

"I know," I replied.

The sale of UWF to Crockett promotions was either going to catch fire or flame out. I had a feeling we were going to find out quickly as to which it was going to be.

"So how badly are you going to tell people that I beat you?" Dusty asked as we shared the last beer on our walk back toward his Mercedes.

"I'll tell them you whooped my ass," I replied.

"Smart."

"I'm not dumb enough to beat the booker."

"Really smart."

Chapter Twenty-Four

LET THE GAMES BEGIN

1987

I rented a condo in Dallas that had a communal pool, and that communal pool was frequented by ladies, which meant I was always feeling communal for some reason. I was making good money—roughly the same six figures I was making with Bill—and working a much lighter schedule. I was in the sun, meeting new people, enjoying my Crown Royal and the occasional herb, while hoping a permanent place would present itself for me on TBS.

As I lay poolside with the sun beating down on me, I couldn't get a simple sentence out of my head: "Oh, you're renting? I thought you were one of the smart guys in this business, Jim."

Jimmy Crockett, my new boss, had made the passing comment a few days before and it started to bother me.

Did he think I wasn't committed enough to buy a house in Dallas because I didn't have faith in his company? Did he think I wasn't smart enough to see the benefits of buying a house? Did he think I couldn't afford it?

Whatever it was, my ego and paranoia began to double-team me. Perception was truly reality in the wrestling business. That's why the parking lot outside Crockett's new Dallas office looked like a Cadillac dealership. Everyone on top of the organization was "living the life"—none more so than Crockett himself. Limos, fur coats, Rolex watches; the company even had *two* private planes. One an older, 14-seat Gulfstream—the "Jabroni Jet"—that sounded creaky inflight, and the other a 10-seat Falcon that Crockett called "Startdust," after booker Dusty Rhodes.

I had no jet. No Rolex. No limo. And no house.

Exactly one week later I still had no jet, no Rolex, and no limo. But I was moving into my new house—a house I didn't need and didn't want. Perception was everything, and I wasn't going to let it be said that Jim Ross wasn't smart or dedicated. Even if it meant spending every last penny I had.

* * *

For two companies whose public faces were not to view the other as competition, Jim Crockett Promotions and WWF sure didn't act like it. Both sides traded swift and damaging blows to their openers, with McMahon very much coming out on top.

As Crockett got ready for our company's first pay-per-view (PPV), Vince McMahon primed his reply from his Connecticut offices. Crockett's "Starrcade" had been the lone Thanksgiving-night wrestling show since its 1983 debut—but everything was changing in the wrestling business, and old traditions didn't mean anything to the man who was running WWF.

Starrcade was about to get head-to-head company.

Cable companies at first saw an opportunity to market a wrestling double-header—Starrcade from Crockett and a new concept called "Survivor Series" from McMahon. But Vince, of course, had other ideas. The WWF head honcho was coming off the incredible success of WrestleMania III, with Hogan defeating Andre, so he had the clout to tell cable providers that they would have to choose between offering Survivor Series *or* Starrcade. However, any company that chose Starrcade over Survivor Series would not be able to carry next year's WrestleMania IV.

I felt it was a bluff, because there was no way Vince was going to stop his baby, WrestleMania, from being carried by every single company that could air it. His national expansion had not yet paid off to the point that WWF could afford to sacrifice the cash flow that a widely-aired 'Mania could bring. Of course, the cable companies didn't know if McMahon had the balls to stick to his guns or not, so of the dozens who had committed to airing Starrcade, only five actually did—and the loss of planned revenue crippled Crockett out of the gate.

Also, it didn't help that we were main-eventing with Ric Flair versus Ronnie Garvin—but with Flair in the unusual role of challenger. Garvin had won the belt from Flair couple of months before, which I thought was a mistake—and not because of Garvin's ability, as he was a hell of a worker, but because Ronnie just wasn't terribly charismatic and didn't project a lot of personality in interviews. And the way the run up to the match was booked did Garvin no favors either. Crockett announced that Garvin would have a 45-day period of no title defenses to allow him time to prepare for the Starrcade cage match against Flair. Garvin, who won the title with zero buildup beforehand, needed to be seen defending the belt to give him credibility as champion. Instead, it looked like he was getting protection from the promotion.

To make matters worse, not only was Vince hobbling Starrcade, but Crockett's own booking was doing a good hatchet job on the event as well. When Flair pinned Garvin to regain the belt on November 26, 1987, at Starrcade, the Chicago crowd roared its approval—even though Ric was the heel.

It only got worse two months later, when Crockett attempted his second pay-per-view, "The Bunkhouse Stampede." This time McMahon partnered with USA Network, the home of WWF's *Prime Time Wrestling* show, to air a free special called "Royal Rumble." Again, on the same day. That move hurt not only Crockett financially, but the cable companies as well. Those companies missed out on their share of pay-per-view revenue due to a free special that netted them *nothing*.

The battle spread to the venues, too. Vince dispatched Ed Cohen, who was a rock star in the arena management world, to negotiate a "prime tenant" clause in all WWF contracts with the buildings. This meant no other wrestling company could use those venues for 60 days before and after WWF was booked in them. This, of course, put huge strategic pressure on Crockett. It made the touring aspect of his promotion way more difficult that it should have been. If he could find the right venue, then he found it hard to get the right dates. If he nailed down the right dates, he'd find it hard to find a venue that hadn't already signed an agreement with Vince.

Cohen even tried to sew up Louisiana by going to see the athletic commission appointed by the Governor there, Edwin Edwards. Now, I had personal knowledge of just how Edwards and Louisiana operated, as I visited him a couple of times when I worked for Watts and McGuirk. The State of Louisiana, through the State Athletic Commission, only sanctioned one pro-boxing license and one pro-wrestling license per year. In the early days, I was sent to Edward's office with an envelope to make sure the wrestling license wasn't an issue. I was around a business where charisma paid the bills, but Edwin Edwards was by far the most charismatic man I had ever met at that point in my life.

"I'm a little concerned for you coming down here with cash," Edwards said to me once. "Tell your people I'll take a check from now on."

He was concerned for *me*. Not himself, but me. Edwards considered himself untouchable and above any move to highlight just how corrupt he was. But *me*? Well, I might get caught. So I wasn't surprised when I heard that Ed Cohen was literally laughed out of his meeting with the Louisiana Athletic commission. Apparently, they found it hilarious that McMahon sent a Jew to see them instead of his Southern wife, Linda. Vince was winning street-fight battles all over the US, but Louisiana was a tougher nut to crack. So the WWF's boss put his focus back on PPV.

WrestleMania IV, WWF's biggest show of the year, came shortly after, on March 28, 1988, live on pay-per-view. And, lo and behold, Crockett and Dusty decided that would also be the perfect day to run a free special of their own on TBS, called "Clash of the Champions." They also decided that this would be my first TBS, primetime event to commentate on. I knew this provided me an opportunity to help launch my broadcasting career on a national level. Dusty and Jimmy Crockett tapped me to work with Tony Schiavone—which was a bold move considering that we both were play-by-play guys—but our duo worked nicely. Tony and I had chemistry that couldn't be artificially produced, which I felt was always the key to any broadcast team. It was also the first time I'd work in the famous sports cathedral known as the Greensboro Coliseum.

Going live in prime time, on free, nationwide TV was a huge rush and felt like one of the highlights of my career so far. As I stood there looking around, I knew I had come a long way from the KTBS TV studio in Shreveport. The size, the scope, the majesty of it all made me think I'd made the right decision in coming to Dallas. Unfortunately, my UWF brothers weren't fairing nearly as well. They were booked to look inferior to their Crockett/NWA counterparts. The UWF belts were made to look meaningless and, soon after, wrestler after wrestler began jumping ship to Vince's WWF or looking for work elsewhere.

The Clash of the Champions card was stacked with the main event pitting world champion Ric Flair against Sting, the face-painted powerhouse who was the hottest young star Crockett had. The match went 45 minutes with the only downside of the match being the finish. Three judges sat at ringside, who would score the match and determine a winner if it went the full 45-minute time limit. When it ended, one judge voted for Flair, one for Sting, and the third ruled it a draw. Even when we had Vince on the ropes, we ended up punching ourselves in the balls with flawed creative.

I was happy with my debut on Crockett's national TV show, though. I knew I could do better, but felt I did enough to be kept in contention.

Even the flat finish couldn't negate the Clash's ratings success or change the fact that we had siphoned millions of dollars from WWF's biggest show. At that point, the cable companies did step in because these "free event versus pay-per-view" showdowns were costing them big, no matter which wrestling promotion won the day.

Vince turned his stance around and used his influence to point out just how much Crockett's free show had cost not only him, but the cable carriers, too. Turner suddenly had to field calls from his friends in the cable TV business about how TBS running free shows was hurting their bottom line.

To Vince, wrestling was everything. To Ted, it was just another thing. That simple fact made me kind of nervous for who just might win out this battle in the end.

There were no WWF tactics to contend with when we held our next pay-per-view, "The Great American Bash," but a combination of those costly PPV battles and some poor business decisions by Crockett had already put the company in a dire financial situation. That dire situation was only exacerbated by the fact that Crockett's own accountant—a long-time family friend—didn't report the promotion's five million–dollar hole for nearly a full year after it appeared, or so we were told.

All the talk of money owed and sudden cutbacks made me nervous. I saw in Crockett what I had seen in Cowboy before him. There was a particular look a man got when he was racking up debt, losing a fight, and looking for a way to move on.

Crockett's company had become like a men's club, with hundred-mile journeys that used to take place in packed cars, now taking place in the company jets. The West Coast loops were purposefully based out of Las Vegas where Stardust could fly the Boys to a show, and then back to Sin City to party all night, only to repeat again, over and over, show after show. Vegas became the hub of the West Coast. I was becoming more and more curious as to the company's future even though I got paid according to my contract. My money was late a few times, but they always told me about it ahead of time. Still, I was preparing myself financially and psychologically to take a pay reduction. A blind man could see that Crockett Promotions just couldn't continue as it was. Within months, rumors quickly started floating that TBS was looking to either bail out Crockett or buy the promotion outright.

The wars with Vince, coupled with the out-of-control spending and some curious booking decisions, were destroying the company before it really found its national feet.

Chapter Twenty-Five

RETURNING HOME

1988

I hadn't been home in a while, but I knew what was going on. Or least I knew *one* side of what was going on. My father and I hadn't been on the best of terms since he and my mom separated. I thought I could give it a shot at maybe getting them back together. No one asked me to, but I decided to give it a try anyway.

I met my dad in a greasy spoon restaurant in Stilwell, Oklahoma, "The Strawberry Capital of the World." He was living there now, and seeing another woman in the area. As per usual in our relationship, we made small talk and avoided anything too deep or meaningful as we ate. I paid for lunch. I wanted to. I wanted to show my old man that I had moved on from my failures and had money in my pocket; I wanted him to see that my decision to leave "and run away with the circus" was paying off—at least for now.

My dad and I both finished our meal without me saying what was really on my mind. Outside we had separate cars and I was heading back to Dallas, him back to his new home. He waited for me outside the front door as I put on my jacket and followed him out.

"Well, it was good to see you," he said.

"You too," I replied.

"You take care, son."

There was a moment between us where he left me enough time to say what was obviously on my mind, but I couldn't even form the words properly. Words that I had been rehearsing in my car the whole ride there. He nodded and turned to leave.

"How could you do it?" I blurted out. He stopped. There were a couple of people walking by. He waited for them to pass before replying, but I jumped back in before he could. My heart was racing now; adrenaline flowing. "How could you do it to Mom?"

"There's two sides to every story, son," he said. "Now, I'm sorry that things ended up the way they did between me and your mother, but—"

"But what?" I said, interrupting him. "What the hell was worth this?"

I felt nervous at even cussing in his company.

"You don't know all the facts," he calmly said.

"Like hell I don't," I shouted. "You . . ."

He took a step toward me. People were starting to notice our "conversation."

"Listen, son. You need to know that if you keep talking to me the way you're talking, then there'll be consequences to those words. Son or not, you've no place sticking your nose in. You understand me?"

He waited for my reply. There wasn't anything I could say. He was right. Who the fuck was I to lecture anyone on relationships? I'd only heard my mother's side of things and, in a town as small as ours, she was embarrassed by my father's actions. It broke my heart to think of her putting up with that small-town humiliation every day.

"You got anything else you want to say to me now?" my father asked.

I shook my head. I was still pissed at him, but what was there left to say? He hugged me. "Let's leave it there then," he said as he turned and walked for his pickup truck.

He headed home to a house he obviously wanted to be in with a lady he loved, and I headed back to the house I didn't want, alone.

Chapter Twenty-Six

LAST DAYS OF CROCKETT

1988

"Don't worry, they won't replace you as an announcer," Cowboy said over the phone. He was out of the business, but people like Watts never truly stop taking a keen interest in what's happening.

"What makes you so sure?" I asked as I stood in the house I didn't want and couldn't afford without a monthly check.

"They do TV," he replied. "If Turner buys, he's doing it because he sees it as a TV product. And they're not going to find anyone they like better than you."

"I'm not sure about . . ."

"They're not going to want to disrupt operations," he said, interrupting me. "You've already established yourself. You should probably feel as secure as anyone there."

Coming from someone who understood wrestling and television as well as anyone ever had, that made me feel a lot better. And, as usual, he was right.

"And, Jim, you're going to love Atlanta. It's like the New York of the South."

Bill had lived there while working for Georgia Championship Wrestling in the early '70s. I could hear in his voice that he was missing the hustle of the business a little.

"New York of the South, huh?" I said.

"It's like Sodom and Gomorrah come to life."

Now that I could handle.

While a lot of the Turner Broadcasting suits looked down their noses at wrestling, Ted Turner himself liked it and saw it as the programming that had helped build his UHF Channel 17 in Atlanta into cable Superstation TBS. It had been on the network since the '60s. TBS had always been built on the Atlanta Braves, *The Andy Griffith Show*, the MGM movie library, and wrestling. Ted also liked the notion of competing with Vince McMahon. Plus, the shows always got good ratings, and wrestling provided three hours of first-run programming each weekend.

So as Crockett was going under, I was confident that wrestling would remain on TBS, in some form or fashion. But I didn't know what that form would be—or if it had room for me—so I quietly started exploring other options. I made some inroads with Atlanta radio stations and the Atlanta Falcons. I was getting ready to move again.

For eighteen months, my Atlanta experience had consisted of the drives between the airport, the hotel, and the TBS studios where we taped our weekly programs. After hearing Watts's assessment of the place, I was even more excited to get out of the house I bought and just move.

"Any more word on my 5 percent?" I asked Watts before he hung up. Truth was I already knew the answer. Jim Barnett, the flamboyant former wrestler turned famed promoter, had already given me "the dirt." "Jimsy" loved to gossip about what was going on in the business.

"Well," Cowboy said. "I didn't get my four million, so you won't get your 5 percent either."

"So what will I get?" I asked.

It took me several months to get my answer. I would receive a $10k check from Bill, but he insisted that I fly from Dallas to his hometown in Tulsa to buy him a high-dollar dinner to get the money.

So, from the industry changing deal I initiated, where I got a fraction of what I thought I would, I bought Cowboy a great meal and the rest to finish financing divorce number two.

Who was I to lecture my father on relationships indeed?

PART FIVE

WCW

1988–1993

Chapter Twenty-Seven

HERD, FLAIR, AND THE LADIES IN THE LIMO

1988

"You're dragging the good name of this organization down," my new boss, Jim Herd, shouted at me from the other side of his desk. "You can't go out into public and do whatever you like," he said, as he threw his hands in the air. "I want to know what happened in that limo, Jim?"

I sat there having been informed that Herd already knew full well what happened in the limo. As with a lot of times in my life where my boss was chewing me out, Ric Flair was involved in the story somewhere.

A couple of months before, I had again packed up my dark blue Lincoln Continental and driven myself, and everything I owned, to Atlanta. TBS had taken over operations of Crockett Promotions—and they did so without skipping even a week of production. There was a short meeting, led by a couple of Turner executives, who said there would be some changes made, but it would be a good thing as they were bringing wrestling in as a division under the Turner Broadcasting System's corporate umbrella. For me, it meant becoming a full-fledged employee; receiving corporate retirement benefits and health insurance for the first time in my career. For a guy who started off in the business fetching whiskey and cigars, everything was going great.

The move to the bigger, more modern Centre Stage was an improvement, too, as it immediately changed the atmosphere and look of the show. We still had the benefit of remaining in a controlled environment, but with more people generating more energy, which translated better to TV. On the corporate side, though, World Championship Wrestling—as it was now being called—was the red-headed stepchild of the TBS empire, so the line wasn't exactly long with Turner execs looking to run the company. This is why Jack Petrik—the top TBS executive assigned to WCW—hired his "St. Louis happy hour" friend, Jim Herd, to run the day-to-day operations. During one of their happy hour gatherings, Petrik learned that Herd had directed, among other things, "Sammy" Muchnick's successful St. Louis weekly wrestling show. When Turner came looking for someone to run a "rasslin" company, Petrik knew just the man.

Jim Crockett was moved into a "consulting" role while maintaining a small share in the company, and Jim Herd was assigned the role of WCW Executive Vice President.

Straight off the bat, Herd had a reputation for being gruff and unlikeable; traits that got *me* heat. Yeah, Herd's way of working got *me* shit with the Boys. Right from the start, it seemed that I was the only one who could get along with Herd, so that separated me out from the eh . . . herd. The Boys figured that they didn't like the new boss, so I shouldn't either.

The one thing I had learned from living with my father and working for Bill Watts was that the last thing you want to do with an alpha male is butt heads. Particularly if that alpha signs your checks or puts a roof over your head.

No one found this out quicker than booker Dusty Rhodes.

Dusty and top star Ric Flair had regularly crossed swords over the years. It was a product of both men feeling that *they* knew best and both men feeling *they* were the best. It was a healthy struggle that boiled over every so often— and that "boiling over" helped shape both men's careers.

In the new WCW, Dusty wanted Ric to drop the NWA World Heavyweight title in a short match to Rick Steiner. Flair wanted no part of losing the title—and certainly not under those circumstances—so the Nature Boy made noises about leaving the company just as it was trying to find its feet. Herd, not wanting to lose his biggest star, intervened and overruled Dusty. The match was changed to be Flair vs. Lex Luger at Starrcade with Flair retaining the title. Not only did Dusty lose face, but he also felt he was being held back with the new corporate policies of WCW—one of which was *no blood allowed*. Telling someone like Dusty that they couldn't use a little "color" was like telling a master chef that they couldn't use garnish.

A couple of months later—while I was on commentary—Dusty booked the huge, aggressive tag team of The Road Warriors to come out to the ring, double team him, and stick a spike from their shoulder pads into his eye. Dusty bled. Badly.

I couldn't help but think, as I watched the blood streaming down his face, that this was Dusty's "screw you" to his new boss. Herd immediately removed Dusty as booker—and soon after as talent. And just like that, Rhodes was gone from WCW.

And that was the beginning of how I found myself at Herd's desk getting chewed out. When he asked me, "What happened in the limo?" I knew Flair had already been asked the same question. I also knew that Flair had told Herd the full story and escaped with not so much as a raised voice or a slap on the wrist. Ric could say just about anything he wanted and Herd would grin and bear it. But me, I was no Ric Flair. Herd was looking to take out his frustrations on someone—and that someone was me.

"Well," I began. "It happened after you left. Flair walked into the bar just as I was about to leave, and we started talking business."

"It didn't end up that way," Herd said.

Herd knew Flair and I had things to discuss because, when Dusty was let go, George Scott, who was half of The Flying Scotts tag team in the 1950s and '60s and a talent executive for Vince McMahon, was overseeing "creative" for a little while before Ric became booker. Herd then set up a committee around the Nature Boy to ensure fairness and balance to proceedings. It was a sound theory, I suppose, but horrible in practice.

It began with Flair, Jim Cornette, Kevin Sullivan, Eddie Gilbert, and me. I was the only "office" person involved. I was the only one who lived in Atlanta, so as soon as the meetings began the rest of the committee would be itching to leave so they could catch their flights home, or go to the gym—or to the next party. I didn't have much to leave the office for, so I stayed behind often to finish my work.

Better to die of use than rust.

Herd also spent his weekdays in Atlanta before traveling back to his wife in St. Louis on the weekends, so a couple of times a month he'd pop his head into my office and say, "You fancy a meal on Turner? He can sure afford it." I wasn't really set up in Atlanta yet, so I was happy for company. I think he was, too. We talked football over stout liquor and red meat. As much as I tried to avoid it, talk inevitably turned to work. This got me heat with the rest of the committee, because when Herd would talk business, he'd usually finish up with notes he wanted me to bring back to the booking meetings.

But for now, he still wanted to know what happened in the limo.

"You and I had dinner," I said. "And then you left to go home."

"And I thought you did, too," Herd replied.

"I was on the way out the door when I heard Flair calling me from the other side of the bar," I said.

Herd rolled his eyes. He wasn't long in the wrestling business, but he knew Ric Flair + bar = no one was going home early.

"And I didn't want to leave because I'm already seen as 'the office' or 'Herd's boy'—so I stayed for a drink," I said. "To be sociable."

"Sociable?"

"Yeah, well that was the plan," I replied. "It's just that Ric is a little more sociable than most."

When Flair called me at the door of the Omni Hotel bar, I knew there was no way I was leaving. Before even saying hello, he said he had two flight attendants at his table. "One for me, and one for you."

I looked over his shoulder and saw that both ladies were way out of my league. "I think I'll just go home," I said.

"You're going home to sit in your empty apartment like a cat lady, Jimbo? Not happening," he replied as he turned and walked back to his VIP table. "Follow the Naitch."

"And then what happened?" Herd asked.

"Well, I felt a little stupid walking to the table. The two ladies in question didn't even seem all that interested in Ric, never mind me."

"Ladies," Ric said. "This is Jim Ross, the greatest wrestling announcer of all time."

Before I could challenge Flair's introduction he was already waving at the barman to bring another bottle of Dom Perignon champagne. I was a little shy and a little rusty. A man knows before he even sits down if he has a shot or not, and I had more chance of winning the world title from Flair than I did with either lady at the table.

"What do you think our chances are?" Flair whispered into my ear.

"I'm going home," I said in reply.

"That bad, huh?" he said. Flair stood up again and increased his champagne order.

Herd was sitting across from me with his head in his hands. "And the limo?" he asked, not really wanting to hear the reply. "What happened in the limo?"

"Well," I said. "That was outside. At the end of the night we were a little more than tipsy, and Ric asked the ladies if they wanted to go to an after-hours place."

I walked outside with Ric while the two ladies walked arm-in-arm ahead of us.

"What do you think our odds are now?" Flair asked me.

"I don't know. Maybe for you the odds are good but for me—"

"We'll have to do something to raise the odds," Ric said with a twinkle in his eye and a look of devilment in his face.

We got into the limo where both ladies sat opposite us. It was a little dark, but I could still see that the lady in front of me wasn't interested in me whatsoever.

"How long is your layover until you have to fly out again?" I asked her.

I could see her eyes weren't in my direction. She was squinting, like she was trying to make out something in the dark beside me. Flair, ever the gentleman, turned on the overhead light to help her out. Her jaw fell open, so did her friend's; both women were stunned. I turned to Flair to see him smiling, proud as punch, from ear to ear at what he'd done. He nodded down to his crotch, and I instinctively followed Ric's gaze down to see his erect penis standing to attention through his zipper.

"What in the name of God are you doing?" I shouted.

Both ladies scurried out of the car in disgust as Ric just sat there, basking in his Nature Boy-ness.

"He just—whipped it out there?" Herd asked me.

"Yep," I replied.

Herd could only shake his head. Flair had already told him. Flair had already told me that he had already told Herd. Didn't matter, Herd still couldn't understand why. That made two of us.

"What did you do that for?" I said in the limo as Flair put his gun back in the holster.

"I was trying to increase the odds for you, Jim," Ric replied. "That works about fifty percent of the time, and that's fifty percent more chance than you had before I pulled my dick out."

"And you went home?" Herd asked me.

"I did," I replied. "Last thing I saw was Flair strutting back toward the bar, and I got a taxi home."

"What was he thinking?" Herd shouted. "That bar is the corporate bar. Those ladies could have sued. Could have went to the papers! What was he thinking?"

I knew Herd was saying to me all the things he wished he could have said to Ric. He was also probably pissed that he just missed out on all the "fun" himself. Herd proceeded to rip Flair limb from limb for another twenty minutes before he finally ran out of steam and sat back down at his desk again.

"Jim?" I said. Herd looked up from his desk. "Is this a bad time to talk about my money?"

Chapter Twenty-Eight

BOOKING COMMITTEE

1989

Of course no matter who ran the company, the characters backstage were always the same. Some tried to "peacock" their way around, others kept to themselves—but having time to kill far away from home made most of the Boys lose themselves a little. I got to know a lot of the roster in different towns and situations all the way up. Some I knew well, some I didn't. Others I thought I knew, but didn't.

"Hey Jim," I heard a familiar voice say, as I parked my car outside.

I turned to see Dick Murdoch calling me. I was on my way to a booking meeting, but I always had time for Dickie.

"Look at this," he said as he reached into his billfold. I thought he was going to pull out some weird brand of condom or the $1 check he kept from Watts. "You ever seen one before?" he asked, as he showed me a Ku Klux Klan member card.

"No, I have not," I replied.

And that was it. No follow up. No discussion. No recruiting. Dicky just felt compelled to let me know that he was a member of the KKK. I wasn't sure if he was just seeing if he could get a rise out of me or if he was legit; he was always hard to read in that regard. This was the same man who told a lie about going to West Texas State so many times that not only did he start believing it, but the university actually believed it themselves—to the point where they invited him to play in the varsity alumni game.

He never even went to school there.

"OK then," he said, as he walked off.

I looked around, waiting for the Boys to come out of the woodwork to tell me it was a rib—but no one ever appeared.

And that was how I'd feel for a lot of my WCW run: standing in disbelief, waiting in vain for someone to tell me what I had just seen was a joke.

The booking committee went through so many changes and permutations, I couldn't keep them all straight in my head. One thing that remained true was the heat I was catching from the members—no matter who they were—because I was usually the one who had to deliver the changes that Herd wanted made back to the committee. I got to the point where I didn't care if the guys on the committee were mad at me or not. I was just doing my job. And getting it from both ends.

Herd would storm into my office, throwing the format onto my desk and saying, "Who wrote this?! What the hell is this shit?"

"Well, that would be Saturday's show," I'd reply.

"Well, it's not going on this way!" he'd say.

And I knew that I was going to have to bring his changes back to the booking committee. They were pissed when Herd changed stuff, and Herd was pissed at the committee's approach. I was the "office" guy in the middle.

Generally, Herd thought there was too much talking, too many interviews. His experience was from directing some episodes of Sam Muchnick's long-tenured promotion in St. Louis. That promotion had heavily emphasized matches, with few interviews. That made St. Louis the exception. To Herd, however, that was how wrestling should be.

But those on the committee all knew that a lot of times the interviews were better than the matches. We also knew that interviews were vital for selling tickets and pay-per-view events, as well as getting across the wrestlers' personalities. Our roster had some of the best talkers ever and an interview with Terry Funk or Jim Cornette was going to be more entertaining than the one-sided squash matches that were the norm on TV.

I knew all of this. I knew the booking committee knew all of this. I knew Herd didn't know this. And I knew that I would still have bring the changes back and get shit for it—then bring the new format to Herd and get shit for that, too.

My take was: If you're going to work with somebody on a daily basis, you have to coexist in some sort of professional, amicable, tolerable manner. If you're in a contentious relationship, no matter if it's personal or professional, it's not good. It's not good for your health. It's not good for anything. So I tried to get along with Herd the best I could. I knew he didn't have a lot of product knowledge, but I also saw a booking committee that had their own agendas as well.

From the get-go, WCW had problems that were so obvious that they could have easily been fixed, had one of these senior VPs or executive directors made WCW a priority. I began to think, "Somebody's going to see some of these things that I'm seeing."

But as the days and weeks and months went by, they didn't. What they did was, they applied to WCW what they thought worked for TBS: they'd turn the decision-making over to a committee. TBS was just setting us up to fail on a creative level. I knew you couldn't put active performers on a booking committee; you'd never get any long-term planning done if everybody in power had a dog in the hunt.

People just looked out for themselves and it stopped us from going down creative avenues we should have been going down.

Like pulling the trigger on Sting.

I tried to tell Flair that he was so big and so over that he didn't need the world title to be a really significant asset. When I voiced that same opinion at the booking committee meetings, I caught flak from some of the others who wanted Ric to be happy. I even had my words twisted around to the point that I had guys asking me why I thought it didn't matter who the world champ was.

My thoughts were simple: Ric was better than the title. He had spent most of the last decade as heavyweight champion of the world. Flair would still appeal to fans, as long as he was featured and put into a personal issue, where he could cut a passionate promo about it and then be made whole by the end of it. It was best for WCW to have two major drawing cards in Ric Flair, plus Sting as the world champion—and Flair wouldn't have been hurt either creatively or financially, as he wasn't getting paid extra for being the champion.

But I knew Flair looked at the creative end just like he viewed being the traveling NWA champion. As booker he was the one responsible for the attendance, the TV ratings, the casting and the storytelling. He wasn't going to get grades to let him know how he was doing; keeping business strong was how he was going to be judged. He certainly wasn't going to get fired, but if business dropped while he was booking he would have been known, at least in his own head, as a failed booker. That led him to the decision that a lot of bookers had made over the years—he could depend on himself more than he could anybody else. So he filled out a roster with people he felt he could rely on—his buddies. He was doing them a solid, getting them good bookings on the card, and they would then have his back in political situations.

Sting would have to wait.

Chapter Twenty-Nine

ROTATING ANNOUNCERS

1989

I got my meeting with Herd and his boss, Jack Petrik. I wanted to talk money and they wanted to talk about my role in the company. When I entered the office, Tony Schiavone was already sitting opposite Herd and Petrik, with an empty seat waiting for me. Tony and I heard through the grapevine—telephone, telegram, tell-a-wrestler—that the meeting was coming, so I wanted to be prepared. I found out the salaries of the announcers who called Turner's Atlanta Braves baseball games; Tony also told me his best year was at $20,000.

I sat down and kinda took over. I didn't even mean to, but I was that passionate about what we did as the voices of the show that I memorized ratings of the shows we did, the hours we worked, and the miles we traveled compared to other announcers in the Turner corporate family. We outworked them all, but we were getting paid far less. Plus, we had no off-season.

Herd and Petrik listened and nodded along as I made a case for Tony and me to get a bump in salary. When we were done, or when I was done, Herd and Petrik asked me to step outside while they spoke to Tony.

"Can you give us twenty minutes with Tony?" Herd asked.

"Of course, no problem," I replied.

As I closed the door, leaving the other three men in the office, I thought I was finished; it was the classic wrestling paranoia kicking in again. Maybe my mouth got the better of me, and Tony, who stayed more or less silent during the meeting, was the kind of person they wanted on board.

I took a walk around the floor and on my way back to Herd's office I saw Tony at the payphone, and he had a smile from ear to ear. He gave me the thumbs up as I passed.

I knocked on Herd's door and entered to see Petrik was still there, too.

Herd got straight to the point. "Jim, we want to offer you a fifty percent raise and make it a three-year deal."

Now I knew why Tony was smiling so much.

"Yes sir," I said.

"We have a deal?" Petrik asked.

I put out my hand to shake on it. "We have a deal," I replied.

As it turned out, our meeting to discuss money was only the first of two meetings that Herd and Petrik wanted to have with Tony and me. The second meeting was about *where* the company saw us plying our trade.

Once again I found myself sitting opposite Jim Herd and Jack Petrik with Tony Schiavone beside me.

"The brass has decided that one of you is going to be the voice of syndication, and the other is going to be the voice of TBS," Herd said. "Now, they decided that it's going to be you, Tony, on syndication while Jim here goes on TBS."

I immediately knew that Tony was not happy with coming off of TBS, after nearly four years of hosting that show, and losing that national exposure. The syndicated world still offered a lot of exposure, but doing it market-by-market was a slog instead of doing overlay.

I said, "Well, look, it doesn't matter. I'll be happy with syndication, and Tony can do TBS."

"You both got the same contract, the same money," Herd said. "It's the same work for the same pay—just in different directions."

I tried again. "It doesn't matter to me . . ."

Herd said, "It's not up for discussion or debate. This is the way it's going to be."

It was tough to see Tony hurt. He and I grew close doing the TBS post-production work for Crockett in Atlanta, earning just $35 a day each. As a way of saving money we shared a room and a car. We were ecstatic when they built a new Fairfield Inn at the Atlanta Airport because a standard room had two double beds—and because it also had remote control TV. We didn't even fight over the remote. It was just the general theory that being able to lay in bed and change channels was just too good to be true.

Now we found ourselves on opposite sides of a situation that neither of us wanted.

We could both see that Herd and Petrik were done; meeting was over, there was nothing left to say.

A week later, I heard through the grapevine that Tony had taken an offer to go work for WWF for even more money.

* * *

Rotating announcers wasn't a new concept in wrestling. Freshening up the voices was routinely one of the first things a new boss or booker might try to make their mark on a show. Wrestling was a business of newness—new champions, new matches, new markets, new announcers.

Just like when I brought a voice from the past back to TV.

Gordon Solie was a role model for me as an announcer. Bill Watts did a lot of business with Eddie Graham, Solie's mentor, so we would get tapes from Florida where I heard a lot of Gordon's work. Even before I got into the business I heard Gordon call the Danny Hodge-Hiro Matsuda title change a hundred times. His voice was etched in my mind as the greatest announcer in wrestling history.

But he got forced out at TBS in 1985 when Jim Crockett took over and wanted Tony Schiavone and Jimmy's brother, David Crockett, to be the voices of his national wrestling show. Gordon's drinking was an issue, and Crockett felt it was time for something new. Unfortunately, Gordon got unceremoniously pushed out. I thought that someone who had given that many years, been that loyal, and worked so diligently to bring some class and decorum to the show deserved better.

So we created a role for Gordon in WCW. He was kind of like a Walter Cronkite commentator. We called him the Dean of Wrestling Broadcasters. He liked hearing everyone use his new moniker, and soon it was "here comes the Dean" and "good morning, Dean."

So we created a deal where we would write two minutes of commentary— an idea I got from Paul Harvey, an iconic radio newsman who did "And now, the Rest of the Story." So Gordon would basically give you his thoughts on an angle. We would write it and Gordon would edit it if he chose to, giving him editorial control. We put it in the prompter and away the "Dean" went.

Gordon lived in Tampa—so we'd fly on Delta—and because he was a "million-miler," he always flew first class. Of course, in first class, you drink free *and* he was a lifetime member of the Crown Room, which meant he also drank free at the airport. At about midday on his first day in, Gordon was due to arrive at the CNN Center to meet me and go over his segment. By the time he arrived, I think it was fair to say that he'd had a little too much to drink. He'd been "over-served," as he liked to say.

Keith Mitchell, who was head of production, called me and said, "You need to come down here. We have a problem with Gordie."

I replied, "Okay, I'll be right down." I was on the twelfth floor, so I rushed to an elevator, went down, and immediately saw my friend was a little more than "over-served."

"Gordon," I said, "the storyline's changed and the bookers are working on the new direction upstairs."

"What?" he said. His speech was slurred, his eyes watery and somewhat glazed over.

"I don't want you to have to do it two or three times," I said. "If it's all right, why don't you just spend the night and we'll do it in the morning?"

I didn't want to scold a man I greatly respected or embarrass him on his first day on the new job. Instead I checked him into the Omni Hotel—while he disappeared into the bar.

We rolled tape at 9:00 a.m. the next morning and he was just fine. So from then on, that's what we did. Gordon flew in late evening, just in time for him to get a nice dinner and a beverage, and then we'd get up first thing in the morning and nail down his segment. It was good to see him back, and his appearances always got great feedback. The fans loved having him be part of a TBS wrestling show once more.

Gordon had an issue with the booze; it wasn't a well-kept secret. His health was deteriorating and, unfortunately, his best friend and his life partner, his wife Smokey, was very ill, too. Watching her fade away was killing him. I wanted to do something to say, "thank you for steering me in this direction." I wanted to give the best in the business a reason to put on a suit and come in front of a camera again. For many, many wrestling fans, he was a voice of their childhood, and to hear him back on the air, even for two minutes a show, was a pleasure.

A short time later, we were doing *TBS Saturday Night* show tapings, and I was lacking a color man. Gordon was very, very apprehensive about doing color because, to be truthful, he didn't want to go four-plus hours without a drink. I sent a stagehand out and got an Igloo cooler and we filled it partly with orange juice and the rest with vodka. Gordon sat beside me all night and drank screwdrivers for four hours and just filled in the blanks. Drink or no drink, I loved working with him. It made me feel like I did something right for the business that he got to come back and step out of the dugout for one last run, and tip his hat to the crowd.

Chapter Thirty

STEAMBOAT AND FLAIR

1989

I was excited when I learned that Ricky "The Dragon" Steamboat was coming in. George Scott had pushed for Ricky hard in his short stint as booker. He knew, as we all did, that Steamboat could help us a lot because he still had "it." Sometimes when guys step away you don't know if it's a lingering issue physically, or they can't hold up as they once could. But one look at Steamboat and it was easy to see that he was healthy and motivated. I had never called any of his matches before, but I'd seen him on tape numerous times. During his classics with Flair for the title, I could tell he hadn't lost a step; smooth as silk, at times, almost too smooth. He was really, really talented and always gave the audience superb match quality.

His run with Flair was bringing out the best in both Ric as champion, and Ricky as challenger. At Chi-Town Rumble we flipped both men's roles as Steamboat pinned Flair in an amazing match in Chicago. We knew switching the belt would only help prolong the feud, where everyone would benefit.

Of course, we as the booking committee didn't do Steamboat any favors, creatively, by putting his wife and son with him in the storyline. His wife really wanted it to happen, but I didn't want Ricky to do it. The ultimate family man with his wife and little boy, versus Ric Flair, the king of adultery and dalliances and Learjets and diamond rings and limos. Normally having both guys so polar opposite—one with family values and the other materialistic and arrogant—would be a great idea, but we were heading into a time of defiance in our audiences. Bringing your wife and your little boy to the ring was hard for some young males to swallow. If they were going to live vicariously through somebody, it seemed they wanted it to be the jet-flying, limousine-riding son of a gun.

Whatever about the creative surrounding both men, when the matches started it was poetry in motion; absolutely spectacular. Steamboat was as good of a seller in the ring as anybody I ever saw. He made me wonder, several times during commentary, if he was really hurt. And I knew if I was genuinely and authentically concerned about his welfare, and if that rang true in my voice then the fans watching at home would get even more involved in the story.

I made a point of talking to Ricky shortly after he arrived, as part of the due diligence, to find out some biographical information to make sure it was accurate. I wanted to know about his amateur wrestling background. Was he really trained by Verne Gagne? Was it really that daunting? Things like that. As far as what he was going to do during the match? Or, how he was going to get heat? I didn't care about that.

As a broadcaster, I knew I had great story tellers in there and I couldn't wait to help them tell their story. I didn't want to be affected with too much knowledge; I wanted to go on the same ride that the audience was on, except I'm going to be voicing it over as we ride along together.

Just as Flair and Steamboat were always looking to change *their* dynamics, it seemed change was part of my job, too. For Clash of Champions VI, I was joined at the announcer's booth by none other than NWA Legend, and first time announcer, Terry Funk.

Terry was always great on the mic but taking in the details and direction of announcing sometimes caught even the best promo guys off guard. But not the Funker. Within minutes, I was pleasantly surprised at how good

Terry was. A lot of wrestlers that get the chance to do color commentary are more concerned about putting themselves over, or memorizing specific lines. It's like hearing the guys talking about putting their matches together: "Well, I need to get my shit in," and knowing that's what the match turns out to be: shit.

Before he arrived, I had no idea what to expect from Terry. He showed up nicely dressed even though it was counter to his "crazy Texan" persona. That little detail alone led me to believe that Terry wasn't coming to get himself over, but to get the matches over and the "pomp and circumstance" of a big event over.

In wrestling *matches*, the heel usually calls the match; in wrestling *commentary* it's the play-by-play guy in the lead who he calls the match. Terry had that great ability, no different than he would have in the ring, to listen to what I did and come right with me. To go out and do a live, two-hour broadcast is challenging for the most experienced broadcasters, much less someone that's new at it, but Funk was a natural. His instincts took over; his understanding the fundamentals of the game took over; his passion for his business took over.

Terry offered the perspective of a former world champion, in terms of how a world champion carries out his strategy to keep the title. He was always a great in-ring psychologist, and that mindset and skill-set was invaluable to him in his role as an announcer that night. We gelled well and added the lyrics to the music that Flair and Steamboat were providing in the ring. Terry Funk was another pro wrestling treasure who quickly became one of my favorite TV partners.

My partners were always changing, but I was happy to use my experience, and confidence in what I was doing, to try and add as best I could to every event we were putting out there.

Calling all the matches, I felt like we had a better in-ring product than WWF. But sitting on the booking committee, I also knew just how fragile our shot at becoming number one truly was.

Chapter Thirty-One

STARRCADE

1989

I was so stoned that I couldn't command my own hands to function. That's a lot of stoned. But I was *legally* stoned. Or so I thought. I was on my way to "Starrcade: Future Shock," but had just been through another dental ordeal—my fourth bridge in a month—and needed a clear head. Nitrous oxide and in-house pain pills weren't a good mix, but I thought nothing more of it as I got a cab back to my CNN Center office.

I sat at my desk and waited for the effects of the dental visit to wear off. I had paid the dentist $10,000 up front on my first visit, whilst also under the effects of nitrous oxide, to get that perfect TV smile. I was finally at the end of three root canals and four bridges, and ready for my close-up—except I couldn't stop dribbling on myself. The effects of the gas and pills were starting to subside, but the numbing agent was still in full effect.

My office phone rang, and the receptionist downstairs said there was someone here to see me.

"Clan ew foot them off faw a howerur, please," I said.

"What?" she replied.

"Caaewwfloot . . ."

"Flute? What? Is this a bad line?"

"Caaaaaneeeewwww . . ."

"I'll send him in. Thanks." Click.

"Fuut sake," I said as I hung up the phone.

I didn't want anyone to see me like this; I was a bumbling sloppy mess. So I did what any grown, rational man would do . . . I ducked out of my office to hide. I was sure whoever it was could wait, or find me later at the venue. I just wasn't in the mood or space to talk wrestling—or talk in general.

I walked around for twenty minutes with a sheet of paper in my hand to make people think I was too busy to stop. I presumed whoever was looking for me would surely now be gone, but when I returned to my office I could see a very serious looking gentleman waiting outside for me.

"Are you James Ross?" he asked as I approached.

I still wasn't sure of my speech, so I nodded. He introduced himself as a DEA agent. "Can I come in?" he asked.

DEA? I could immediately tell this wasn't a rib. I didn't want him in my office, but I also didn't want anyone in the corporate company seeing someone for the Drug Enforcement Agency "questioning" me, either.

Again I nodded, and we entered my office. I took a seat behind my desk and prayed to the good Lord in the sky that my tongue and speech had returned to their normal selves before I spoke to the DRUG ENFORCEMENT AGENCY.

He took out a small pad and pen. "Did you have some dental work done today?" he asked.

I knew I had to answer, but I didn't know what my answer would sound like. "Yes," I quickly replied. My reply sounded good, but it was too short to tell if I was 100 percent. I had no idea where he was going but his general demeanor was intimidating.

He watched me closely and leaned forward. "And did you get any prescriptions made out in your name today?"

"Yes," I said. I was kinda sure my speech was okay, but not sure enough that I wanted to try to make full sentences if I didn't have to. If this guy was

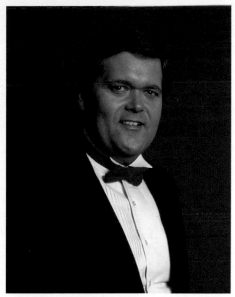

St. Pete, Florida, in 1976: Beginning our journeys at Bill Kinnamon's MLB Umpire School, with MLB umpiring legend Tim Mc-Clelland and college baseball's Tony Gisondi. I'm using my "wrestling" face. (Photo courtesy of the author)

Mid-South days in the first tux I ever owned. Cowboy facilitated it from his pal Ed Beshara's Men's Store in Tulsa, Oklahoma. (Photo courtesy of *Pro Wrestling Illustrated*)

Very proud of my work being noticed. (Photo: George Napolitano)

Dr. Death was #76 for the OU Sooners on the gridiron, but he was #1 in many hearts—including mine. He was $2 steak tough. (Photo: Dr. Mike Lano, wrealano@aol.com)

My mentor, Cowboy Bill Watts, who was a pro wrestling genius and a man who redefined the term "tough love." (Photo: George Napolitano)

The Stinger and "Gentleman" Chris Adams verbalizing their case and why fans needed to buy a ticket to see them perform.

Was there ever a better three-man team than The Fabulous Freebirds, led by the talented Michael P. S. Hayes?

(Photos: Dr. Mike Lano, wrealano@aol.com)

The greatest to ever do it . . . The Naitch! Ric's passion to be the best separated him from his peers.

Dusty Rhodes's charisma, the "it" factor, can be defined by his attire at this televised event on which we teamed. Did I borrow my black hat "gimmick" from The Dream?

Hall of Fame level talent's Mark Calaway (The Undertaker), Teddy Long, and Dangerous Dan Spivey in WCW. Some in WCW thought Calaway "would never make it." Now that's pet coon goofy.

(Photos courtesy of *Pro Wrestling Illustrated*)

New set for *WCW Saturday Night*, the flagship broadcast for years on Ted Turner's TBS.

Custom-made suit thanks to "Uncle Ted." Broadcasting on TBS on Saturdays at 6:05
p.m. EST was awesome for this fan.

(Photos courtesy of *Pro Wrestling Illustrated*)

The Dream and me doing pay-per-view work. Rhodes loved to invent new words on live TV . . . if you will. (Photo: Dr. Mike Lano, wrealano@aol.com)

Jesse "The Body" Ventura was amazingly talented, but our team never accomplished what we should have due to my ego. Sorry, Governor. (Photo courtesy of *Pro Wrestling Illustrated*)

Tony Schiavone was one of my favorite broadcast partners in my career, and is now producing UGA Bulldog football and basketball games, as well as being the voice of the Gwinnett Braves and hosting a successful podcast. (Photo courtesy of *Pro Wrestling Illustrated*)

My wrestling broadcaster role model, the best to ever man a mic: Gordon Solie. (Photo: George Napolitano)

Quite the dangerous duo, The Barbarian and Mrs. Foley's baby boy, Mick. Lots of top talent passed through WCW. (Photo: George Napolitano)

Dusty Rhodes, Jim Crockett, and me at a breakfast meeting where The Dream was holding court. Looks like we were coming off a long night. (Photo: George Napolitano)

Jerry "The King" Lawler and I seemed to gel from day one, but we strived to get better with every outing. Jerry was the star of our team without a doubt. (Photo courtesy of the author)

I thankfully no longer smoke!

Joel Watts and me during our days broadcaster for Joel's step-father, Cowboy Bill Watts, in Mid-South Wrestling. Joel was a brilliant video editor.

(Photos courtesy of *Pro Wrestling Illustrated*)

Steve Borden, a.k.a. Sting, is one of my longest standing friends in the wrestling biz. Always charismatic, athletic, and exuding integrity and class. This pic was taken at OklaMania in 2016.

Well . . . not all creative concepts are hits.

(Photos courtesy of *Pro Wrestling Illustrated*)

My first WrestleMania, in 1993, with Bobby "The Brain" Heenan and "Macho Man" Randy Savage outdoors at Caesars Palace in Las Vegas, Nevada. The start of an amazing journey. (Photo courtesy of the author)

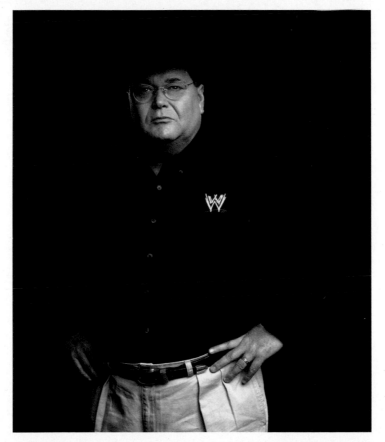

Attitude Era attire, complete with a 200X Resistol hat, which was a Christmas gift from Steve Austin. (Photo courtesy of the author)

(Photo: Dr. Mike Lano, wrealano@aol.com)

Nothing beats hearing my "Boomer Sooner" entrance music at a WWE event and the fans responding in kind! That live feeling cannot be replaced. (Photo courtesy of the author)

Can't explain what these two HOFers, JJ Dillon and Jerry Brisco, have meant to me—both personally and professionally—in my career. (Photo: Dr. Mike Lano, wrealano@aol.com)

My career has been blessed with many outstanding broadcast partners, including these two who I met working first for Jim Crockett Promotions. The great Bob Caudle and the talented Tony Schiavone. Bob is the classiest pro I ever met in the biz. (Photo courtesy of the author)

Happy days with our WWE family, including a young Dwayne Johnson, Bruce Prichard (a.k.a. Brother Love), Olympian Mark Henry, and my late wife Jan who was my "secret weapon" in talent relations.

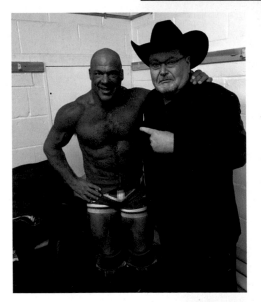

With your Olympic hero in England. Pittsburgh's own Kurt Angle was one of our all-time great signees. No amateur great ever made a smoother and impactful transition to the pros.

"Stone Cold" Steve Austin and yours truly with a lovely Oklahoma Sooners football fan at the OU game in Norman.

(Photos courtesy of the author)

More recognition, this time from *Pro Wrestling Illustrated*. (Photo courtesy of *Pro Wrestling Illustrated*)

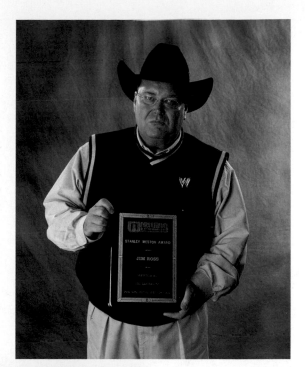

Enjoying my Sooners winning the Big 12 Championship in Arlington, Texas, against Nebraska before politics and egos pillaged the league. (Photo courtesy of the author)

I don't think that a woman could love her man more than my angel Jan loved me. I miss you terribly. (Photo: Dr. Mike Lano, wrealano@aol.com)

suspicious of me for some reason, dribbling all over myself while slurring my words was going to make things a whole lot worse.

"It seems that there have been a lot of prescriptions made out in your name over a very short period of time," he said.

And then it hit me. My dentist *was* very pill friendly, and I *did* get a lot of prescriptions from him over a four-week period. Luckily for me I didn't fill any of the prescriptions past the very first one. In my drawer I had what some people in the wrestling business might call an Aladdin's Cave of scripts, that gave me access to high-caliber painkillers. But I was never that guy, so there the "un-cashed" prescriptions lay, waiting to bail me out of a potentially tricky situation.

"Let me slow you these," I said.

"Slow?" he asked.

"Show," I replied, as I corrected my tongue and took out the prescriptions. "I can explain everything."

The agent was astonished I had all the scripts in my top desk drawer and that I was never going to fill them. "How are you dealing with all the pain from your dental work?" he asked.

"Crown Royal," I replied, showing him my new $10,000 smile. He wasn't one bit impressed. Our meeting lasted 30 minutes—or 25 minutes more than necessary. The script-happy dentist was next on his list. Starrcade was next on mine.

I came up with the round-robin concept that some people in the back loved, and others not so much. We were looking for a different theme for the upcoming pay-per-view and everybody was pitching new ideas in the booking meeting. We wanted a kind of a sports oriented theme to stick with our more sports geared presentation. The idea of the round-robin itself posed political issues because some guys didn't want to lose, and others simply didn't understand it. I got the sense backstage that it probably caused too many political issues to be fully embraced by the talent. When I heard the guys putting their matches together and arguing over the finishes I couldn't help but feel like I should have kept my mouth shut and let someone else come up with another idea. But, unfortunately, nobody else had any good suggestions even though management asked us to come up with something completely different. The brass wanted a "concept pay-per-view."

So I came up with babyfaces versus babyfaces and heels versus heels—all in the spirit of athletic competition and new matches. As a wrestling fan I was intrigued by The Road Warriors versus The Steiners.

My rationale was: it was a new concept, something different for that pay-per-view, and we were coming to the end of the NFL season—so everyone was talking football. So I thought it would be kind of cool to give us some match-ups that we had not seen in a tournament setting that meant something. I thought the concept of a tournament that began and ended on the same night it began, gave you a payoff for the investment of the pay-per-view dollar was a logical idea.

But the idea wasn't a good one. The talent didn't buy it and the rest of the booking committee didn't spend any time trying to "sell" it to them. There were too many political agendas, too many people playing favorites for it to have any real impact.

At least I had a great smile to help me convince people that I didn't want to scream and pull my damn hair out.

Chapter Thirty-Two

SOME OLD FACES RETURN

1990

Change was in the air. It nearly always was in WCW. The booking decisions, and playing favorites, was starting to catch up to the house show business, which was in the toilet. Word was that Herd wanted Flair out of the booker's role, and that Ric's replacement was imminent.

As I boarded my flight to the next town and the next show, I saw a familiar face looking back: Tony Schiavone. I had heard that his time in WWF wasn't the easiest, and moving his wife and five kids to the far more expensive northeast was taking its toll. But I had no idea he was back in WCW until I saw him on the flight. I was happy to shake his hand and see him back—I think we all were.

The new booker though, now he was a different proposition to people.

Ole Anderson was a gruff, no-bullshit, no-hand-holding type of person. I was glad he was going to be the new booker because at least there was now one guy that we could go to and get clarification on a question. His reply probably wasn't going to be the most genteel, business-like corporate response, but you would know exactly where you stood. Like the old saying went: You can go the horse's head or the horse's ass. At least by going to

Ole, you went to the horse's head. I knew I wouldn't always agree with his mythology, or his style, or his presentation skills, but I never, ever wouldn't appreciate and respect his knowledge of the business.

I knew very quickly that he and I were on the very same page. He'd give me the broad brush strokes and expect me to be professional enough to connect the dots. He never once produced me in my headset, leaving that to Keith Mitchell, who was a joy to hear because he, too, let me do my job.

My theory was simple: if somebody on the roster was better than me, then hell, put them in my spot. I knew that's what life is about. I enjoyed the competition, but I didn't need to be spoon fed basic fundamental things; that's wrestling 101.

Ole was one of those guys who wanted you to *feel* it and he wanted you to see what you call and call what you see. Have the ability, the talent to put it in the right tone and inflection on the air, and that's what I did. He was more concerned about the Boys and the in-ring product than he was about the announcing. But that's because he was spoiled when it came to the announcing. He had Gordon Solie during his peak years and Bob Caudle in the Mid-Atlantic. Ole had the luxury of working with some really good story tellers that were low-maintenance guys—and I wanted that trend to continue.

Ole came into the job frustrated and stayed that way because of the intrusions and the idiocies of TBS upper management who thought wrestling was so simplistic that any idiot could manage it, produce it, announce it, and perform it. The majority of the executives that had the stroke didn't understand why Ted had bought Jim Crockett to start with. And the deal was that most of the guys in the blue suits didn't have the balls to go to Ted and express their concerns, they just lashed out and were corporate bullies to those of us who worked in WCW.

Ole would write the main TV shows, and the secondary shows Tony Schiavone and I would write. He then gave feedback and kept us in the loop as to what was coming up in the storylines, so that when we did go on the air, we were clued in as to where he was going.

It was off air that was harder to see where it was heading.

Chapter Thirty-Three

BUILDING STING

1990

Almost from the start, the eventual goal was for Flair to pass the torch to Sting and Sting be the babyface champion. Then the WCW creative would be in the process of building viable heels to chase the champion babyface, again playing off what WWF had done with Hulk Hogan, Watts with JYD, and Eddie Graham with Dusty Rhodes. It was a simple philosophy. Some territories are heel territories, where you've got a heel champion and the babyfaces chase, and some are the opposite. I wanted Sting to be our flag bearer and for more heels to be created to chase him. But for that to happen, we first needed Flair to pass the torch.

Then, during the main event of "Clash of Champions: Texas Shootout," Sting blew out his patella tendon trying to get in the steel cage. In the very same match where Flair had turned on him to start their feud. So, of our top two heroes, one had turned villain, and the other got injured. It was a disaster, so we needed to turn Lex Luger back, even though he had been heating up as an arrogant villain.

Luger wasn't cast in any one role long enough for people to get in a groove about how they really felt about him. Pro wrestling wasn't Lex's natural calling, because he didn't have an innate aptitude for it, so adapting to those multiple changes didn't come organically for him. With help and time he improved on his promos and, while never being great, he was always good enough to get by because of how he looked. Having watched him closely for months, I thought he could have learned more, absorbed more, when he was with the Horseman. There wasn't a better place in the wrestling world to be if you wanted to learn how to make money. Lex was with a perfect entity to just be quiet—to watch and learn.

I had dealt with guys I enjoyed working with more; Luger was never rude to me, but I found him to be somewhat aloof and arrogant at times. He placed a very high value on his look, which is fine, as I understood that in the wrestling world you have to do that to maintain your sanity sometimes—but he just wasn't as advanced as he thought he was. He never met a mirror that he didn't embrace and really, that was his big priority: the look. He thought "the look" was going to get him farther down the road than it actually did. It certainly got him noticed, and he always looked the part without question, but his in-ring skill set was not advanced to push him up to that next level.

So with Sting out, Lex was put in the "Capital Combat" pay-per-view with Flair, while Sting appeared with an unusual guest in RoboCop.

"Fucking RoboCop?" I asked backstage.

Keith Mitchell just nodded.

"From the movie?"

Keith nodded again.

"We had no choice. Turner's Home Entertainment division cut a deal with the studio."

"What are they expecting us to do with RoboCop?" I asked.

"We have to figure it out," Keith replied.

Well, there wasn't much to figure out. RoboCop was essentially useless— not just as a character, but as a prop, too. He couldn't do a "run in" because he couldn't move faster than a snail in his costume; he couldn't walk up steps so we couldn't get him in the ring, and he couldn't throw a punch or take any moves because the suit was so restrictive.

So we had to come up with a wrestling angle for a guy in a full body cast.

The executives wanted us to be seen as "Hollywood friendly" just like Vince was in WWF. During the introduction of Sting and RoboCop, our hero Sting was pushed into a cage by three of the dastardly Four Horsemen, where he had to wait for RoboCop to shuffle down the aisle and rip off the cage door to free him.

"They gave us a plate of horse shit and we have to make it kinda edible," Ole said.

RoboCop aside, Sting was ready to be champion. He wanted it, the fans wanted it. But others didn't.

Ric Flair had a lot of allies. He was the best performer in the world; one of the top three I had ever seen. He was already a made man, a legendary figure, so with the title or not he was going to be a huge part of the shows and a huge draw for the fans. Problem was Flair saw himself as "the champ." He didn't like the idea of not being associated with the "big gold belt."

It wasn't the first time that Ric had put the brakes on a potential new champion. A few months earlier I had mentioned Japanese star, The Great Muta as a possible future champion, too. Ric was having none of it. Jim Herd curiously heard about my suggestion afterward—even though he wasn't even there—and simply said, "there's no way we can get people to cheer a Japanese guy."

A few months later, at The Great American Bash, Sting did get his victory over Flair. It was a huge moment that was again dick-punched by events outside the Stinger's control. Bad booking, overly complex finishes, and no red-hot heel waiting to "chase" the new champion hurt Sting's ability to cement his place at the top of the card. As fellow booking committee member, Kevin Sullivan, said: "You never saw a knight become a knight by slaying a salamander; he's got to kill a big dragon to be a hero."

But Ole had a masterplan to bring Sting his dragon to slay . . . and that dragon's name was the Black Scorpion.

Actually he didn't have a masterplan. He had half a plan, and even that half of the plan was just a "screw you" to everyone. When the management said they wanted a big angle for their TV and PPV's, Ole decided to give them just that. He started an idea, with no plan on how to finish it.

"I can book what I want," he said.

"But what's the plan?" I asked.

"We'll figure it out when we get there."

At that point, Ole wasn't getting along with anyone, and kind of isolated himself from outside points of view. In trying to block out the bad advice of the upper management, he simply blocked out all advice. Black Scorpion was going ahead, whether there was an end for it or not. And Ric Flair was coming with him.

Flair, of course, hated the idea. The Black Scorpion was some masked, mysterious man from Sting's past who sounded like Ole—because Ole did his voiceover on TV. He was also a different height and weight every time he was seen because he was being played under the mask by different wrestlers. Flair hated it so much he refused to have anything to do it—right up until the last messy seconds. Ole was an old school "do what I say" booker, and at the back of it all, Flair was an old school team player. The Nature Boy, like any performer or athlete, was anxious about doing something so out of his comfort zone that a little guidance or coaching might have made all the difference.

When the Nature Boy finally pulled off the mask to reveal himself as the Black Scorpion, he made the very best of a bad situation—but also talked about quitting. Again.

Chapter Thirty-Four

LADY ON A PLANE

1990

"You know I introduced you to her, Jimbo," Flair said. We were about to board another plane, to hit another town. Of course, I knew just who "her" was. Nothing lit up Flair's memory of Jan quite like a US Airways flight.

"How long did she last?" he asked, as he sat down in his first class seat.

"We're moving in together," I said, as I sat down beside him.

He was shocked. "What? Is she crazy? She must be."

I thought the same.

A few years before, Ric and I boarded a US Airways flight from West Virginia to Atlanta. It was only a small flight with just four first class seats. Nature Boy and I were the only passengers that sat in two of the four available.

"I'm really sorry," said the first class attendant. "They told us there weren't any first class passengers on this flight, so there's no breakfast to serve."

"Is there vodka and orange juice?" Flair asked.

"Yes," she replied.

"Then there's breakfast, sweetheart," Ric said. "And bring a Baileys and coffee for my friend."

I smiled at her with my $10,000 TV smile, and she smiled back. Ric immediately leaned into her line of sight. "Can you also hang up my $20,000 robe? Cause I'm the world's heavyweight champion."

Jan took the robe and disappeared to make the drinks.

For the next 30 minutes the Nature Boy wheeled out his "best" lines to try and catch her attention. "You want me to put on the robe for you, honey?" Flair asked.

Luckily she refused, as I knew that "put on the robe" meant *just* the robe. I had already seen Flair's private parts way too many times. Thankfully she stuck to her job, kept the drinks coming, and generally faded into the background. But I couldn't help notice how beautiful she was and what a great sense of humor she had, as she told us some great jokes.

When we landed, I readied my business card.

"Is that for her?" Ric asked.

"Yeah," I replied.

He burst into laughter. "You really think she's going to go for you when she's been showing no interest in me?"

I put my card back in my pocket. Maybe he was right.

"Thank you guys so much for flying with us today. Hope you have a great day," Jan said as she handed Ric back his robe. Naitch gathered together his things and walked towards the door.

"Can I . . ." I mumbled as I searched for my card again. "Can I . . ." I couldn't find my card.

She had her own business card waiting for me.

"Is it okay to call you sometime?" I asked.

"My number is there," she replied.

It was because of that meeting on that flight that Ric claimed he set Jan and me up on a date.

"And now you're moving in with the flight attendant that gave you her card, Jimbo?" Flair asked.

"Yep," I replied.

Ric could sense I was a little wary. He ordered some drinks. Not to celebrate, just because he wanted to drink. "You ready to be tied down again?" he asked, as he held up his glass to toast.

I clinked my drink off his, not knowing how to answer. I knew I loved Jan and didn't want to lose her. I also knew what a horrible husband I had been in the past. "I'm not sure," I replied.

I knew my dilemma didn't really affect Ric. To the Nature Boy, his wives were married but he wasn't.

Chapter Thirty-Five

HEYMAN

1990

Paul Heyman was an ambitious, aggressive, in-your-face, never-back-down pain in the ass—and I liked him immensely for it. I knew he was money because he was a born heel with the guys in the business hating him nearly as much as the audience watching the show. He didn't genuflect for no one and always called bullshit on the segments, people, or interviews he thought were bullshit.

He hadn't been long fired from WCW, filed a lawsuit, and even met Vince about going to WWF. But I wanted him back. Unfortunately, I was surrounded by people who despised the "New York Jew" so much that they simply didn't want him around, no matter his value to the company.

"What if we brought him back and then beat the shit out of him on air?" Jim Barnett asked. "That would shut his mouth."

Heyman once described Barnett to me as "a flamboyant, evil son of a bitch; a cross between Truman Capote and Darth Vader," so that might have had something to do with Barnett's plan.

"I'll take him," I said. "He can come with me and I'll be responsible for him."

The small cabal who were trying to figure out Heyman's next step all shrugged their shoulders. As long as they didn't have to deal with him, they were fine with my suggestion.

"Just keep him away from us" was the general consensus.

I called Heyman and said, "I know you haven't signed a deal with Vince yet, and I want you back here."

About six months before, Flair sent Heyman home for being a pain in the ass, but WCW wouldn't release Paul from the remainder of his contract. This left Heyman in quite the spot, as he couldn't come back to WCW because Flair wouldn't have it, and he couldn't go to WWF because he was still under contract. Paul felt he had no other recourse but to sue Turner and WCW.

"Jim," Heyman said to me over the phone, "I'm not going back there. They haven't paid me in six months and Ric Flair will make my life hell."

"I can't get you back as an announcer," I said. "They hate you too much to put you front and center just yet. But I can get you back as a manager."

"I'm not interested. But if I was, who would I be managing?"

"Mark Calaway."

"Oh, he's money."

"He sure is," I said. Mean Mark had already debuted with Teddy Long; both men had zero chemistry and Ole was looking at the big redheaded Texan as a write-off.

I could sense that Paul was tempted. "What if I worked out something that got you paid your six months that they owe you?"

"What about Flair?" he asked.

"If you don't pick a fight, I've got your back." I could hear some shuffling down the phone line. "What do you say?" I asked. "You come back now, do your six months on your contract, and then if you want to leave WCW you'll be doing it with a clean slate. So when WWF is done with you, you can come back here."

"OK," he said.

"You're in?" I asked.

"I'll see you tomorrow."

"Paul, before you hang up . . ."

"Yeah?"

"How's your driving license?"

"It's clean."

"Good."

"Why?"

"No reason. Pick me up at my house tomorrow."

From there, he drove me everywhere, and during those rides I passed on to him what had been passed on to me. All the lessons I'd learned from Watts, Ak, and Hodge, all the stories, all the psychology. Every chance I got, I'd bring Heyman on commentary with me as a "guest." Our chemistry was undeniable. We would say the worst things to, and about each other—but we always kept our eye on *why* we were doing that. We wanted to pull the audience in, and then use our platform to enhance the action in the ring.

With Paul at my side, I began to show him the ropes. I showed him how to fill in TV sheets and explained the rundown of a show. I thought it was a simple run-of-the-mill type gesture, but Paul didn't think so. When I looked up from the sheet I could see Heyman was a little emotional. "Thank you for showing me this stuff," he said. I tried to bat his sincerity away with a joke, but he was deadly serious. There was something in him that really appreciated me taking a risk on him and showing him how a TV show was put together.

As the months went on, I fought for Heyman to come with me on the Saturday night show, too. Everyone else railed against it, but I was adamant that he and I had something WCW could desperately use.

We had believability.

"Get a suit," I told him. "And dye your hair."

"Anything else?" he asked.

"Show up ready to fight for your life, because they're all rooting for you to fail."

"Good," he said. "Fuck them."

The next day, Paul collected me in his car and we started our drive to the office. As we pulled out onto the road I could see Heyman looking at my car, dusty, in the driveway.

"Paul," I said. "How much do you learn from me in our preparation?"

"I get the rhythm and psychology," he said. "So, a lot."

"And how much do you learn in the car?"

"I get ten percent in the building, fifteen percent around the locker room, and seventy-five percent from you in the car."

"Exactly. That's why you drive me around so much."

I could see Heyman smiling. He wasn't buying it.

"What?" I asked.

"Oh, *you're* doing *me* the favor by having me drive you everywhere?"

"Exactly. That, and the fact my license is suspended."

Heyman slapped his steering wheel with excitement. "I knew it! I knew something was wrong!"

Even though he and I were in his car alone, I still looked behind me to see if anyone could hear what I was about to say. "I got caught on a second DUI. They suspended my license for ninety days."

"I won't say anything."

I felt like shit for even putting myself in such a lousy position. I should have never driven while drunk—I knew it, and learned my lesson. As well as taking my license, they also made me pick up litter from the side of the road for six weeks. Even though I'd wear a semi-disguise of baseball cap and sunglasses, sometimes people would honk when they saw the chubby-headed man from TV filling his plastic bag with soda cans.

"I'd happily drive you around for as long as you need it," he said.

I believed him, too.

And then he was gone again. Another fight with higher-ups, which resulted in Heyman going home for another stint. I still had my eye on him, though. I knew I could help direct his energy and passion in the right direction.

I just had to wait until this round of heat had left Heyman's name. As soon as I saw an opening, I was going to pitch to bring him back in again. I couldn't let someone special like that just float off to the competition.

Chapter Thirty-Six

CHANGES, OLD AND NEW

1990

Near the end of the year, Dusty Rhodes returned to replace Ole as booker. I heard that Ole quit, then heard he was fired, then that he quit, but, no, he was fired. Either way, the wrestling world had changed around Ole, and he didn't seem to have the tools to deal with it. WCW wrestlers had guaranteed contracts, which meant that got paid no matter if they were "injured," not working hard, *or* taking his direction. This created a standoff—one which Ole couldn't win. His style of booking wasn't as painful to me as it was to other guys. I was used to that kind of person all the way along my wrestling journey. It was like my brain had evolved a way of dealing with confrontational, abrasive, combative alpha male types. I knew as long as I did my job well, I would get paid either way. And that's all that mattered.

I had enjoyed working with Dusty in the past because he was funny and he was low maintenance. He knew what he wanted: he wrote the show; he was doing the booking. The sense around the company was that people were happy to hear Dream was coming back. Dusty was a "hit-maker" in the sense that he had crafted many, many memorable and money-making angles and characters with Crockett—and in Florida before that with Professor

Eddie Graham. We were all hoping he could come back and again catch that lighting in a bottle.

In addition to him being booker, Dusty was also going to join me on commentary, too. It was no surprise to me when he fit right in. He was charming, quick, knowledgeable of course and most of all, entertaining. He wanted to do well because that's just that wrestler ego—he wanted to do better than all the top names in both WCW and WWF. Dusty wanted to be better than Jesse Ventura, Jim Cornette, Bobby Heenan, or Paul Heyman.

And he had all the tools to do it.

I sat back when he was on a verbal run, and listened to him just make words up. He'd say things like, "He was oogly. He wasn't ugly, he was oogly. That's worse than ugly." You then add in his energy, delivery, and slight lisp and Dusty was a unique package on color. We had fun and he had no issues if a match was real slow, or whatever, to kind of subtly jab the talent in the ring about it, because what are they going to do—he's the booker.

Dusty probably was about as stress-free to work with as anybody that I worked with. He didn't want a pregame; he didn't want a production meeting as far as me and the announcers were concerned. He'd already thought the show through, gone over it in the truck with the director, gone over it with the talent and the agents. By the time it came down to him and me, he was tired of going over it, which suited me fine. I knew enough to not get caught out with anything. Everything else we called on the fly. If I made a left and I should have made a right, he'd get us right back to where we were going, and I would hear it and I would adapt. In between matches we'd make each other laugh and elbow each other, and he'd remind me of the time he beat me at HORSE, over and over again.

"I'm still not stupid enough to beat the booker," I said.

"You're still smart then," he replied.

Of all the matches, and all the talent we saw, both Dusty and I agree that there was one kid who had something special. He reminded us of a linebacker in the way he looked—big, rugged, blond hair. You could tell he was an athlete: he walked like an athlete, carried himself like an athlete.

He was intense from the get-go. I couldn't tell if it was just nerves because he was new and had gotten a big break from starving in Tennessee, or whether he was always that intense. He'd come up from Dallas, or "Peyton Place" as it was called because there was always some drama, some soap opera down there. That territory was unraveling with all the issues that were going on with personal lives and the lack of institutional control in the booking office and things of that nature. Steve Austin probably was happy to get away from some of that insanity—little did he know that WCW bathed in its own brand of craziness.

He was motivated, excited to compete. You could tell from the beginning that his mindset was "I'm going to become somebody."

WCW was a fresh start for him, but he never struck me as a guy who was just "happy to be there." He always had his game face on, and I think that came from a lot of the fact that he was an over-achieving football player who was a big star in high school. He played linebacker at Wharton Junior College in Texas, and then he got that scholarship to North Texas State in Denton, Texas. Then he got the wrestling bug after watching the World Class Championship Wrestling. He saw commercials for the Chris Adams Wrestling School and he took a job on a freight dock to earn the money to attend. That not only got him trained, but booked, too.

Steve told me he lived way outside of Atlanta, kind of away from everybody. He was a loner. I could see that he had made friends with Brian Pillman, which I thought was kind of the odd couple. Pillman was loud and extroverted and Steve seemed to be a bit more reserved, a Cool Hand Luke kind of a persona. As time moved on, I thought they made a very good team on and off screen.

The Dangerous Alliance was a big break for Steve, because he was very non-political. He needed something to give him an identity and give him a little bit of a political foundation, and having the re-hired Paul Heyman as his spokesman meant he was always going to get great ideas, because Paul was always thinking. He had a group of guys there that were good independent thinkers as well—Rick Rude, Larry Zbyszko, and Arn Anderson, who had been big stars in their own rights, and you add Steve to that group, the youngest of the crew, who was kind of really the guy that was going to get the big rub at the end of all that. Then you had Madusa adding sex appeal and the female component to the mix. And with a great, young manager in Heyman. It was a very good booking by Dusty.

You had Larry, who WCW had nothing for. You had Austin, who they had nothing for really to speak of, in lieu of some of the stuff with Pillman for a while. And Dusty had confidence and knew about how good Arn was. Dream knew Heyman was a heat-seeking missile as a manager—and there weren't a lot of women, so adding Madusa to the group was a great move as she was a brilliant heel. If they had stayed together over a longer period of time, they probably would have gone and been considered one of the more prolific factions ever.

And Austin was a keeper. He just had something. Something that was worth keeping an eye on.

It seemed Dallas was a rich vein for new talent around that time but WCW didn't have a great track record of bringing that talent along and getting the most for their money. WCW was good at hiring guys with potential, then doing nothing with them.

Mark Calaway was a great example of this. He was wrestling in Dallas as the Masked Punisher, but I knew no one in that promotion was making a lot. I saw money in him right away. You don't see too many 6-foot-9 guys that could move around as athletically as he could. With us, he was making about $150 grand a year downside, and his contract came up for renewal. Ole was booking at that time and I said we needed to address Calaway's contract.

"Well, he's never going to draw a dime," Ole said.

"Well, if that's your opinion you're going to miss the boat on this guy," I replied.

"I don't want to hear another fucking word about it."

I talked to Mark, and the word on the street was that McMahon was romancing him. I couldn't understand Ole's thinking and it was the only time I pushed him so far that I thought he was going to punch me. As I saw it, you can't coach big. He was a legit athlete. He was 6-foot-9, 300 pounds. The kind of guy that walks through the airport and everybody looks at, so he's what bookers generally clamor for. He was a head-turner. And Mark was a great guy, very down to earth and very unpretentious. He was kind of laid back, actually. Ole thought that Mark was just another big guy that hadn't found himself, and therefore wasn't going to draw any money.

"You think they're going to give me anything here, Jim?" Mark asked.

"Well, if the booker has no faith in you, *why would you stay?*" I said. "I don't need to know your business, and I don't want to know your business, but if you have the opportunity to go someplace else, based on what I know, I would explore it seriously."

Soon after, I saw him on WWF-TV working as The Undertaker.

Dallas TV also brought a young Mick Foley to my attention. I was in equal parts fascinated *by* him and worried *for* him. He did the running elbow off the ring apron to the floor that was one of the coolest and riskiest moves I had ever seen. In the context of the show, it looked devastating for Mick's opponents. In the context of it being a human body facilitating the move, it looked devastating for Mick Foley. As part of my job, I used to watch wrestling shows from the other territories in marathon sessions. Hours and hours of TV, countless moves, wrestlers, promos, and personalities—and Mick Foley stood out. And it wasn't just his risky moves and daredevil dives. It was his persona under the "character." Mick Foley as Cactus Jack worked equally well bell-to-bell or on the microphone. He was compelling with the volume up or down.

I knew I wanted him to come to WCW.

Chapter Thirty-Seven

JAPAN

1991

Jan and I were kinda moved in together. I was still an asshole afraid to commit, so she moved out again. I missed her more than anything, and I knew I was in danger of losing who I was and what I wanted. She was eager to move our relationship forward, but as someone in the "twice married, twice failed" club, I was in no rush to pull that lever again. As usual, just as she was packing her bags, I was packing mine, too. It was for my first trip to Japan for WCW's co-promotion with New Japan Pro Wrestling, "WCW/New Japan Supershow."

"Will you stay until I get back?" I asked her. "We can talk more about this then."

She was quiet, but resolute. "I know what I want from life, and this isn't it," she said.

Jan went her way, and I went mine. I didn't want her to go. Not even a little bit, but I couldn't help but hear my father's voice saying, "Son, you're not the marrying kind."

On arrival in Japan, we were split into groups and assigned a host who would "look after us" during our trip. Ours had a partly missing digit, which

I would grow to learn meant he was a "made man"—a representative of the Yakuza. My group was Ric Flair, Rick and Scott Steiner, Tony Schiavone, and myself. On the night before the big show, we were taken to a great place for the best steaks I have ever tasted. From there, we were taken to the bathhouse to get a massage. Some of the women that worked there were second- or third-generation and had a very strict set of rules. For instance, they would not tend to anyone with tattoos, which would have left the Steiners out. Our host, however, had a "friendly chat" with the owner of the establishment and the rule was relaxed for the evening.

When we left the baths, we went to a nightclub where Jim Herd, our boss who chewed me out for damaging the company's reputation, got up on stage and drunkenly sang Chuck Berry tunes.

At this point, I just wanted to go to the hotel. I was in this haze of drink, noise, women, decadence, and debauchery, and it didn't sit well with me. I didn't know if I was uncomfortable because this *wasn't* who I was, or because it *was* who I was now. Just as the parade of ladies was being led into the bar, I found our host and asked him to arrange a ride for me back to the hotel. I was just looking for a cab, but he arranged a bodyguard and a driver. Outside the place, my car pulled up, a Corniche Rolls-Royce convertible, and I was driven around the city by my driver with a bodyguard right out of *The Sopranos* sitting snuggly against me in the back. They made sure they put the top down, even though I was freezing my ass off. I smiled at both men all the way back to my hotel, through chattering teeth.

The lights, the buildings, the food and drink. The ladies, the money, the travel, the car—it was never more apparent to me just how far away from the farm I was.

* * *

Thank God I was not involved in any of the political nightmare finishes the next day. NJPW's local star, Tatsumi Fujinami, was going to win the NWA title from Flair in the packed Tokyo Dome.

Tony Schiavone and I did some wraparounds from up in the upper deck with the camera shooting us where the backdrop was the fans and the ring, and from those seats the ring looked like a little dot way down in the middle of the building. It was an amazing scene. We could relax and soak it in because we didn't have to voice-over the show until we got back to the States.

As I watched the main event, I couldn't understand the political issues that we had on our end about Flair losing to Fujinami. New Japan wanted to get in bed with WCW and they wanted to work with Ted Turner as a group. I couldn't understand how it would hurt our champion, or our title, to lose to somebody else's finish. Especially when the plan all along was for Flair to get it back at a pay-per-view the following month.

In the middle of all the political nonsense, the finish of the match ended up being confusing and overly complicated. Flair lost, so the Japanese audience believed the "NWA" heavyweight title went to their local hero. But the US audience was told that Fujinami was already disqualified for throwing Flair over the top rope before the pinfall, so the belt didn't change hands. In the US Flair kept the belt, but in Japan he didn't keep the belt.

It was just a train wreck.

WCW should have trusted Schiavone and me to "protect" Flair in losing. We could have told the great story of Flair's travel, and the matches he had before he left the States; the jet lag, and Fujinami having home crowd advantage. We would have sold it like Fujinami barely caught Ric with a 1, 2, 3, that could have gone either way. We could have built it to a huge rematch the following month.

The long-term relationship of New Japan and WCW was adversely affected by the politics of the day involving the NWA title—and Flair was talking about leaving.

Chapter Thirty-Eight

FLAIR LEAVES

1991

Flair finally left.

The primary issue was that Ric and Dusty had a nice professional rivalry that they generally kept subdued and under control, but the wild card in that whole equation was Herd. Herd had definite feelings about Ric.

Herd wanted changes and wanted younger and new stars developed and we kept feeding the viewer the same show—the menu never changed. And Herd, for the sake of change, wanted change. To change for the sake of change isn't good business as a rule. So if you want to change, what's our plan? Well, change into what? That's going to make us better, why?

Herd wanted to change Ric's persona, and Ric was offended by the fact that he wanted him to change. I totally saw Ric's dilemma. It was like asking Sandy Koufax to start throwing right handed, and he's the greatest left-hander of all time in the eyes of many. That's how Ric looked at his game. I'm Ric Flair. Why do *I* need to change? Herd didn't have the same feel for the business. He looked at Ric Flair like he was a long-time incumbent and it was time for him to pass the torch. There was a very distinct, stark difference in philosophy and opinion between the two men. Their lack of communication with each other allowed the problem to manifest itself into an unsolvable issue, where eventually there was no solution left on the table.

And their tensions were present in the company every day. The people in the office got it from Herd and the people on the roster got it from Flair. In the end people got tired of it. It almost alienated Ric from a lot of people that worked there because they had to live with Herd. Ric was in Charlotte at his mansion working with his lawyers, while a lot of us were sequestered on Herd's floor at the office, so it just got to be unbearable. *Solve the problem for God's sake. Fix your issues. Come to some sort of middle ground. Can you compromise? Is there anything whatsoever that can be done to eliminate this problem? Get a mediator. Do something, instead of just continuing to wear it out with rhetoric.*

"Ric Flair is no longer with this company," Herd said to me.

"He's gone?" I asked. Even though I knew of all the troubles between both men, I was sad the great Ric Flair had finally been broken and forced out.

"He's gone. Good riddance," Herd said. "By the way, you ever hear of anyone walking with the title?"

"Why?" I asked.

"No reason."

Ric left all right, and took the heavyweight title with him. As in the actual belt itself. He had laid a $25,000 deposit on the "strap," per the instruction of the NWA. Ironically, it was an older "rule" that was born out of paranoia that a heavyweight champion could walk once he won the title. In Flair's mind he paid for the belt and it was his. I don't think Herd even was aware of the deposit or the legalities of who owned what.

It was a sad day when Ric left. It was also unfortunate, and we were all going to miss him because he was one of those social guys that loved to have fun and was always the life of the party. He was the company social ambassador and a large part of the face of WCW, and with him gone a huge part of the NWA legacy . . . and had now gone to work for the competition. It just didn't feel right.

Chapter Thirty-Nine

CHANGING OF THE GUARD

1992

Not surprisingly, Herd was the next to go.

"It's just not worth it," he said as he packed up his desk. "This place has taken years off my life. I'm going home."

I knew the constant internal battles were tearing him up and that he was reaching the point of having to step away. He was butting heads with Dusty as booker and getting frustrated with WCW in general. Herd was facing a near-impossible task for someone who had years of wrestling experience—never mind someone like him who had none.

After he left, TBS named K. Allen Frey as WCW's new lead executive. I liked Frey, who asked everyone to call him Kip. He was a smart guy, having earned a law degree at Duke University. He was a big basketball fan and was a genuinely nice man, who immediately tried to foster a positive work environment. Unfortunately, he lacked the one thing he needed most in his new role: he had virtually no product knowledge and was easily manipulated.

He had never been a fan. I don't mean that he hated the business, as so many of the holier-than-thou Turner executives did. Wrestling simply had never registered with him. And for a guy who was so bright, he probably thought nothing of having to manage a crew of wrestlers, beyond the fact that he got to be a department head, which would, in turn, be a stepping stone to something more significant within Turner Broadcasting. Kip's other major problem went hand-in-hand with not being familiar with wrestling—managing the wrestlers. He was too trusting, not understanding that when you had a roster of wresting talents in that era, it was going to have its fair share of con-men. A lot of the guys had the instinct to spot a weakness and the willingness to pounce if they thought they could get something out of it. Some of the guys got contracts or perks that would never have flown with someone more savvy to how the business operates.

Frey was one of the first in wrestling to offer guaranteed contracts, which would prove to be a disservice to the company and even to the wrestlers themselves. Paying wrestlers based on the strength of business gave the wrestlers the thing all athletes needed most: the motivation to keep getting better. WCW's guaranteed contracts paid as much for an empty arena as for a sellout.

I thought it was a concept that wouldn't work that successfully. However, he did create an incentive that was new and innovative: he gave bonuses for the guys who delivered the best performances at the pay-per-views and Clashes. This helped level off some of the "comfortable" matches that guaranteed contracts helped usher in.

Kip also scored something of a "get," when he brought in Jesse "The Body" Ventura to be color commentator on pay-per-views. Although he wasn't the first commentator to advocate for wrestling's villains—Watts had Mid-South villains filling in as early as 1980, and Roddy Piper was doing the same a year later on TBS for Georgia Championship Wrestling—Jesse was the one who popularized the role.

I left Oklahoma with the plan of never living with regret, but the way I handled my working relationship with Jesse was something I regretted and wasn't proud of. Frey signed Jesse to an extraordinary salary for which Jesse would only have to work a small amount of dates. He was only fresh in the door and was earning a huge amount more than I was, even though I was doing all the PPVs and 52 weeks of TV shows a year. The disparity made me furious and as a result, I was standoffish with Jesse right from the start.

I don't know why I blamed Jesse for getting the big money. I should have blamed myself. I didn't have the right negotiation plan in place. I should have had a plan for how to talk to Frey about how much money Ventura was earning versus what I was earning for the amount of work I was doing.

Ultimately, it was wrestlers taking advantage of Kip which led to his exit. He was always doing his best to appease everyone. But in our business, that just means the guys are going to walk all over you.

In May 1992, after only a short time with the company, Kip told a handful of folks individually that he was leaving. I was still working in the office all the time, in addition to broadcasting, so I was one of those he personally told.

"What would you think of me going for the job?" I asked Jan. Ever since we'd split up, I would call her off and on. We became better friends over the phone than we seemingly did when we lived together.

"The department head?" she asked.

"Yeah. Frey says he's leaving, and I think I have the experience now to make something good of the company."

"I think you should do it," she said.

I was a little embarrassed even bringing it up. Wrestling, and my obsession for it, was one of the reasons that Jan and I had split.

"You think I could do it?" I asked.

"Jim, I've never met anyone who loves their profession as much as you love yours," she replied. "Why not you?"

She was right. Why not me, indeed?

"You miss me yet?" I asked.

"Yes."

"You want to try again?"

"No."

"Can I ask you again sometime?"

"Yes."

I loved her and I missed her. And I could hear she missed me, too.

* * *

I walked into the CNN building with my plan laid out and my "pitch" in mind. A lot of people didn't even know Kip was going to leave so I felt that I might have a step ahead of whoever else was considering throwing their hat in the ring.

I really felt that learning all those different roles under Bill Watts in my early years made me as good a candidate as anyone to be the next head of WCW. I had many years of experience in virtually every area of the business, from the communication, handling public relations, writing publicity stories and radio ads, to working with the building managers, recruiting talent, negotiating with talent, booking live events, doing the pay-offs, booking PPV cards and writing and formatting television shows. I did all those things; even within the unique world of wrestling, my education was novel. I hadn't heard of too many people in the business who had experience in all those different departments.

Not a lot of people knew Kip was leaving, but none of us seemed to know that his replacement was already in place.

"Cowboy" Bill Watts.

Since Bill sold the UWF in 1987, we had tried to stay in touch with each other, but with him out of the business for five years that dwindled to where were stayed in contact about as much as anybody in the wrestling business stays in touch—not much.

I found the wresting business funny that way as far as relationships go. I still remember my first road trip with Danny and Akbar when they told me that even after a long career, once I got out of the wrestling business, I would be lucky to be able to count my good friends in the wrestling business on one hand. I thought they were just crabby bastards. Lo and behold, now that I was almost twenty years into the business, I was the crabby bastard saying that to the young wrestlers. When people in wrestling separate, especially geographically, they rarely stay in that close of touch because everyone is focused on the new job, the new roster.

Bill and I would talk sporadically, maybe three or four times a year on the phone, but my relationship with him was different than most because he was a genuine mentor to me and taught me principles of the wrestling business that I had used for my whole career.

And he was now sitting in *the* seat in WCW.

"Jimbo," he shouted when he saw me in the doorway.

"Bill?"

"Come in." He could see I was a little bewildered. "I wanted to call you and tell you," he said, "but they made me give my word that I wouldn't tell anybody, so I kept my word. You know how that goes." I nodded because that was always true of Bill. When he told you he was going to do something, then he was going to do it. "Take a seat," he said, "and tell me about this place."

I gave him the lay of the land as best I could: about job descriptions, telling him who people were, etc. He asked a lot of questions about everything under the sun: the booking, when the deadlines were for ads and promotional stuff, a lot of the fundamental things.

"I don't care what they think here in these offices," he said. "I'm going to do it my way, no matter the cost." And I knew with those few words that Bill's time in WCW wouldn't be long. He had an old-school wrestling mentality in the new-school corporate world—and I had already witnessed how that worked for Ole. "They want me to cut costs around here. Big cuts."

"Where are you going to start?" I asked.

The system of Cowboy's new department, and how TBS structured it, was built for failure. The upper management just didn't seem to care who had answers, or if there *were* answers. They were just thinking about how much money WCW was losing, and when some suit in the north tower decided the guy on top of WCW had lost just about enough, TBS would just replace that guy with another guy.

Watts was the new "other guy."

I also saw my own potential headaches when various Boys in the locker-room began saying things like, "Why didn't you say something about Bill coming in? I can't believe you didn't tell me."

I said I didn't know. 'Cause I didn't know.

The reply was some variation of "Aw, come on. You're Watts's boy."

They couldn't believe it, but I had no idea. Now all of a sudden I was looked at suspiciously. On one hand they wouldn't believe me when I said I didn't know, and on the other hand I was now seen as Watts's lieutenant who was double dealing, or hiding things from the Boys.

Everyone knew there was a new sheriff in town and things were going to change. How things were going to change, nobody could guess—but there was definitely change in the air. And they wanted me to tell them *exactly* what those changes were, even though I had no clue.

Everyone could tell that TBS hired the wrong guy with Jim Herd. He was truly a decent man who had some ill-advised ideas: Hunchbacks, Ding Dongs, some of that stuff. At the end, he wanted the great Ric Flair to become the Gladiator, cutting his hair and wearing an earring. Whatever WWF was doing that Herd saw and thought he might be able to copy, then that's what we did—or he wanted to do. Watts, on the other hand, had plenty of experience and product knowledge. But his first task set by the company wasn't anything to do with the wrestling end of things; his marching orders were to reduce the budget and the losses immensely, and to do it yesterday.

This made Cowboy very challenging to work for.

Bill was so accustomed to calling the shots and not being second-guessed that, in his own way, he was as unprepared to deal with the corporate people as the corporate people who came before him had been unprepared to deal with the wrestlers. Watts immediately butted heads with Bill Shaw, one of the TBS executives who sat higher on the corporate food chain than us peasants in WCW. Bob Dhue, who had managed the Omni—Atlanta's premier indoor arena, and the site for major wrestling shows in that area—ended up being the buffer between the two Bills.

Dhue loved to have a cocktail and play golf. He took things with an attitude of "easy come, easy go," which also meant he was usually happy to take the path of least resistance. But he didn't know a damn thing about the pro wrestling business either, though he was a hell of a lot better to deal with than Bill Shaw. Shaw was like an evil Andy of Mayberry from *The Andy Griffith Show.*

He managed a number of divisions for TBS, and the last thing he seemed to want to do was lower himself into having to deal with the carnival freaks of WCW. I thought after one of his visits he'd have hand sanitizers installed outside the door of the WCW offices so he could cleanse himself on the way out. Shaw used to tell us how other people at TBS didn't understand why Turner was in the wrestling business at all.

But the ratings were very competitive, and it was wrestling programming, which meant it was somewhat cheap to produce and was first run, original programming.

Watts was reducing the costs, but making waves everywhere he went. He even restructured my contract to give me more work on the office side of things. He got my job description listed on my contract and put in a significant pay bump which reflected my new responsibilities. He clearly wanted me to fill into my old Mid-South slot of being his "man on the ground" but I could see from a hundred miles away that it was a poisoned chalice.

I didn't want to tell Cowboy that I just couldn't see how an individualist like him was going to work out long term. I saw him more as being a great consultant, coming in and working for a week or a month, troubleshooting problems, offering some creative quality control and helping get things restructured when they went off the rails.

Bill did some good things; he also did some things that people didn't understand. I loved Bill; he was my mentor and family to me. He was the most influential person I'd known in my career. But his tenure in WCW really was detrimental to me professionally.

It was guilt by association.

There was always volatility and hostility. He came to work angry a lot, and I was his confidant, I was his guy—which I wasn't ashamed of. There were also some swirling statements that Watts made some years before that were coming back to haunt him. I sat under Bill's learning tree and knew he wasn't a racist. I saw the very personal relationship he had with his black booker Ernie Ladd, and his top star, another African American the Junkyard Dog, which other white promoters would never do in that era. He was also proud to put the WCW World Title on Ron Simmons.

But him leaving was all about TBS, and nothing to do with anything else. He'd come in, shook up the entire division (in good ways and plenty of bad), literally pissed off the 12th floor balcony when he felt like it, and then left again.

And when he was gone, I was ostracized.

The guy that taught me more than anybody in wrestling was the guy who inadvertently derailed my WCW career. There was absolutely no way the brass was going to consider another "Watts type" wrestling person in the vacant position and—fairly or not—that meant my career in that direction was dead in the water.

I needed to start thinking about another path.

Chapter Forty

MY LAST DAYS AT WCW

1993

Watts's vacant role ultimately went to Eric Bischoff.

Eric was a "wrestling guy" who came from the AWA, but very smartly sold himself as the exact opposite. After having Ole and Watts at the helm, Turner had no appetite for another old school, headstrong type leading the charge. So Eric pitched himself as a brand builder; a businessman with an overall vision for consistency after all the changes to the company. He was young, handsome, and just the type of antidote to Watts that the brass wanted. He had served his time in WCW as an announcer who mostly worked on the lower shows, but when the time came to make his case for the head of the department, he positioned himself brilliantly. Eric had street smarts and amazing ambition.

Bill Shaw brought me over to his office and told me about the various gripes he had with Watts: from his bombastic nature, all the way down to WCW booking Cowboy's son, Erik, as a wrestler.

"Bill Watts has cast a big shadow around here," he said. "And you're still standing right under it."

"I'm my own man," I replied. I kinda knew that trying to argue my case was useless. I had already said everything I could say, and did everything

I could do. But it was like my nearly twenty years in the business didn't mean anything. I was being judged by another man's actions.

Shaw continued, "So here's your options from here on out. You take six weeks off, to let things cool down . . ."

"I don't want to . . ."

"Just hear me out," he said. "We'll continue to pay you and you come back when the bad taste is gone out of the place."

I didn't want to go anywhere; I knew what it would look like if I followed Watts out the door—even short term. "What's my other option?" I asked.

"Well, you accept a reassignment. You keep your official title as vice president of broadcasting . . ."

"But?"

"But you'll be working in syndication sales, traveling nationwide to market WCW shows to various local TV affiliates across the country," he said. "You'll also be working behind the scenes with the announcers on the Sunday WCW show on TBS."

The show I had created. I felt like Leroy McGuirk's smoldering testicles.

He continued, "If you take the six weeks, I might be able to get you back on the air when you get back."

Shaw knew that was the position I wanted to keep most. "How are you going to get me back on the air," I asked, "when Bischoff specifically said he doesn't want me calling the shows?"

"You don't have to worry about Bischoff," Shaw replied. "He works for me."

I immediately saw how this would work out. I could have turned the meeting into a confrontation—and he would probably have put me back on the air—but it would have been some Mickey Mouse, obscure, demeaning role, which would not only piss me off, but would piss Bischoff off as well because Eric didn't want me on anything. I was around since day one and seen as the "old guard," one of the "wrestling guys." Eric wanted a fresh start, and I understood that completely. Ironically, Watts a few months before had wanted *me* to fire *Eric*. Eric was our C-announcer who handled the smaller shows and did the "grunt" work in terms of announcing.

"I don't like him," Cowboy said. "He's an asshole. An asshole who answers to you, so get rid of him."

"What did he do?" I asked.

"Nothing. I need to send a message."

"Well then, I can't do it," I said. "Eric does a good job, and we have no reason to give corporate for firing him."

Eric stayed. And now I was on the chopping block.

Shaw said, "Look, this is what I would do if I was you. I would take the six weeks off. We're going to pay you anyway, and see what you think then. You don't have to take the syndication thing, but we're offering you a job over here that needs some help. And if you don't want to do the syndication job, then just take another six weeks, because we're going to keep paying you."

The company didn't want me to stay, but knew I had a contract, which raised a major problem for TBS. When they'd re-signed me under Watts, a raise was not all I got. I also received a guaranteed deal to be the voice of the Saturday night TBS show, the Clash of Champions specials, and the pay-per-views. At the time, TBS had wanted to lock me into those roles so their own lawyer put in writing my job specification. When my lawyer looked at it, he said, "You need to sign this right away, because you're locked in to prime time. It's like being the host of *Monday Night Football* and that's your gig, and if they don't want you to be the host of *Monday Night Football* anymore, they have to pay you your full contract."

By having me out on vacation, or traveling around with syndication sales, I simply wasn't going to be around the company. I was being sent out to the hinterlands to be forgotten until my deal ran out three years later.

So I took the six weeks and went to Jamaica. Alone. Bad idea. After I stumbled back to the States, the mere smell of rum made me ill. It was the first vacation I'd taken in years. Problem was, I was bored just two weeks in.

I called Jan a lot, and I felt like we were getting even closer. I told her what was happening, and she was an amazing confidant who I missed dearly. I looked forward to talking with her above just about anything in my life.

But I wasn't the kind for sitting around.

I didn't want the money for nothing, I wanted to work for it. I wanted to earn it. *Better to die of work than rust.*

When I came back, I decided to give the syndication and production job a try. I did get to keep one of my "broadcasting" jobs, too. Little did I know that my weekly report on WCW's 900 number on Saturdays was making a small fortune, and, of course, I got none of that money. Traveling around and going to the local TV stations, and pitching the WCW syndicated programming was soul destroying. I knew where I wanted to be, I knew I had much more to offer on TV. I'd gotten enough attention from fans of my work over the years that I ended up getting the same question over and over: "Jim, how come you're not on TV anymore?"

It just became embarrassing, and I had enough.

I'd watched talent after talent, person after person travel north to WWF over the years. It was my turn to try and do the same.

PART SIX

WWF

1993–1999

Chapter Forty-One

VINCE

1993

I decided to make two calls that would change my life.

The first to Jan, and the second to Bruce Prichard.

Jan and I were communicating a lot more, talking on the phone and occasionally meeting up for drinks. I didn't know how she and I would do back together, I just knew that I wanted to find out. Once Jan knew I was serious, she made up her mind, too. I was ready to marry the kindest, most understanding woman I had ever met, and she was ready to settle down with a high-maintenance wrestling guy who was away from home a lot and obsessively committed to his job. I was nervous that I would be a bad husband again, but Jan was too beautiful and too smart for me to let go again.

"I'm a little worried about how I'll be as a husband," I said to her.

"You want to find out?" she asked.

"More than anything."

"Well, me too."

I also realized that, professionally, I needed to be back to where I felt I belonged: on air calling matches and helping the talent get over. I knew that, with Eric in charge, WCW wasn't going to allow me to do that. So I rang my old friend from Mid-South, Bruce Prichard. When Bruce first came on the scene, Cowboy didn't like him and didn't want him in his company. Bruce and I got along great, however, so even though Cowboy was wary I hired Bruce to do the syndication interviews after the Sunday night Tulsa shows.

Bruce did really well considering he had never done much promo work on screen before. I helped him the best I could, and he was always loyal and trustworthy to me. So as I figured out what I was going to do—and I realized I couldn't drink all the Crown Royal in Atlanta or smoke all the "mysterious" tobacco in Georgia—I gave Bruce, who was now a higher up at WWF, a call.

I was basically sitting alone in my apartment every day and needed to do something. I had the itch. Even though I had a radio show, *Wrestling with Jim Ross* on AM750 WSB, I really wanted to get back into the day-to-day side of the wrestling business. I wanted to see if I could make it in the big show. Every step I'd taken, every piece of advice I listened to, and every lesson I'd learned was all leading me to New York. To Vince McMahon. To WWF.

I drove my navy blue, two-door Lincoln Continental Mark VII from Atlanta to Augusta, Georgia, to have my first in-person meeting with Vince McMahon. I thought about the only other time I had spoken to Vince, which was on the telephone when he called the UWF office in Bixby, Oklahoma, looking for us to release Missy Hyatt. Watts didn't care to talk to McMahon so I handled the call and agreed to the release, as Cowboy had nothing creatively for Missy at that time.

I was hurtling down I-20 East loading myself with breath mints and dabbing myself with cologne; I didn't want to arrive to what was essentially a job interview stinking of the cigarette smoke that was wafting around in my car.

When I arrived, I parked in the back of the arena where the TV trucks, talent, and crew parked; I worked that same building with WCW so I knew my way around. I walked down the ramp to the backstage entrance of the arena without having to show any credentials or ID. The local security were the same so they knew me and thought I was just there to say hello to a few old pals.

The first guy I ran into was Jerry Brisco. Jerry was the promoter for the town and was told to keep an eye out for my arrival.

Jerry knew me, and I certainly knew him because both he and his brother, Jack, were fellow Okies and legends in the business.

"You here to see Vince?" Jerry asked. I wasn't sure how to answer, as I didn't know if our meeting was "secret" or not. "It's okay," he said, sensing my reluctance, "I'll go and get him for you."

Vince wanted to talk before the taping started so he could then get on with producing three TV shows before a packed house of 8,000 fans.

I heard McMahon's familiar voice talking to someone as he approached. I instinctively pretended to be cool by whistling softly while looking in the opposite direction, like this was no big thing.

"Jim?" Vince said as he got closer. Before I could answer, someone from production asked Vince a question, then someone passing shook his hand. The Steiner Brothers, who I knew from WCW, walked by and said "hi" to both me and Vince. We were standing in the corridor where all the talent arrived.

Bam Bam Bigelow, Terry Taylor, Tatanka, and "Hacksaw" Jim Duggan all stopped to say hi as well. It was great seeing old friends, but I was anxious to get my own time with Vince to see if I could land *myself* a spot in the company the Boys were already working for.

I could see by Vince's interaction with his roster that he was the kind of man who liked to get to the point. He was polite and respectful to all who passed, but didn't really engage in much small talk. He struck me as a guy who wanted to know what time it was, not how to make the watch.

"How about we go outside?" he said.

"Sounds good," I replied.

My thinking was that McMahon and I could have our talk and then I could slip out in my trusty Lincoln and head back to Hotlanta.

"I appreciate you taking the drive down," he said. "I'm glad Bruce could get us two together."

"Me too."

"Tell me about how you got in to the business," he said as he stopped in a quiet spot away from the building. I knew he didn't have long before his taping began, so I launched into my history and what my various roles were under Cowboy. He cackled at some of my stories and seemed to get a real kick out of certain people and wrestlers who crossed both of our paths. We talked about a litany of philosophical matters, booking approaches, and my ongoing job as VP of Broadcasting for Turner Broadcasting's WCW.

"What do you think we could do here to make people more aware of what we're doing?" he asked me.

"Radio," I said immediately. "Nobody in wrestling is using radio properly to market their events."

"Really? How so?"

"You have the talent, you have the announcers, *and* you have fans who want to hear more from them." I could see he was really taking in what I was saying. I continued, "For instance, you could broadcast live radio from the house shows. Give people a real taste of the excitement and the energy that comes from experiencing the matches live."

I saw McMahon opening up more and more as our talk continued. Behind the name, the title, and the stories I'd heard, Vince was just a redneck from North Carolina who liked to joke, curse, and talk about wrestling. I knew I was really getting somewhere when he didn't leave to produce his shows. It was unheard of that "hands on" McMahon wasn't front and center for his own TV taping—but something in our conversation made him stay. I felt some of my ideas had struck a chord with Vince, and his vision for how he wanted to build the wrestling business damn sure motivated me. I was less concerned about what position I was going to play in WWF—I just wanted to be issued a jersey.

After almost three hours of talking about life, family, and a lot of wrestling—in the parking lot—Vince put out his hand. "I can't match your WCW salary, but I can get very close," he said. "I can also give you a signing bonus of fifty grand. What do you say?"

"Deal," I said on the spot.

And we shook hands.

"Great! I want you to start at WrestleMania."

"WrestleMania?"

"Goddamn, what a way to introduce yourself."

Vince and I shook hands once more and that was that—we had a deal. I would be starting roughly a month later, at WrestleMania, in a yet to be determined role.

"I appreciate the opportunity," I said as he walked toward the building and I walked toward my car.

"You're going to fit right in around here," Vince replied.

I felt an immediate connection in some crazy, rasslin' way to the genius known as Vinnie Mac. I was buying what Vince was selling and I decided there and then that WWF was the company I wanted to finish up my pro wrestling career with. And if the boss said I was going to fit right in, then who was going to question him?

Maybe the asshole that punctured all four of my tires in the parking lot.

Someone obviously spotted me parking "Ol' Blue" and either decided to "rib" me or simply be a tool and slash all of my tires. I was 150 miles from my Atlanta home, with four flat wheels, on a weeknight, with no phone booth in sight to call anyone—or no one to call even if I could find one.

Thankfully, one of the friendly security guards knew a local service station where they sent their wrecker to tow me to their shop. I bought four used, mismatched tires, which were barely good enough to get me back to Atlanta.

As soon as I arrived home, I had a call on my machine from Bruce Prichard. I called him back.

"Vince is pissed," Bruce said.

Panic hit me all at once, as I thought he'd changed his mind. "Why?"

"Cause he heard what happened to your car, Jim."

I was relieved to hear it wasn't anything to do with our meeting. "Really? Tell him it's fine and that I'm looking forward to coming to work with you guys."

"Vince wants to pay for the damage. What did it cost you?" Bruce asked.

Through Bruce, I politely refused Vince's generosity. It was my issue, and I wanted to get that negativity off Vince's radar as soon as possible. I got my dream job and couldn't wait to launch the beginning of the next, biggest, most daunting part of my career.

"Vince said I'd fit right in," I said to Bruce over the phone. "You think so?"

Bruce paused. "Eh . . . yeah?" he replied, obviously lying.

Chapter Forty-Two

WCW RADIO

1993

When my deal with WWF became official, I wanted to make a big splash with the news. I thought, *I'm not going to be a part of the Turner family—except getting their nice checks every other week—so I want to elevate my radio show by opening it up a bit.* WCW was a sponsor of *Wrestling with Jim Ross*, but they didn't own it. They had no claim to my guest list, and no further claim to me.

I knew WSB wasn't a minor station, either. WSB was *the* station in Atlanta, and the second word got out that WWF Chairman Vince McMahon was coming on the show, my phone started ringing. I heard from Jim Barnett and the TBS lawyers, who wanted to know what I was doing; they had the mistaken belief that they owned or controlled my show.

"None of the contracts with the advertisers were in WCW's name," I explained. "The deals were all cut between me and the advertisers directly."

I knew a guy like Bob Hughes, who became a great friend and was in charge of the massive advertising budget of Georgia Power, was irate that WCW were treating me like dirt. WCW couldn't have moved his advertising from my show with a stick of dynamite. Not a single business cancelled advertising after WWF personalities starting appearing on the show—not least of which was the WWF chairman himself—who came live on air to tell the wrestling world that I was their new signee. Vince said that I was the business's premier announcer, and that Christmas had come early for his company. "It's the equivalent of John Madden jumping from CBS to NBC," he said.

I got calls and mail from listeners in 37 states who said they were in wrestling heaven because my one-dimensional WCW-centric show was now bringing on the Superstars from "the other side."

The station had a meter which could measure how many people were calling, or trying to call, and we had the most called radio show on the station. It was an amazing hit because wrestling fans finally had an outlet to communicate.

Of course, the WCW lawyers began to push it a little too far, so someone in WCW had to step in; they had to come clean. The reason Jim Ross could jump ship so cleanly was because the management of WCW screwed up. WCW had reassigned me, therefore voiding their own terms and breaking their own contract with me.

I was free to jump and be welcomed with open arms to the WWF.

Chapter Forty-Three

WRESTLEMANIA IX

1993

"You sure you're okay wearing that, pal?" Vince asked me. I was standing backstage at Caesars Palace wearing a toga and some sandals.

"It's the world's biggest toga party, right?" I said, referencing WWF's theme for the show.

"That's right!" Vince said.

"Then I'm sure as hell joining the party."

I was ready to debut for WWF at their biggest event of the year, WrestleMania IX, where the company drew inspiration from their "Roman" surroundings to create a Colosseum theme.

They hired actors to play Cleopatra and Julius Caesar, I saw elephants backstage and ostriches, buzzards, centurions, and "vestal virgins" walking around. There were costume designers and rehearsals, lines to learn for the show opening, and a new broadcast team to work with.

I was a long way from home.

Apart from me, Howard Finkel had a costume, Gorilla Monsoon had a costume, and Bobby Heenan had a costume. The only person that didn't wear a period piece was "Macho Man" Randy Savage. I don't know if that was because he refused or it went against his gimmick, but either way I was too busy to think about it. It was my first week on the job, my first ever WWF PPV—a WrestleMania—and I was ready to show an entirely new audience what I could do. It didn't matter to me what they dressed me in, I was solely focused on what the audience was about to hear, not see. Vince even gave me the option of wearing a suit if I was uncomfortable in a toga.

"You ready?" asked a familiar voice from behind me. It was Gorilla Monsoon.

"I'm just trying to remember my lines," I said in reply. Gorilla was a huge man, a legend in the business, and the voice of WWF. But he didn't look well. His health wasn't strong in general, but it had certainly slid further after his son and WWF referee, Joey Marella, died in a car crash ten months before.

Gorilla smiled and said to me, "You're going to do great."

Monsoon's words were a huge comfort. We had a big production meeting the day before and I wasn't exactly welcomed with open arms by the vast majority of WWF employees. I was known as the voice of "the enemy," but Gorilla stood out as being friendly and helpful right from the beginning.

"Energy," Vince reminded me. "Give me energy out there!"

As we went live, Monsoon's voice was the first to be heard on the WrestleMania IX broadcast. He would have done the play-by-play as well, if he wasn't so clearly ill. He got into his costume, did the intro at the very top of the show, and then pitched it down to the newest member of the broadcast team: Jim Ross.

It was showtime for me, in the biggest wrestling company in the world. "It will be a day of firsts, ladies and gentlemen," I said with all the excitement and passion I could muster. "My very first WrestleMania. First time that yours truly, from the great state of Oklahoma, has ever been in toga myself. This is quite an impressive outfit, and I, too, could get used to this. What do you think of these gold shoes?" I said, showing the camera my perfectly appointed golden sandals. "How would those play in Tulsa?"

As I took over, Gorilla went back to his room to rest. I wrapped up my intro, ran down the top of the card, and nailed all the lines I had to remember. I moved down to ringside and waited for my broadcast colleagues, Bobby "The Brain" Heenan and Randy Savage, to make their entrance down the aisle.

My head was full of little things to worry about. I wasn't so much concerned about getting the wrestlers over or calling a compelling match, I was more worried about it being daylight and outdoors, which would cause glare on my monitor. Or making sure I facilitated both Savage and Heenan in their role, as I had never done a three-man booth for a whole PPV before. And certainly not one that just happened to be the biggest event of the year for the company and the entire business.

I was aware of all the changes, all the things I had to get used to as we went live across the world. I was also aware that I was on top of the world. I loved feeling the rush; the fact there was no safety net. As I settled at ringside, Bruce Prichard introduced himself in my headset, the music hit for the first match, and I sat down in my seat to lead my two, vastly different, new colleagues into the fray.

Randy was challenging to work with right from the get-go. I could hear right away that I was going to earn my money with Macho. He kept me on my toes—and not in a negative way—as soon as the PPV began. I had no idea where exactly where he was going in his commentary so it was hard for me to "direct traffic." He was wound tight at the best of times, but this was WrestleMania, and he didn't seem to like the fact he had to get used to a partner, me, live on PPV. I had heard that Savage, historically, was not an overly trusting individual; it was just the nature of his personality, so he committed to working his own style, and I had to follow.

Heenan, on the other hand, was just the opposite. He was loose and funny and made my job easy. I knew Bobby was good from watching his stuff on TV, but I had no idea *just* how good he was until I sat beside him and "went live."

When I thought of all the tools that someone can bring into the wrestling business, I could see nobody who had more to offer than Bobby Heenan. I was a huge fan of his wrestling and on-air role as a manager, and now after working with him as an announcer I left that booth looking at Bobby as the best total-wrestling-package ever. I knew he was extraordinarily under-rated in-ring talent. He took the greatest ass-whippings in the history of the sport, and could feed a comeback as a heel to make a babyface look like Superman—as good as any heel I ever saw. Then, the very next week after being mutilated and disfigured, he'd get back on the microphone and talk his heat right back to where it was. He was an artisan. When it was time to step back from the ring he became a broadcaster with no broadcast training. I don't think he even had a high school degree, but the Brain was a genius commentator.

Our first outing at WrestleMania was enough proof for me that Bobby and I had natural chemistry on screen. But I would soon rely on his friend-ship off screen to help navigate the confusing world of WWF.

Chapter Forty-Four

GROWING PAINS

1993

I got the feeling, almost immediately, that the people in WWF hated my guts. Not *me* the person, but *me* the guy Vince hired from the competition and didn't tell anyone about. McMahon was the alpha male and he didn't often ask for people's feedback or suggestions—he simply hired me because he thought I could contribute to the success of his company. What that meant on the ground was some people in the production and television side were reluctant to open up and didn't want to lower their guard and trust me. I was a WCW guy to them, coming over to take their spot.

I knew I had to prove myself—and was waiting outside the Stamford Studios to do just that—when a big Cadillac pulled up. The license plate read: **KAYFABE**. Inside I could see the smiling face of Gorilla Monsoon looking back at me. I stubbed out my cigarette and walked toward his car.

Gorilla was a former main event wrestler and a trusted confidant of McMahons who was so well respected that they named the backstage section just behind the curtain, "The Gorilla Position," after him.

"Nice ride," I said.

"You like to drive?" Gorilla asked me.

"I started out driving for Leroy McGuirk in a car like this one," I said as I looked the Cadillac up and down.

"Well, I'm more or less blind now, Jim. How about we ride together when we go out on the road?"

"Love to."

"If we're renting a car, I need something with leather seats. I can't get out of the car if it has regular cloth seats."

"Got it." I was just thrilled that someone with so much clout was taking a shine to me.

Gorilla opened the door for me to enter the building. It was my first weekend of TV, and Monsoon was already looking out for me. I was there to team with Bobby "The Brain" Heenan for a show called *Wrestling Challenge*, which was one of the two syndicated shows that WWF produced. I knew when I entered the studio that the reception for me was cool to say the least. Some would say it was hostile. Gorilla, feeling it too, smiled and ushered me in.

"What do I have to do to let people know I'm not the enemy?" I asked him.

"You want the truth?"

I nodded.

"I'm not sure," he said. "This is pretty bad."

Little did I know that it was the mixture of Bobby, me, and the catering guy that would turn my fortunes around with the crew.

After a couple weeks working with the Brain, he leaned in to me and said, "You know, they used to hate you around here."

"I know," I replied. Then it hit me. "Wait a minute, *used* to?"

"It's the catering," Bobby said.

"The food?" I asked, confused as to what Heenan was alluding to.

"Vince and Savage are here the day before us," he explained. "That means pasta, salad, and chicken breast. Then me, you, and Gorilla come in to do our show—" Bobby waited until I caught up with him. "Nothing but desserts, meatballs, potato salads, and soda. The crew can't wait for you to come back every week. They love you!"

"They do?"

"Well, no, but they tolerate you. That's a start."

He was right, it was a start. I had nothing to do with the menu, but when Heenan, Monsoon, and I were there, the catering guys would order the food we liked: hideously bad, fattening, carbohydrate-loaded foods . . . and a chocolate cake to finish.

The food got me some love to begin with, and then the crew began to see Bobby and I had great chemistry, we didn't overthink things, and we hit our marks and got the job done. We would normally do all three hours of our TV in just four hours of taping. That included pee breaks and dinner breaks. I quickly learned that nothing will endear you to a hostile crew like unhealthy food and shorter hours.

On the other days, when Vince was involved, the time needed would go into the evening hours because McMahon had so many interruptions between takes. He was chairman of the board and had a lot of irons in the fire; when someone would call over, they'd have to interrupt the voice-overs so Vince could take the phone call or fix a problem. The tapings were stop and go, stop and go, stop and go. Bobby and I, we just nailed our business with no fuss and no waiting around.

I quickly came to love working with Bobby and Gorilla, and they both accepted me because they liked how I started in the business—working for little money and paying my dues. My story seemed to resonate with the two veterans, who then would communicate that to the people who worked for WWF. I needed all the help I could get, as the crew weren't my only detractors. I was even "shunned" by other broadcasters, like Lord Alfred Hayes. Hayes was an Englishman who was a good wrestler and heel manager before settling in WWF as a broadcaster in his later years. I'd never even met him, didn't know him, but still he treated me like I had malaria or some other infectious disease. He was rude and unprofessional until Monsoon and Heenan got wind of it.

Gorilla had a quiet word to his Lordship, after which, Alfred and I became famous friends. We had fun and drank together; he loved to drink wine and regale us with the stories of his days in the UK or his time working for Bob Geigel, the NWA promoter who was eventually bought out by Jim Crockett. We soon found we had mutual friends that we'd met on the territory circuit. Bit by bit, person by person, I could feel I was making ground in the company.

Bill Watts had told me years before that Gorilla Monsoon was one of the truly good guys, and he was right. Heenan and Monsoon both knew I wasn't some kid fresh from broadcasting school. I was a territory guy. I rode up and down the roads with the guys, getting my hands dirty. I refereed. I was one of the ring crew. I was one of the Boys.

But that didn't protect me from everyone.

* * *

It was an odd feeling getting pulled out of a studio by a volatile former WWF champion. At first I panicked at the sheer sight of his wild eyes as he stomped toward me. Then the second before he grabbed me I thought he was joking because he seemed to be "in character." One thing I soon learned about "Macho Man" Randy Savage was: he wasn't a character. What you saw on TV was him. He was that intense first thing in the morning till last thing at night.

All that's all well and good, until he turns that intensity in your direction.

"Get out!" he shouted as he pushed out through the door of the studio into the hallway.

All I could think was, *I'm about to get my ass beat by the Macho Man. Holy shit. It's happening.*

"Who put you up to it?" he shouted in my face. "Who got you, yeah, to bring me in here to do all this work?"

I whispered through my dry mouth. "I don't know what you're talking about."

He didn't like that reply at all. He shouted, "You keep bringing me in here to do these interviews and I'm not even booked to be here!" Clearly someone had been in Randy's ear, stirring him up. "Are you goddamn ribbing me, Ross?"

"Randy," I said. "You're a household name. I want to get you on TV to help get these angles over for—"

"Shut up!" His eyes were wild, and he was talking a little to himself and a little to me. "You think it's funny bringing me up here to do this shit? Do you?" And then the surreal got dangerous. He stuck his finger in my face and put his other hand around my neck and began to squeeze. "'Cause if you think that you're—"

"Randy," said a familiar voice from down the hallway. "The boys are working you."

I managed to tilt my head a little to see Gorilla walk toward us.

"This asshole," Randy said to Gorilla about me. "He's bring me in to do these promos because he thinks it's funny, yeah, to bring the Macho Man in to do promos. Yeah."

"Jim is just doing his job. It's the Boys who are ribbing you," said Gorilla.

Macho looked right back at me. He already had me pinned against the wall and pretty much peeing on myself. He leaned his head in against mine until we were nose to nose. "I'm going to find out," he said. "And when I do . . ."

"You're not going to do anything," Gorilla said, standing behind Randy. "I strongly suggest you take your leave."

Randy was breathing deeply, the veins in his neck were popping out and the finger he had in my face was nearly pushed through to the back of my head.

"I mean it," Gorilla said. "Let him go."

Macho released his grip and turned to Monsoon. I certainly didn't want Gorilla, at his age, to get into anything physical. I don't think Randy did either. Macho stood down out of respect for Gorilla, then stormed off.

"You okay?" Gorilla asked.

"I'm fine," I said. "Lucky I'm wearing dark trousers."

"He's intense, isn't he?" Gorilla said, laughing.

"I'm learning that."

"Let's get back to work."

Gorilla was like the uncle I never had. I didn't dislike Randy at all; he was just so amazingly unpredictable and talented, I had never been around anybody like him before.

"I think I might stop booking Macho on interviews," I said to Monsoon as he walked slowly back to the studio door.

"I think that's best," Gorilla answered.

Again, the most powerful weapon in wrestling came out: the eraser. In the wrestling business, I learned we all worked in pencil, so I erased Randy's name, put somebody else in there, and went about my business.

"Not *everyone* here dislikes you, you know," added Gorilla.

I knew that. I had already made some interesting friends.

Chapter Forty-Five

MAKING FRIENDS

1993

I found myself in a basement full of pot smoke, sitting in a chair under a light, getting a haircut. For all the unwelcoming people in WWF, there was also an amazing counter-balance of people who welcomed me like one of their own. Pat Patterson was one of those guys.

Pat was a territory guy who overcame giant obstacles within the "good-ole boy territory network" to carve out a Hall of Fame career for himself. He was a French Canadian who left his home in Montreal as a boy—without knowing a word of English—to come to the US for work. He earned some money and learned to speak English along the way, until he found his calling in professional wrestling. Pat was also gay, and homophobia was as prominent as racism back in the day—particularly in the wrestling business. Still, he made himself a star in the ring and invaluable to Vince outside the ring. Pat had a brilliant mind and was a wonderful sounding board for Vince, as McMahon was really heavy on sizzle and creating an attraction, while Pat was more rooted in the fundamentals of wrestling. Pat was a showman too, but he had infinite knowledge of the business and wouldn't deviate too far from what got people over.

For me, Pat's house became a sanctuary; a welcoming home in a new city where the door was always open. Jan was a flight attendant for US Airways and was gone a lot. Her flight schedule rotated every week *and* she was based out of Philadelphia, which meant she took the train from Stamford to Philly, and then would catch her flights and go to work.

With Jan gone so much, it was nice to have somewhere to go that didn't involve a bar or an airplane. Pat's long-term partner, Louis Dondero, was an amazing host, as well as generous, funny, and a licensed hair stylist.

"How's Jan?" Louis asked me as he looked for his scissors.

I was down in Pat and Louis's basement in the "barber's chair" while Pat looked on.

"She's doing good. Traveling a lot," I replied.

Louis joked, "Now, it was a perm you asked for, wasn't it?"

Beyond the haze of Louis's pot smoke, I could see Pat laughing. Pat never smoked—he liked a vodka cocktail—but I never saw him smoke even a joint. Louis, on the other hand, was something of a connoisseur.

"If you can find enough hair to perm, you go right ahead, Louis," I said.

"I'd love to see you ride back to Oklahoma with your hair permed," Pat laughed. The visual got everyone laughing. "What do you think old Cowboy Watts would think of that, Jimbo?"

"I don't think Bill would be too impressed," I said. "As I remember it, he wasn't too big on men with perms."

"Unless you were a Freebird," Pat howled.

And once again it struck me just how far I was from home. Even though I was a grown man, I still missed my hometown. My mom and my dad, the cinema, and the dollar for a haircut. But I was sure I was in the right place. I loved wrestling. I loved working for the biggest wrestling company on earth. And I loved being with friends.

"You got any plans to make an honest woman out of Jan?" Louis asked me.

"I do indeed," I replied. "Just got to let things settle down at work first."

"Are you fitting in okay?" Pat asked, as he slid his chair in closer.

"It's been quite the journey, Pat," I said, trying to be as diplomatic as I could. "But some days I go to lunch and people won't sit with me; won't even talk if I say hello."

"Ah, fuck them," Pat shouted. "You're here with us now."

Nothing annoyed Pat more than someone being singled out.

"And Vince has been hinting at me becoming a 'character' too," I said. "I'm not sure how to handle that one."

Pat smiled. He took a second before deciding he could confide in me a little. "Some of the thing with Vince," he said, his accent still struggling with plurals, "I'm not keen on. Everybody has to be a character. You have policeman, or a garbage man, or whatever."

"He wants me to wear a cowboy hat," I said.

He replied, "He's not going to let go, you know. If he sees you in his mind in a cowboy hat, then you're going to be in a cowboy hat."

"I don't think so," I said, defiantly.

Pat laughed and shook his head. "Okay," he said, "we'll see."

Chapter Forty-Six

IN SICKNESS AND
IN HEALTH

1993–94

Jan and I got married at the Little White Chapel in Las Vegas on October 12, 1993. That was also where such luminaries as Steve Austin, Michael Jordan, Mickey Rooney, and perhaps most luminously of all, Bruce "Brother Love" Prichard had also gotten married.

We left the hotel, went to the courthouse to get a license, and made a reservation at the chapel. The whole deal took just an hour. It was my third wedding and Jan's first, but neither of us was interested in a big church wedding. We just wanted to be married.

Of all the things that had happened to me during my years in wrestling, that little wedding was the best. There was no match, no WrestleMania, no contract that exceeded marrying Jan. I was ready to start the new phase of my life. New job, new wife, new home, new start.

And I couldn't wait.

My fifty thousand dollar signing bonus arrived in the mail, which turned out to be for $32 grand. Uncle Sam helped himself to eighteen thousand dollars in taxes somewhere along the way. "Welcome to reality," I thought.

Still, I'd never gotten a $50,000 check before in my career, and I'd already been in business for nineteen years.

After WrestleMania IX, I worked the "King of the Ring" PPV, after which Vince came back on TV and I went to the bench. I went from debuting at WrestleMania to doing some international voice-overs and grunt work in booking the syndicated promos, and the talent that went with them.

I watched the shows, heard the commentary and wondered what Vince had in store for me. I began to judge myself harshly. *Was it my look, my accent, or maybe I wasn't talented enough?*

One thing I knew for sure: I was hungrier than ever to get back on TV and show Vince and the wrestling world what I could do. I was very aware that my contract was only for twelve months, and I didn't want to run down the remaining months sitting on the sidelines unable to prove my worth. I wanted to re-sign and felt that nothing was going to get in my way of doing that—or at least nothing I could control.

* * *

"The doctor said I have Lyme's disease," I said, sitting at home.

"Lyme's disease?" Bruce Prichard asked over the phone. "Don't you get that from licking rocks?"

"I don't think so, Bruce."

The first attack happened in my sleep, the morning of Super Bowl XXVIII, and I didn't even know it until well after I'd woken up. I went into the bathroom to brush my teeth and when I looked in the mirror my face was hanging and one of my eyes was drooping lower than the other. I didn't feel anything; I didn't even think anything was wrong until I looked in the mirror but, when I saw what I saw, I thought I was having a stroke.

Jan was en route home on a train from Philly, so I packed myself into the car and drove to the ER as fast as I could. Along the way, I'd catch glimpses of myself in the rear-view mirror and startle myself all over again.

My face had no symmetry; my eyes didn't line up and my mouth drooped down on one side. It was a scary thing to see my features change so dramatically and not even know why.

"But I found out today, when I went to a neurologist, that the doctor who said I had Lyme disease was wrong," I continued.

Bruce replied, "If it's not Lyme's disease, what is it?"

I picked up the report from the neurologist and read the words "Bell's palsy" down my phone.

"I have no idea what that is either," Prichard said.

"It's facial paralysis," I said. "They don't know what caused it but he says that most people get over it in a couple of weeks."

"So you're going to be okay?" Bruce asked.

"Six to eight weeks and I'll be good as new," I said. "Tell Vince I won't be down for long."

Chapter Forty-Seven

IN AND OUT

1994

"Vince needs you to come in." It was Lisa Wolf, head of Human Resources for WWF, on the phone.

"Today?" I asked.

"Right away," she replied.

It was icy, snowy road conditions; the only thing that was open was I-95 because the side streets hadn't been plowed yet. It was one of those days where the weatherman would say, "If you don't have to get out, don't do it." It was a Friday and they couldn't seem to wait until the next Monday when the weather cleared up. I only lived about twenty minutes away from the office, but it took me over an hour because of the driving conditions.

I didn't want to go anywhere. It was less than two weeks since I'd had my Bell's palsy attack, and I was in bed when the call came. My face was still paralyzed, and I was suffering from blinding headaches, poor vision, and numbness across the left side of my face.

When I sat opposite Vince in his office, I knew something wasn't right. Lisa was there, too, which was an indication. I knew from experience that it's never a good thing when the boss and the head of HR sit you down.

His words to me were very simple: "I'm changing my plans and you aren't in them, so I'm going to let you go."

My contract wasn't up for another four months or so. I said, "When are you letting me go?"

"Now. Today," Vince replied.

I constantly wiped my eye and mouth because of my attack. I said, "Well, what about my contract? I don't understand you letting me go with no notice."

Vince hesitated in the answer. That's when I said, "I've always heard you were a man of your word. I made a commitment to stay here through May, and even though you don't want me, I am surprised you're not going to honor your end of the contract."

Before McMahon could say anything, Lisa said, "Well, that's something Vince and I will discuss."

"We're not talking about another year," I continued. "We're talking about a couple more months until my contract is up. It will let me figure out what I'm going to do. And I thought you'd want to keep your word."

Both Vince and Lisa didn't commit one way or the other. And then I left.

I got back in my car and drove home on the frosty, slick I-95 to tell my new wife I'd been fired. We'd been married just four months, moved to Connecticut, set up a new home, and now I was let go.

At first Jan thought I was kidding her, but she quickly saw there was no joke in what I was saying.

"Why?" she asked.

"I'm not sure."

"Is it because of your face?" Jan wondered.

"I hope not," I said. "I'd like to think Vince isn't that cruel."

"Me too."

"It might have been because I was reluctant to play the character they wanted, the good ole Southern boy with the cowboy hat."

"Honey," she said, "don't worry, it will be fine, and we're in this together. We'll figure something out."

"I think we should move back to Atlanta," I said.

She agreed. Jan liked Atlanta, and by moving back there she could commute out of Atlanta as opposed to going from Wilton, Connecticut, by train to Philadelphia. It would be a lot easier on her.

"I'm sorry," I said. I was just about all beaten up. I'd lost my dream job not even a year after getting it. It brought back up the sickening, familiar feelings of being a failure. Jan hugged me, but I didn't feel like a very good husband. I was bringing all these issues into our new household: my illness, unemployment, two ex-wives and the complications that brought. Jan acquired a lot of baggage that I didn't want her to inherit. I just didn't know where I was going to earn the kind of money that would continue to put my two daughters through school and college, while keeping enough to support my life with Jan too.

The only thing I could think of was that I had a lot of business contacts in Atlanta and the housing market was much more affordable than in Connecticut.

A few weeks later, I met Jan at the Westchester County Airport and we had all of our stuff already on the moving van on its way back to Atlanta. She and I embarked on our journey and we drove most of the night, stopping somewhere in the Carolinas to eat and sleep. We made it back to Atlanta and within a couple of weeks bought a townhouse on Sheffield Glen Way. It had a two-car garage and was part of a larger complex; it was very reasonable compared to Connecticut. There was no yard work and it was only about a five-minute drive to Fat Matt's Rib Shack. There's always a silver lining.

Once we got settled, I made an attempt to get back with WCW. Unfortunately, Eric Bischoff was not interested in bringing me back. We had one meeting at a place not too far from the WCW offices, a little restaurant. Eric didn't give me any false hope, I'll give him that. He said, "I wanted to meet with you because I just don't think it's going to be happening." I was a little taken aback by his forthright take, but appreciated his honesty all the same. He continued, "I don't know that it fits anymore, and to bring you back would upset too many people."

I didn't know which "people" he was talking about, but knew it could have been a few different factions. I had been in the wrestling business about twenty years and knew full well that sometimes the political winds were at your back and other times they were gusting right in your face.

At that point, I just washed my hands of the wrestling business. I had a good run and felt it was time to move on.

But not before I did a favor for an old friend.

Jim Cornette had left WCW a few years before after a final blowout with Herd and Ole. Corny wasn't the kind to sit idle, so within a year of his leaving he opened up Smoky Mountain Wrestling. When he heard I was a free agent, he offered me $300 to come and tape two one-hour shows for him. It was a six- or seven-hour drive one way, so it wasn't like I was on easy street. Between paying for gas and food, I couldn't really justify a hotel. I just sucked it up and drove up there and drove back, getting home at seven the next morning. I was happy to help a friend while having some fun doing a little old-school wrestling. It was very nostalgic for me, and I enjoyed being around JC. The guys were happy I was there. I had had a pretty good run as an announcer by the time I started doing Smoky Mountain Wrestling—I'd done clashes and pay-per-views and WrestleManias—so I had a little bit of street cred. They had some amazing talent "hiding" out there, too, including a guy named Glenn Jacobs.

Glenn was Unabomb with a mask. He had that great look, was college educated, soft-spoken, and classy. I thought if Vince could see this guy he would want him on his roster. Underneath the size and potential, Glenn immediately struck me as a model employee. I knew it would be a benefit to both Glenn and Vince to meet up some day.

It was in the car on the way home from the Smoky Mountain tapings that I started to replay my meeting with Vince and Lisa Wolf over and over in my mind. They paid me the remainder of my contract, but it was Vince's words that I couldn't shake: "I'm changing my plans and you aren't in them, so I'm going to let you go."

Vince was now facing a federal trial for allegedly distributing anabolic steroids to WWF wrestlers. The news was everywhere in the wrestling world, as well as the mainstream media.

I got home at about seven in the morning, and Jan had gone to work. I decided to do something. I was worried about not making enough money to keep my family secure. I was worried that the door had closed on my dream of working long-term for the biggest wrestling company in the world. I was worried about being forgotten.

So I wrote a letter.

May 24, 1994

Dear Vince,

I hope all is well with you and your family. I'm sure that during these trying times that their support has been an inspiration.

I am sorry that we did not get the chance to talk before I left Connecticut. I called a couple of times but, as usual, you were very busy.

I must let you know that everyone was very kind to me as I was leaving, especially Lisa Wolf and associates. The only disturbing thing I have heard is that you perceived me to not be loyal to you and Titan Sports. This is absolutely not true and runs deeper than I need to get into here. I take a great deal of pride in being in our business the past twenty-three years, and I am especially proud of my work ethic. I have told many people that my experience working for you was a positive experience.

Because of the lingering affects (sic) of Bell's palsy, I am having to be creative in finding something to do to provide for my family. I am in the process of launching a mail-order-based home business whereby I will be responding to fan mail via audio cassettes. The primary promotional vehicle will be direct mail to wrestling fans and this is where I need to ask this favor. Would you allow me to use the mailing list you have developed via magazine subscriptions? This could prove to be invaluable in helping me kick off my home business.

If at any time I can be of assistance to you either as a radio or television talent, producing or consulting, please keep me in mind. My travel benefits allow for some very economical commuting.

Thanks for your time and consideration. I look forward to hearing from you soon.

Sincerely,

(signed)

I sent the letter to his house in Greenwich, because I knew at the office, Vince's staff wouldn't put it in his "need to see" pile. I also didn't want anyone else but him reading it. I didn't think I'd ever hear back from him; I thought that ship had sailed. I'd had my Tony Schiavone experience—almost a year there—and I figured that's just the way it was meant to be. Onward and upward; I'd have to figure out something else to do.

But at least I got to say my piece, and hopefully he would take the time to read it.

* * *

With Vince consumed with his trial, WWF had a King of the Ring pay-per-view from Baltimore where the announcers were Gorilla Monsoon, Randy Savage, and former NFL great Art Donovan. I watched and knew it was a train wreck. Within days, my phone rang asking if I'd be interested in coming back and doing *Monday Night Raw*.

"Sure," I said.

I worked with legal about my contract where I got a nice bonus for working "SummerSlam," too. Not knowing how long I'd be needed, and knowing that SummerSlam was a high priority, I negotiated a very healthy five-figure payday.

Then, fortunately, Vince got exonerated.

I thought the whole case was ridiculous. For Vince to be charged with distribution was laughable. The jury must have agreed. It also didn't hurt Vince to have the best attorney I'd ever met in his corner. Jerry McDevitt was a badass attorney, boy. I knew that if I ever found myself in deep trouble, I'd be calling the 412 area code and talking to McDevitt.

Vince's fortune, however, became my misfortune. After McMahon came back, I was out again. I wasn't even the quarterback that went back to holding the clipboard on the sideline—they took my jersey and playbook and sent me home once again.

This time, I wasn't caught by surprise. I knew that when Vince came back, he was going back on *Raw*. If they had something for me then they would discuss it with me, but more than likely they wouldn't. I just showed up and did my job, enjoyed every minute of it, and saved my money. I also got a lump sum when they exercised the option to let me go. I knew it wasn't a firing this time because it was built into the deal and I got a nice payout and everybody was cool.

Once that was settled, I went back to Smoky Mountain to replace my old friend, Bob Caudle. As much as I loved the old school feel with Corny, I knew where I wanted to be.

Chapter Forty-Eight

VINCE AND GOOD OL' JR

1994

"Jim, it's Vince. Are you ready to go back to work?" The boss called like nothing had ever happened. It had been about four months since they exercised their "out clause" on my contract.

I was a little surprised to hear him on the line. "Sure!" I said.

"I want you to come back as a producer, and be JJ's assistant in Talent Relations. Sound like something you'd like to do for us?"

JJ Dillon was a former manager for the Four Horsemen in WCW, who transitioned to "the office" when his time on TV was over at WCW.

"I can do that," I said. "Absolutely."

Vince said my role would be to do some producing at the TV studio and help the other announcers.

Before I knew it, he even had me producing him at *Raw*. I was in his ear with lines and information, and although I wasn't announcing myself, I was just happy to be back on the team.

It seemed like Vince was happy with me, too. "Jim, you ride with me," he said after a few weeks of *Raw*. In the parking bay of the building, Vince had a big Cadillac waiting. I could tell the second he started the engine that this was going to be a little bit of a "white knuckle" ride.

"What music do you listen to?" he asked.

"Eh . . . well I . . ."

Before I could answer McMahon blasted AC/DC through the car speakers, the sound of which made everyone turn to see who the asshole was. When they saw it was the chairman's car, they all smiled and waved. We reached the road outside the building and Vince floored it. I honestly thought I was going to die before we even made it to the highway. I was stuck to the back of my seat praying to the good Lord himself for a safe journey. Beside me, Vince was singing at the top of his lungs, punching 90 miles an hour on a secondary road, all while "dancing" in his seat. "I'M AN AMAZING DANCER FOR A WHITE MAN," he shouted over the music.

"I CAN SEE," I shouted back.

Any car he met along the way, Vince drove inches from their trunk until they moved over. Sensing my utter terror, he leaned into me, taking his eyes completely off the road, and shouted in my ear, "I'VE GOT AMAZING DEPTH PERCEPTION. DON'T WORRY, PAL."

"OK."

Vince continued to gyrate in his seat as he weaved through traffic. He then stopped the song mid solo. The silence, after such a jarring burst of sound, was deafening. His demeanor completely changed. He went from bombastic and animated to somber and quiet.

"I want you to hear this," he said in a low voice.

"Hear what?" I said. I was afraid I'd miss whatever it was Vince was letting me in on. He seemed pained, almost confessional.

"You can't hear that?" he said, putting his finger to his lips.

I didn't want to sound like a jackass, so I listened as carefully as I could.

"You hear it, Jim?" he asked, a little more impatiently.

I thought I heard something in the trunk. My first thought was: they've put long-time employee Howard Finkel in the trunk as a rib. "Is it the car?" I asked.

"Jesus Christ, listen will you?" he growled.

I closed my eyes and listened as hard as I have ever listened for anything in my life.

"Here it is," he said. And then he began to fart. A long, bass-filled flatulence that eventually finished with a smile of pride from the chairman. "You hear it now?" he asked, and then cackled with laughter.

I made a split decision not to "sell it" in any way. I sat facing forward like nothing had happened.

McMahon was so happy with himself. "You know how I get the longevity and smell, Jim? Protein. I eat nothing but fucking protein, pal."

"Yeah, it wasn't that impressive," I said.

Vince's head swiveled in my direction like I'd just insulted his wife or something. "What?" he asked with menace. He was serious. Offended, even.

I couldn't back down now. It was a test. I was sure it was. "Well, I've been around the business for over twenty years now, Vince. Robert Gibson . . ."

Vince locked the windows and let another one go. Twice the volume. Twice the smell. He watched my reaction intently as we continued to tear along the highway at speed. His "creation" was putrid, but I knew if I told him that he'd just keep doing it. So I sat still and waited for the smell to stop burning my lungs.

"How about that one?" Vince asked. He hated to be beaten at anything, even farting competitions.

He studied my reaction until the blue lights in his rear view mirror caught his attention. "Ah, shit," he said as he pulled over. "Was I speeding, Jim?"

"Just a tad."

"Why didn't you say something, goddammit, pal?"

The Ohio State Trooper approached and McMahon rolled down his window. I took a covert, life-saving breath of fresh air as the trooper asked for the license and registration.

"We just finished producing our national TV broadcast, *Monday Night Raw*," Vince said as the trooper looked over his license. "I'm Vince McMahon," he said before pausing for effect. "And this here is Good Ol' JR beside me."

Good Ol' JR? I thought. *Have I not got a real name?*

"So, *you're* Vince McMahon?" the trooper asked as he leaned in the window a little.

"I am," the chairman said, proudly. "Vincent Kennedy McMahon."

"Well, I guess that makes me the Big Bossman then," the trooper said as he handed McMahon a speeding ticket. "Have a good night."

Vince put his window back up and I was expecting the chairman to explode. But instead he turned to me and said, "You're doing real good for us. I wish I could clone you."

It was a compliment out of nowhere.

"Thank you. You're better at farting than Robert Gibson, too," I said as he took us back onto the road.

"You don't mean that," he replied.

"I do."

Vince watched the cop car that pulled him over disappear and then floored the pedal again.

Chapter Forty-Nine

THE NEW AND THE OLD

1995

Bruce rushed up to me backstage at *Raw* and said, "Hey, can you do some voice-overs tomorrow for us for the UK?"

I said, "I can't do anything. No I can't. I can't do it."

"Are you working?" he asked.

"Yes, I just can't do it."

He was confused. "What do you mean, you can't do it?"

"Vince brought me back specifically telling me that I would not be a talent. He told me not to go try to leverage my way into getting a talent job, that he wanted me to be a producer and to help JJ."

"Well, we need you to do some packages for SKY TV," Bruce said. "Do you mind if I ask Vince and get his take on it?"

Bruce was off looking for the boss before I could give an answer. "There's a meeting in the locker room," he shouted back to me as he rushed away.

The passion to get back behind the mic had subsided. I'd come to grips that it just wasn't going to happen. The chubby-faced boy with the Southern accent wasn't going to get the job done in WWF. I knew it and was fine with it. You dance with what brung you. Quite frankly, I enjoyed learning stuff from JJ Dillon and working with him and seeing how the payroll was done and how he handled talent issues and things like that. It was refreshing because JJ was a lot more even-keel than Bill or Ole were in that mentor role.

JJ was a workaholic. He was on time every day and would often eat lunch at his desk so he didn't miss a call. He was totally committed to doing a good job—but it was a thankless pursuit. When the phone rang, or a talent wanted to talk, it was usually because something was wrong and it needed to be addressed *now*. Or *yesterday*. But preferably *last week*. And JJ was such a gentleman in handling it all. He didn't have those nose-to-nose confrontations that you sometimes see in a baseball game where the umpire and the manager go kicking dirt all over each other. JJ was a calm, cool, collected veteran who didn't need to raise his voice to make a point. I was learning a lot from watching him and happy to pick up the slack and tend to any talent relation issues whenever I was needed. I liked the idea of being involved with younger talent; talent I could help find and shape for the future. I was settling in, enjoying my married life, and coming to grips with my facial paralysis.

I was happy.

As I walked toward the meeting Bruce had shouted back to me about, I thought I saw a glimpse of a familiar frame walk into the locker room ahead of me. It was a little like déjá-vu when I saw that Cowboy, again, hadn't said a word to me about coming in—but there he stood in the locker room, side by side with Vince.

We all crammed in to listen to what the boss had to say. Vince announced that he was stepping more into the executive side of the business, while Cowboy was here to run the wrestling end of things.

"The only one who can overrule Bill is me," Vince said. "But I won't."

As WWF continued to grow, and Vince became more fragmented in all of his other responsibilities, it made sense for McMahon to bring in some help from the outside. Bill had experience running a territory, had administrative experience, had practical experience, and Vince needed someone to help him in those exact areas. If you were looking for someone with that skill and background, there weren't a lot of guys to choose from.

I loved Bill, but I was worried that his steamroller management style would double back on me again. Our last run together in WCW didn't end very well for either of us.

Right from that very first meeting, Cowboy was very much hands-on in WWF. He took on a lot of responsibility.

And then he was gone . . . lasting only a few weeks.

He had issues with the HR people—Lisa Wolf in particular. He didn't want her to try to tell him how to manage or handle wrestling issues, and he wasn't the most politically correct individual in the company. She took Cowboy's behavior upon herself as a challenge to change him and correct what she saw as his misbehaviors. It was more or less his profanity here, there, and yon that offended her. "Nobody talks to me the way Bill Watts does," she said in her thick Boston accent. "Not even my fa-tha."

The irony is that Vince was just as profane; he just was more strategic in when he used the colorful language. Bill didn't have a filter; he didn't care. Not about Lisa, and not that much about anyone else either. He came to WWF to make his mark and initiate change.

Just sometimes the "changes" came from an old-school mentality.

We brought in Ahmed Johnson, whose real name is Tony Norris. Tony was an impressive African American athlete who had a great look. We didn't really have any African American megastars, but we thought Tony had a shot at being just that. Bill wanted to name him Buck Johnson. Buck. Buck Johnson—which sounded like a name from another era entirely. Vince saw that Cowboy was back in the Junkyard Dog/Ernie Ladd era with the name Buck Johnson, so he gave Tony a more contemporary name because so many pro athletes were taking on Muslim names. Vince overruled Cowboy and named Tony "Ahmed Johnson" instead.

In that small little decision, the writing was on the wall. Vince *was* going to overrule Cowboy. And Cowboy wasn't going to take it. Vince thought he'd be able to step away from the creative/TV end of his company a bit more, but it wasn't going to happen. Watts wanted to get harder on the Boys;

to bring in fines for lateness and bring back some older ways of working. Vince thought things were working just fine.

At the end of the day, Vince did not feel comfortable relinquishing a lot of the responsibilities to Bill, or anyone else. McMahon was still the boss and needed everyone to know it. There was never any doubt about that. Bill didn't want to be *the* boss, he just wanted to be able to affect the wrestling side. Vince just wasn't going to give up enough power to let that happen. So Bill left his assignment at WWF and Vince took care of him on the way out, financially.

Bill rode off into the sunset in a company-paid-for rental car—which he proceeded to pack with all his things before driving it all the way back to Oklahoma. Who in the hell knows what the drop charges were and the mileage that went along with driving a rental from Connecticut to Oklahoma. Nobody ever said the Cowboy wasn't eccentric and one of a kind.

As quick as he arrived, he was gone again.

Chapter Fifty

MARKET RESEARCH

1995

JJ asked me to go check out a kid in Florida, as both he and Vince trusted my judgment when it came to assessing the potential of green guys for the future. I'd already heard from Pat Patterson that this guy had the potential to be a keeper, so I was intrigued as to how our meeting would go.

My overall sense of talent evaluation was: I wanted to see the prospects in situations outside of the business. I figured I could learn far more about who I was hiring if I got to see them operate in the "real world" first. I wanted to know if they have manners? Are they good with their family? Do they handle themselves well in public situations?

I wanted to use my meetings as market research.

When I met Dwayne Johnson, I brought him to lunch. It was a Cuban place that he liked to eat at—when he could afford to. He wasn't long finished up playing for the practice squad of the Calgary Stampeders in the CFL where he told me he left with seven bucks in his pocket.

Straight away I could see he was mannerly to the staff. He was unique looking, with a black father and a Samoan mother, about 6-foot-4 and a muscled 270 or so.

"I'll have the grilled chicken, black beans, and rice please," he said to the waiter without looking at the menu. I told the waiter that I'd have the same. Dwayne seemed to know the joint well enough to know what was good. "I'm going to be your top guy one day," he said before our drinks even arrived.

"Well, let's see how you handle the training. Then the locker room. Then your first match, and we'll take it from there."

I watched his reaction closely. He was serious; he truly believed he was going to be our top guy—but not in an arrogant way.

He said, "You know I'm broke and living at home, right?"

"Lunch is on me," I replied, being purposefully dry.

"Well, thank you. But I mean that I'm coming in to make an impact, because I have to."

I loved this kind of talk from new talent. I didn't approach Dwayne's confidence as a bad thing because I wanted the Talent Relations department to be run like a major league franchise. I saw my own role as that of a talent scout/player development/coach. I knew most old-timers in the business wouldn't like Dwayne's proclamation of greatness, but I personally loved it. If a completely new guy had his eye on the top spot, I saw it as my job to guide him toward that spot. It was completely up to him if he had the tools, attitude, and good fortune to actually get there.

"The standard contract is for three years at $100,000 a year," I said. He simply smiled and nodded. I continued, "but if it's not working out there's a 90-day termination clause in the contract too."

"I know, I'm cool with that," he said.

"Well, alright then. Let's have a little something to eat, you and I."

Over lunch I could see and hear that Dwayne had the foundation to be a major player. Being a potential third-generation wrestler, he had great product knowledge; he also asked all the right questions about the terms of the contract and what to expect. I watched as the women in the restaurant kept asking if he needed anything more to eat or drink, if he needed some more napkins maybe. I'm pretty sure that a lady or two who didn't even work there asked him if he needed anything. In a "looks" business like professional wrestling, that was a great start. What I saw in front of me was a guy who was hungry, informed, confident—and had "it." Like all my new signings, I just didn't know if his "it" would evolve into something that could make us all money.

He finished his meal long before me, wiped his mouth, and said, "I want to start yesterday."

"I think you have all the pieces," I said. "It's up to you to make them all connect."

"Just let me start, so we can get this show on the road," he said.

I left knowing we had a new "Grade A" prospect on our hands. I had no idea how far Dwayne would go or how long he would last. All I knew for sure was he was going to do everything in his power to become the main event. And we needed more people like that in our locker room. Hell, in life as well.

Chapter Fifty-One

BACK TO ANNOUNCING

1995

"You're back," Bruce said.

"Back where?" I asked.

"On commentary."

And just like that, with no real explanation, fanfare, reason, or logic, I was back out there with Vince and Jerry Lawler. WWF were moving their commentators around, trying to get the right mix across the shows, and my name came up. Vince gave me the nod.

"Just listen to me," McMahon said before the "In Your House 2" pay-per-view show. "And all you have to do is jump onboard when you hear an opening."

Of all the three-man crews I'd been on, I knew this one I could look forward to because I wasn't cast as the lead guy. Vince was in control and that made it easy for me to play off of him. Lawler effortlessly took up the reigns as a pure heel, and I was the counter to his approach. We all knew our roles to help move the show forward without getting in the way of the talent in the ring.

There was clean direction from the boss, lights on and let's go.

Lawler felt like Heenan with his natural timing, wise-ass one-liners, and the zingers. He was just a natural born performer. I can't imagine too many people that were more perfect for the business than Lawler and Heenan. They were seemingly born to be entertaining pro wrestling personalities. King had mastered the art of the soundbite as booker in Memphis for years before his WWF run. He was a top babyface there, and was a top heel, too, so he understood the psychology of being both thoroughly. He had also written television and created characters, so he knew instinctively what was worth highlighting and what didn't need a word. If he needed to get something in, he knew that in a three-man booth it was the soundbite world.

I had to learn the same thing.

I was used to being the lead guy and talking more than I needed to, but now I was the "analyst," or the voice of reason, between Lawler and McMahon. Still, the same principles applied: I needed to learn to talk in shorter bursts that had some substance to them, and not talking just because I hadn't chimed in for a while. I went back in my mind to watching the games on TV with my dad. He too wanted info on the players and teams, but in a succinct way. As I found my footing live on air, I was really imagining how my old man would like me to break down the wrestling business if he were to suddenly become interested in it.

I immediately felt we had good chemistry. It was very hard for me and King to go into business for ourselves because we were sitting with the guy that owned the company, and therefore had blessed all of the storylines we were commentating on.

Out there at the desk I also saw a different side of Vince: a more playful, mischievous side. He was relaxed on TV and acted more like one of the Boys.

I knew he didn't watch any other wrestling shows, so he didn't know the names to a lot of the holds and moves. I'd help him when I could—but moves and submissions didn't light his fire. Storytelling did. Good versus evil, personal issues, and creating value on the title was where he excelled. He learned the fundamental things as a kid, growing up around his father, Vincent J. McMahon, who was also a hugely successful promoter. "Everybody fights to become the champion. The winners make more than the losers. Winning and losing is important."

And Vince took that "winning and losing is important" mantra into his business life, too. His work ethic was off the charts. He'd be the chairman of the company, with all that entails, then literally change clothes, change mindset, put everything else aside, and go out there and be the lead announcer.

Jerry and I had a blast out there because, among many things, "King" needled McMahon about his toupee, which Vince never wore. Lawler then turned his sights on me and some of my clichés and colloquialisms. McMahon, too, got a little jab in at me every now and then for one of my crazy sayings. I fired back by calling Lawler "Henny Youngman," making clear I thought his jokes were stale. It was all in fun, and our three-man booth was the best of its kind that I'd been a part of.

I had no real desire to get back on commentary—until I put my headset down at the end of the show. It hit me all over again just how much I loved calling the action and being a part of the presentation. My trips to the three-man booth didn't last long, however, and I found myself solely in my back-stage capacity again for several months—until an electrical storm hit. Our May PPV, Beware of Dog, was a couple of matches in before the rough weather killed our power. The show literally went dark. All the remaining matches had to be taped a couple of days later, where "Mr. Perfect" Curt Hennig and I got the assignment to work together on commentary.

Curt was a natural wrestler, athlete, and just about anything else he wanted to be a natural at. He wasn't competing in-ring because of a long-term back injury, but was a quick learner who could adapt to a range of other tasks needed for TV. He was lighthearted and very social—which meant he knew all the dirt. He did the greatest Razor Ramon impersonation that there ever was. "Hey, Chico." It never failed to crack me up. He was a big person-ality that I thought had a real future at the announcer's desk . . . and he wanted to learn.

He had been around so many great talkers, including Jesse Ventura, who was kind of like the Godfather of the heel wrestling announcers—even though Roddy Piper did it before him—that he wanted to measure up to the very best.

"What should I avoid?" he asked.

"One of Vince's big issues is the double-negatives, so you never want to describe a talent like, *This guy's mean as a snake and he can't wrestle either,*" I said.

"Cause that would kill the heel."

"Exactly. *Mean as a snake* is good. But the fact that he can't wrestle makes everyone look stupid. His opponent for not beating him, the heel for not being able to do what everyone else on the roster can do, and the company for hiring him in the first place!"

Curt was a gamer, but I could see he was a lot like Flair. He was the life of the party and, unfortunately, being the life of the party got the better of him. He wasn't sure that he wanted to be on commentary long term, but my short run with him, Vince, and Lawler certainly let me know that I was sure. It fit, felt at home, and after my Bell's palsy had subsided a little, I knew my focus for being an on air presence was back.

I just needed to figure out *how* to get a solid spot on the headsets.

Chapter Fifty-Two

CHANGING ROLES

1996

I was standing on the sideline of a stadium in Johannesburg, South Africa, when I heard JJ was gone. WWF had a contractual obligation to run some shows in South Africa, so we brought a skeleton crew and put on a stadium show over the course of the week. Bruce Prichard and I were sent as the "office people" on the tour because Vince's son, Shane, was getting married a few days later.

"JJ is gone," Bruce whispered in my ear. I could see he wasn't happy.

"What happened?"

JJ wasn't happy with cuts in pay versus the responsibility and stress attached to the job. He also had a child with special needs at home who needed more of his care. All of that plus the lack of vacation time, general support within the company, and the cost of living in Connecticut forced JJ's hand. He resigned and left WWF, effective immediately.

"Vince wants me to replace JJ," Bruce said. I could see by his reaction that he thought I might be upset by Vince's choice.

"Of course," I replied. "You're here longer and know the company far better than I do."

I saw what JJ had to deal with, and I was in no rush to take those reins.

Bruce continued, "Vince wants to give us both new roles. He wants to make me VP of talent relations and you VP of wrestling administration."

I didn't know what my title meant, but I presumed it involved a pay bump so I was okay with it. Bruce, on the other hand, didn't look comfortable at all.

"You doing okay?" I asked him.

"I know what that job is like," he said. "JJ found out the same as everyone else does. That job . . ." he said trailing off at the end.

For me, I was just looking forward to getting back home. Home to Jan, home to my own bed, home to the new wrestling war that was brewing with a rejuvenated WCW under Eric Bischoff.

JJ wasn't going to be the last one to leave WWF. Of that I was sure. There were changes coming all over the company, and not just behind the scenes either.

* * *

Poor Jerry Brisco. He'd been through wars as a talent, been through tough times as one of Vince's inner circle, but I don't think anyone pushed him to the limit like I did as he drove to *Raw* in Hershey, Pennsylvania, that night.

My in-ring promo was, for better or worse, one of the first "Attitude Era" type segments, where wrestling storytelling was blended with behind-the-scenes reality. I was to expose Vince as the owner of WWF, instead of the mere announcer that he had always played. It was part of the plan Vince came up with to have me rip him for firing me after I got Bell's palsy.

"You think I like that?" I said, practicing. "You think that I like the fact my left eye don't open . . ."

"*Doesn't* open," Jerry said.

"What?" I asked.

"Your left eye *doesn't* open, not *don't* open." Jerry looked like he was ready to jump out of the moving car. This was the hundredth time I had "acted out" the promo on our drive to the building.

I didn't have a script to work from, just the bullet points of where they wanted me to go. "You think it's any good?" I asked.

"It's different," he said.

"But is it any good?"

"It's different."

"But, is it . . ."

"JR," he said. "We're driving on pure ice. I'm trying not to kill us both. You've been cutting the same promo for nearly two hours. I want to kill you right now. I might not be the best judge."

"Well that's what I'm going for," I mumbled. "I hope the audience wants to kill me too."

Jerry choked the steering wheel with his hands. "You might not make it there to find out."

As he drove at ten miles an hour, I continued to whisper my way through my "grievances" against both WCW and WWF. The company wanted me to hint that I brought in "Stone Cold" Steve Austin, Mick Foley, and Vader to cultivate a WWF that was more to my liking, while letting old stars go elsewhere.

My in-ring verbal assault was all part of the new "Monday Night Wars," as WWF and WCW battled for television ratings. The problem was, at the end of my diatribe they wanted me to introduce Diesel and Razor Ramon; normally an easy thing to do. But not when both men who played those roles, Scott Hall and Kevin Nash, were no longer with the company.

With those departures, the infamous "Kliq" was splintered, with Hall, Nash, and Sean Waltman jumping to WCW and Shawn Michaels and HHH staying with WWF. Not a lot of our locker room were sorry to see the Kliq disbanded, as they were a disruptive force behind the scenes. It got to the stage that when I worked with JJ, there were other talents who were going to take matters into their own hands if the disrespect, pranks, and attitude didn't cease.

The Kliq got their way creatively more often than not because there was strength in numbers and they had a direct pipeline to Vince. The irony was that everybody had that opportunity—they just took advantage of it. Collectively, they were an ornery, mischievous group who played many of the other talents like marionettes.

When I dealt with them, I took the most rational, level-headed one of the group, which was Hunter (Triple H), and would tell him what my dilemma was. More often than not, their stuff was harmless pranks. To some people, the frequency of the pranks got more than they wanted to handle.

The other side of The Kliq was that they all had great wrestling minds. They weren't dumbasses. They would go to Vince when they had some creative that didn't jive or resonate with them and explain another way of doing it. There were a lot of times that Vince acquiesced because they were right.

They came to him to converse, not confront. That was the key.

A lot of talents didn't have the balls to go and have that relationship with Vince. They didn't know how to communicate with him. Vince saw himself a little bit in that Kliq; he understood where they were coming from. He was one of those guys.

And now, three of those guys were gone and fighting on the other team, and Vince once again wanted to say "fuck you."

If Hall and Nash decided to jump to WCW, their personas were staying put—and I got the job of introducing the new Razor and Diesel to the world.

In the ring, the thing I soon found about my "heel debut" was, as I continued my rant, I was getting increasing cheers from the crowd. They agreed with a lot of what I was saying. At the end, on *Raw*, I introduced Razor and Diesel, and WWF sent out Rick Bognar as "Razor Ramon" and Glenn Jacobs as "Diesel," but the fans farted at it.

The point for Vince was: WWF owned "Razor Ramon" and "Diesel," even if the guys who played them went elsewhere. It was part legal posturing, part entertainment and part counter-programming.

Despite everyone's best intentions, the idea was DOA.

Still, Vince appreciated my work. When we got to the back he said, "JR, you cut one hell of a promo. One hell of a promo."

I was just happy that Jacobs got another chance at a storyline. The new Diesel character wasn't going to stick, but I had a feeling that WWF would have something else for him when the came time.

I knew I'd keep him around if it was my call.

Soon, it *was* my call.

Chapter Fifty-Three

THE "JJ ROLE"

1996

Bruce didn't last any length in the VP of Talent Relations role. I don't think he really wanted it, and Vince could see Bruce was more valuable on the creative side of things. So the chairman offered me the job. I knew from shadowing JJ what the role entailed. I saw all the great things JJ brought to the position and I had ideas of my own in terms of how to make Talent Relations more expansive.

Specifically, I wanted to hire younger, hungrier talent. Talent that had something to prove. Talent that were passed over in other companies, or had yet to be discovered. I wanted to feed the needs of the machine and build a foundation for the future. And Vince agreed completely.

"JR, I want you to be Senior Vice President of Talent Relations," Vince said.

"Can I sign my own talents?" I asked. "Or do you want me to run that by you first?"

"I trust your judgment completely," Vince replied. "You run with it."

All of a sudden, my apathy for the job turned to keen interest. I knew I could do something with the right team and some freedom to make my own choices. But before I looked outside, I needed to smooth over some things in-house first.

I made it a policy to treat people as they treated me and gauge them by how they conducted themselves in WWF. If a wrestler got a reputation for being a pain in the ass, I wasn't going to let that reputation influence me. I always told guys they were starting here with a clean slate.

That was one of the first lessons I ever got, my first year in the business. Don Jardine, better known as the Spoiler, was a 6-foot-4 masked man who was one of the top villains in wrestling. People warned me I was not going to like Jardine. They said he was aloof, didn't want to be around the Boys, and was creatively difficult to deal with. But I took a liking to him almost immediately, and saw that what a lot of those bad-mouthers had missed was that Jardine knew better than anyone else how to get the Spoiler over. He also knew that for the claw to get over he needed to get occasional blood from the preliminary guys on TV—matches in which you rarely saw "color." That made Jardine stand out and, if the prelim guys didn't know how to get color, he'd do it for them.

One night in Monroe, Louisiana, I was refereeing Don's match against a preliminary wrestler, and I heard him tell the guy, "OK, it's time. Do it."

I was to hover over the prelim guy to camouflage him blading his forehead—but his hands were shaking and he wouldn't do it. Jardine kept muttering to him, "Come on, come on, do it, come on, come on—"

Finally, Don grabbed the guy's hand and stuck the blade in his forehead. The prelimer screamed like a banshee as he started bleeding. That's when Jardine put his giant hand across the guy's head for the claw hold. The Spoiler was so in control of his working the claw and the timing of everything that he even told me when to call for the bell.

As Jardine released the hold, he told his bloody victim, "Just lay there and sell it."

We did the deal where a couple of referees had to help him to the back, and when we got back there, Jardine told the young wrestler, "Kid, all you've got to do is tell me you've never done it before. I could've gigged you, and it wouldn't have hurt nearly as much as me doing it when you were fighting against it. I didn't want to hurt you."

The "aloof" Jardine offered to let me ride with him to and from the hotel a few times, and what I learned there was that he was driving a big Oldsmobile, which was immaculate. It looked like it had just rolled off the showroom floor. He didn't allow anyone to smoke, eat, or drink in his vehicle, because the Boys—as I found out the hard way—will let your vehicle become their ashtray. He also listened to classical music. Most guys were either country or rock, but you didn't touch Jardine's dials, either the volume or the station. The entirety of Jardine's "difficulty" was the cleanliness of his car and a refined taste in music.

From then on, I would decide on my own who was a prick and who was not, and that served me well in talent relations.

At home, Jan ended up becoming a den mother, of sorts, to a lot of the Boys. Sometimes, when a wrestler had to be at the office early, we'd invite him to stay over at our house rather than have to spend another night in a hotel. Jan really went above and beyond the call of duty, making the guys home-cooked dinners and accepting them into our home.

I tried to approach talent relations the way a coach would approach his players, and if you talk to any successful player who had a great relationship with his coach you'd find that the player also had a good relationship with the coach's family.

A lot of the guys even opened up to Jan about problems they were having—things they might not have been comfortable talking to me about. Eventually, she got to know the wrestlers' wives, and they could talk about how things were going, but in the course of normal conversation.

We'd get calls at all hours, day or night, from wrestlers or family members with problems that could use a helping hand, questions that needed answers. And if I was on the road, those callers were perfectly comfortable talking to Jan.

When I wasn't on the road, I was in the office Monday through Friday with Vince, and those could turn into 14-hour days. Then, every Saturday, we'd be at the McMahon house, where he'd tackle every issue or chore he hadn't been able to get to at the office—looking over TV, the next couple of pay-per-view cards, long-term planning. When the weather was nice, those sessions were always outdoors in a gazebo by the backyard pool. In Connecticut, the window for nice weather is limited, so we got out there when we could.

Those Saturdays were a ritual that Bruce Prichard and Pat Patterson had been part of for years before I came aboard. Bruce and Pat wrote the television and, once their part was done, I'd go through talent issues with Vince: payroll, house show bookings, any talent problems I'd had during the week that I needed his counsel on, etc.

I suggested to Vince that he let me do the payroll and simply submit for his approval, rather than us spend half of each Saturday going through it together. I figured this new system would make both our lives easier.

"Since you've got the final say anyway, this would let you look at the completed payroll at your leisure, and make whatever changes you like," I said.

We started doing it that way, and it shortened our Saturday work sessions considerably, to the point that one day Linda McMahon walked into my office and asked me to step out from behind my desk.

She gave me a hug and said, "I just wanted to thank you for giving me my husband back on the weekends."

Linda had even advised me on my relationship with Jan, when we had been dating for a while. I had strong feelings for her, and Linda encouraged me to think seriously about where we were headed.

"It's really just once in a lifetime, if you're lucky, that you find someone who stirs that strong a feeling and is someone you can relate to," Linda told me. "It's something to think about, because that's not an opportunity everyone gets."

I just saw the change in payroll as part of what might have been my most important job: protecting Vince. He had so much on his mind that I used to take notes on everything he said while we worked together so I could remind him later of what he'd wanted to do about a particular situation. We didn't want to lose a good idea, and we didn't want Vince to be made out to be a liar if he had told something to one of the guys and then forgot all the details of it later.

So, sometimes, I had to protect Vince from Vince.

* * *

Although I didn't announce WrestleMania XII, my talent-relations work kept me busy, and I even produced some of the segments building up to the event. The main event that year was Bret "The Hitman" Hart defending the world title against Shawn Michaels in a 60-minute "Iron Man" match. Whereas most matches ended after a pinfall or submission, this one would go for a solid hour, after which, the man who had scored the most pinfalls or submissions would win the match and the championship.

The match was Pat Patterson's invention where it had first been used a few years prior, during some tag matches between, ironically enough, The Hart Foundation and The Rockers. Pat came out of semi-retirement in Florida just to see the match. It wasn't just a way to honor Pat, though. Having the man who invented the match there, and with Pat being one of the best in the world at laying out a match, was a smart move by Vince. He knew Pat understood the match concept, as well as both Bret and Shawn.

Bret and Shawn were two of the best in the world, but had different styles, and the TV leading up to the event played up those differences. Shawn was flashier and did a good amount of high flying, where Bret did more scientific, mat wrestling.

I went to Bret's family home in Calgary, Canada, to record interviews and training footage. His home had a heated pool, so I thought we could get some footage of him swimming as a way to work on his cardio for the long match, but it turned out the Hitman couldn't swim. We ended up using a clip of him paddling to the pool's edge, as if he were coming in from a long swim.

We also got some good footage of Bret doing weight training, and I wanted to cap it off with some mat training at the family home where he and his eleven siblings had grown up. Bret's dad, Stu Hart, was a top wrestler—and more famously a promoter and trainer—and his basement was known as "The Dungeon," where more than one young wrestler learned the painful secrets of Stu's submission holds.

Bret was always seemingly late, so the day we were to shoot him working out in the Dungeon, Stu and I waited at the kitchen table, until Stu started to get bored and invited me down to the Dungeon so he could show me a few holds.

He wanted to put me in a rear chinlock, where my neck was somewhat crimped. Then, in his raspy tone that was one of the most imitated in the business, he said, "Now, uh, when you start seeing spots, that means your brain is being deprived of the oxygen it takes to properly function. Within a matter of moments, you'll lose consciousness. Some guys also lose control of their bowels and bladder, so as soon as you start to see those spots, you, eh, give me the office."

"Give you the office?" I asked.

"Squeeze my arm when you think you're about to go unconscious," he replied. He said it as matter of factly as an electrician describing how to switch a lightbulb. I had this nightmare vision of trying to conduct my interview with Bret after soiling myself, so once he put on the hold, I quickly "gave him the office."

Fortunately, Bret arrived before Stu got the urge to show me a second hold. Bret was less fortunate, so we ended up with a lot of unusable footage that showed our champion, helpless in the grasp of his elderly father, who was "showing Bret some holds" for his upcoming match.

The training packages turned out well, and the match itself was excellent, aside from the questionable finish. After spending all that time building the idea that whoever scored the most falls would win, the hour ended with a score of zero-zero, neither man having scored a fall. After Bret had walked out of the ring with the belt, returning WWF President Gorilla Monsoon declared a "sudden death" overtime, wherein the first man to catch a pinfall or submission would win. The idea was to create controversy and preserve Bret, who was to drop his title to Shawn. As the hour expired, Bret had Shawn in the Sharpshooter, his finishing submission hold, and Shawn had no way out. When the time expired, Bret released the hold and celebrated as a champion would after retaining his title in such a hard-fought draw. Monsoon ordered them to restart, and Shawn quickly hit his superkick finisher on Bret, pinning him for the victory.

My only problem with it was, no one had ever explained anything about an overtime in the buildup to the match, so it came out of left field for the audience. But it was a great way to keep them both strong, for future matchups. No matter what anyone says about the "Montreal Screwjob" or anything else about the friction between them, Bret and Shawn always had good chemistry in the ring and they made magic on many nights.

Elsewhere on the card, Vince also decided he wanted to beef up his star power by once more doing business with the Ultimate Warrior.

Warrior had left WWF under less-than-cordial terms twice, despite being a huge star. Vince even tried him as champion, giving Warrior a win over Hulk Hogan at WrestleMania VI, but it just didn't work out. I'd first met Jim Hellwig when he was a rookie and one-half of The Blade Runners, a Road Warriors–knockoff tag team in Mid-South. I'd gotten a lot closer to his partner, Steve "Sting" Borden, in WCW, but Hellwig didn't last long under Bill Watts's no-nonsense leadership.

Some of the guys who had been around for the drama and machinations of his previous runs, like Bruce Prichard or Pat Patterson, had an attitude best described as, "Oh, no. Here we go again."

They didn't have much optimism that he had become less volatile in the four years since he'd last been seen in WWF, but Vince's attitude was to give him the benefit of the doubt and hope he had changed. I also wanted to make up my own mind about him.

In my official capacity as head of talent relations, I went to Warrior's home in Phoenix, along with Vince and Linda McMahon and Jim Cornette, who became a member of the creative team after closing Smoky Mountain. As contentious as Warrior's relationship with Vince was, he apparently had always been on friendly terms with Linda. Cornette was with us because we also had shows in the area, and he was a frequent travel partner of mine.

"You ready to come back to work, pal?" Vince asked Warrior as we sat around his kitchen table.

"Destrucity," Warrior replied.

Vince looked at me like "what did he say?" so I spoke up to get the conversation back to business. "We're thinking WrestleMania—"

Warrior just cut me off. "Destrucity is what I want."

"Ha. Ha. What's that pal?" Vince asked.

"It's a word I created," Warrior said. "I want to push it out there. Make the world a different place."

"Destrucity?" I asked.

"It's the new buzz word," he replied, very matter-of-factly.

"Jim," Linda said, "we'd very much like to talk about a comeback."

Warrior nodded. Linda's words seemed to have focused his wandering mind somewhat. Although, maybe not. "Destrucity is a concept that I worked out, top to bottom and inside out. I can own it, promote it, and use it as a pathway to speaking engagements and promotional opportunities."

Warrior could see that Vince wasn't getting the vision. He insisted that Vince incorporate "destrucity" into Warrior's return so people could understand his philosophy. Warrior was so exuberant about this word that he dropped several "f-bombs" while describing his concept. Maybe it was my upbringing, but hearing such indiscriminate use of the epithet in front of a lady made me uncomfortable.

In the end, Warrior didn't seem overly excited about returning to the ring—no sign of passion, anticipation, or anything else.

Still, both Vince and I knew that, if Warrior had his head on right, he was still box office draw. He had great name identity and had been portrayed strongly in his previous runs; I mean, he was a guy who had beaten Andre the Giant in 30-second matches, all through the touring loop. He had clearly kept up his training regimen, as he still had the amazing physique that had been his calling card. And he had a unique type of charisma. To Vince, bringing him back was a calculated risk. If all the stars aligned, we'd be ushering in the return of a superstar.

As WrestleMania XII loomed, I already had plenty of issues with our other major returning star, "Rowdy" Roddy Piper. Piper had become one of wrestling's most beloved characters after a long career in the territories followed by his stint as the leading villain of WWF's national push that started in 1984.

'Mania was Warrior's first appearance back for the company, but would be Piper's last. He had functioned as the on-air authority figure since an "attack" by Vader left WWF President Gorilla Monsoon sidelined, which privately allowed Gorilla to address some health issues. During Piper's stint he'd gotten into an issue with Goldust, the androgynous villain who was really Dustin Runnels, son of the legendary Dusty Rhodes.

I'd never dealt with Piper before; we had just never been in the same promotion at the same time and, like a lot of big stars, he could be high-maintenance. I learned top stars frequently had their own needs and ideas, and a lot of what made them high-maintenance came from the same special thing that made them top stars in the first place.

In my first meeting with Piper, backstage at TV, he was less than forthcoming. Our conversation consisted of little said, short answers, and stiff body language that left no doubt that he was not entirely comfortable working with me. All he knew was that I was this new guy who had what everyone still called "the JJ job."

I asked Jerry Brisco, whom I traveled with a lot, how I could improve my relationship with Piper. Jerry and Piper had been friends for more than 15 years, dating back to their time together in the Mid-Atlantic and Georgia territories.

Jerry convinced Roddy that I was a guy who could be trusted. Piper didn't want to go the Warrior route and deal only with Vince, because he knew that between their strong "Alpha Male" personalities and their philosophical differences a blow-up was inevitable.

Roddy needed a go-between. He needed someone like me.

Piper got more comfortable with me once he learned I was an old territory guy who had started humbly; knowing I wasn't just some "suit" eased
his mind. Once he was comfortable with me, any time Roddy needed something I was the first person he would call. And he called me a lot in the weeks
leading to 'Mania.

His match with Goldust was a "Hollywood Backlot Brawl." The idea was
that Goldust exemplified how artificial much of showbiz was, whereas Piper
had set out from wrestling, a decade earlier, to become a serious actor. Their
match started not in the ring, but in an alley behind what was supposed to
be a movie studio in Hollywood, near the Anaheim, California, arena where
'Mania was taking place. Goldust fled, driving off in a gold Cadillac and
Piper gave chase in a white Ford Bronco. The gag was they showed footage,
supposedly, of Piper racing to the arena to finish off Goldust, but the footage
was actually of the televised low-speed police chase that O.J. Simpson had
led police on, in which Simpson was in, you guessed it: a white Ford Bronco.

Later that night, they would finish the match in the ring, with Piper
winning by stripping Goldust down to his "underwear."

After the show, I was walking Piper to the parking garage area where we
had a car coming to pick him up.

"What are you going to do with the Bronco?" Piper asked me.

"I don't know," I said. "But I can find out for you."

"Would you?"

I realized he was looking for an answer right then and there. I found
Vince and asked him what would become of the Bronco.

"Hell, I don't know," Vince said. "Why?"

"Roddy was asking about it," I said.

Vince seemed a little surprised. "Does Piper want it?" Vince asked. "'Cause
if he wants it we'll get a car carrier to take the Bronco to Portland for him."

I went back to Piper, in the garage, and relayed the message.

"If you want it, it's all yours."

He looked at me and said, "Are you ribbing?"

"Nope."

"Jeez, Champ. I'd love it."

It was nothing fancy, just a low-mileage used Bronco, but it seemed to mean a lot to Roddy.

"Vince says we can get it delivered to your house in Portland . . ."

"No, thank you," Roddy said. "I want to drive it if it's all the same to you."

He got a little teary and gave me a big hug. He drove off, as happy as he could be, and his limo driver got the night off. He drove that Bronco all the way from Anaheim to Portland, Oregon.

From that point on, Piper and I had a great rapport; two guys with a lot of mileage on them bonded over a used SUV with low mileage.

His opponent, Goldust, was one of my first major recruits as head of talent relations. The basic idea of the character came from Vince, Pat Patterson, and Bruce Prichard. The idea was, there was no way to conceal that Dustin was Dusty's son. Dusty was working behind the scenes in WCW, but was still best known for his years as a main-eventer with blue-collar appeal. Since everyone would know who Dustin was, the decision was to acknowledge it in the gimmick, hence the name "Goldust," while making the character as far from "The American Dream" as they could get. The character was the issue, because we knew that his in-ring work would never be an issue. Dustin could GO. The issue was: how could we make the most of the son of the Dream, without being the son of the Dream.

Where Dusty was a rugged everyman who wore cowboy boots in the ring, Goldust was eerily androgynous, clad in a gold bodysuit, with gold makeup on his face and a long, blonde wig on his head. His manager was his real life wife, Terri, and she wore sequined gowns and smoked a cigar at ringside during his matches.

Goldust was the first character we picked to really start pushing the envelope of a new, raunchy product.

WWF was changing, wrestling was changing, and I was changing with it.

Chapter Fifty-Four

TALENT

1996

With Hall and Nash debuting for the competition in such grand fashion and more defections coming, Vince wanted to turn the tide—or at least stem it. The first guy we signed to a guaranteed contract was Brian Pillman, who had been a featured player in WCW since I brought him in, back in 1989.

Brian and Steve Austin had been close since their days as The Hollywood Blonds tag team in WCW. They had much in common—especially that they were starving to be top stars and were willing to go through whatever necessary to achieve that goal. Brian had a brilliant mind and was an extraordinary athlete.

But Brian lived in the fast lane and was a party guy.

Not long after WWF signed him, Brian got into a serious wreck in his Humvee, and it shattered his ankle and left him in a coma. When he regained consciousness about a week later, the only remedy available to fix his ankle would cost Pillman the mobility in the ring for which he was known. Brian never got over the fact that having his ankle fused in place had ended his wrestling career—not unlike when Kerry Von Erich had his foot partially amputated after a motorcycle wreck a decade earlier.

However, we knew that, unlike Kerry, Brian was an excellent talker, and he decided that he was smart enough to figure out how to work around having a fused ankle and still have an in-ring career—but it just wasn't working. He and I broadcast some shows together while he was on crutches. He was exceptional, and I tried to sell him on the idea of being the next Jesse Ventura. He was smart, understood the business, sports, and politics; plus, he had a good look and a unique, raspy voice. No one would mistake him for anyone else. He could have had a gig for years.

But Brian resisted, hell-bent on being a wrestling star, as painful as it was for him to work. The pain led him to some chemical shortcuts, and I got reports from agents at house shows that he was acting irrationally, curling up, and sleeping in the locker room. I even had wrestlers who were friends of his—and those were plentiful, because Brian was as likeable a guy as you were going to find in the business—telling me something wasn't right with him.

It was clear that he needed help, so I had a drug tester show up at a house show in the Pacific Northwest to administer a test for Brian. Late that night, the phone rang at the little one-bedroom apartment Jan and I were renting in Stamford; it was Pillman, and he sounded violently mad. He shouted, "I can't believe you're doing this. I thought we were friends. There's nothing wrong with me. I'm not taking any drugs!"

I just said, "Well, then when the test comes back clean, everyone will know you're good."

Regrettably, his urine didn't back up his words.

* * *

Both Rodney Anoia—Yokozuna—and Vader had weight issues that were every bit as hard to manage as someone else's drug problems. Yokozuna had been with the company about four years, and captured the world title on my first night broadcasting for WWF: WrestleMania IX. At the time, he had mobility that belied his 500-plus pounds, but now he was threatening to break the 700-pound barrier. We sent him to the Duke University weight clinic, one of the most heralded programs in the country, alongside one of his in-ring rivals: Vader.

Leon White was still as tough as ever but, after years of working such a punishing style, he had put on some pounds.

Both men found that intensive weight-loss programs are almost like rehab for drugs and alcohol in that they have you totally rethink how to approach some basic parts of your life. They had to re-learn nutrition and how to power their bodies in less destructive ways. The issue was, any wrestler could be awesome in the ring and charismatic as hell, but if he's not reliable then a promoter couldn't put those attributes to use. And as those guys continued to gain weight, it adversely affected their health and general well-being; I didn't want either man getting into an irreversible situation.

The second issue was the athletic commissions. The weights of these mammoths affected their heart rates and blood pressure, and there was a risk that those numbers would exceed what commission doctors would approve for active wrestlers. If a wrestler was deemed unfit to compete in one state, it was pretty much automatic that he'd also be barred in any other state where a commission governed wrestling. We couldn't keep investing TV time and money in guys who could lose their ability to wrestle with one bad exam—so we had to send them to a place where they could lose weight.

Unfortunately, it didn't work.

We were getting reports back that Leon and Rodney would slip out at night and hit a fast-food drive-thru somewhere. We didn't know exactly what they were doing, but I did know that when I got their progress reports, there wasn't a lot of progress. It was frustrating to learn that they were gaining weight from week to week, as the threat of really bad health, getting barred from competing, and losing the bosses' trust were all peering over their shoulders.

Rodney had an eating disorder, and it was sad that he never got it under control. Of all the super-heavyweights I've seen, Vader was the most athletic, but Yokozuna had uncanny timing and great ring psychology.

But we had these two awesome main-eventers who were on the verge of being declared ineligible. We offered Yokozuna gastric bypass surgery and other procedures, but he had no desire to do it. Vader did manage to get his weight down some, and he came back ready for another run. When I watched him out there, I couldn't help but wish we'd gotten Vader before years of Japanese and WCW world title matches in that "strong style" had beaten up his body.

But we had to let Rodney go. The worst part wasn't the loss of a great performer from our rings; it was knowing that this guy, who was so well liked, was heading for major health troubles.

Even though our roster was beginning to click, we were running out of opponents for the Undertaker. He polished off Diesel at WrestleMania XII, capping off a run of a few years during which it felt like he had conquered every big man in wrestling.

* * *

Although he was 300 pounds, Mick Foley was a different kind of opponent for him. I was well aware that he had tried to get work in WWF on multiple occasions and it didn't work out, but I convinced Vince to hire him for Undertaker.

"Alright," McMahon said. "I'm going to let you bring Foley in, because I want you to learn how it feels to have your heart broken by a character you think is going to be a star—and then it ends up being the shits."

I also knew WWF would benefit by having Mick in the locker room, offering an encouraging word to impressionable young talents, or a little advice, or maybe just a joke or funny story to lift the spirits of the Boys.

Some of our older stars had recurring bad habits that they needed to get a grip on and were barely in a position to lead themselves, much less the locker room. They didn't have the self-discipline you wanted others to emulate. It wasn't everybody, by any means, but there were enough in the locker room that were not the role models that we wanted the new guys to look up to.

Vince and I knew that we needed to get younger, it was one of my challenges to find new talent that we could groom and fast-track to get on that roster sooner than not. But they needed to come to that locker room and be around people that could give them leadership, and Mick was a devout family man. He wasn't a drug user; he didn't have a drinking problem—I couldn't even remember seeing Mick take a drink, ever. He had family values. He had a genuine love for the business. And he had compassion for other human beings. He was legitimate.

You get enough of those guys, then you create a completely different environment backstage.

Another guy I felt could be a leader, in a completely different way, was Steve Austin.

Every time Austin had worked with a top guy in WCW, he had more than held his own. At 6-foot-2 and 245 pounds, he had a good look and was hungry. In my conversations with him, he had a burning desire to be great and was never satisfied with his own work. In terms of recruiting talent, there was zero to not like. The matches Steve had with Ricky Steamboat were spectacular, and Austin was passionate about being a heel.

Plus, he carried himself like a badass. I mean, he walked around backstage, walked into catering like a badass; walked to the ring the same way, wrestled and walked out that way, too. It was real. He was coming to whip your ass, and his face told that story.

Starting in WWF, it was just a matter of finding the right persona for him to find his potential. His first one was "The Ringmaster." The idea was that he was a technician who was "master of the ring," and he was the million-dollar champion accompanied to the ring by manager Ted DiBiase.

Steve didn't like it. He thought the name was hokey, and he didn't want a manager. That had nothing to do with any feelings about Ted DiBiase; he just wanted to cut his own promos.

He also thought the whole thing was a dig at him, a way of saying, "We know you're mechanically sound, but that's about it, because you really can't speak, and you really don't have any personality, so you can be the Ringmaster."

I knew that notion was wrong—that Steve had a marketable personality waiting to come out. He'd shown glimpses of it in ECW, where he'd spent a few months after being fired from WCW. In ECW, he cut funny, bitter promos about how he'd been overlooked for years. It was a different side of him than anyone had seen before, unless you'd been with him and Pillman at a bar, laughing and cutting up. I'd seen it a few times, so I knew it was there.

"Steve, one day, you're gonna be a hell of a babyface," I said to him backstage.

"What did you say?" he replied. By the look on his face you'd have thought I'd just burned his house down.

"You heard me. You're going to make a lot of money as a babyface."

He cussed *at* me, *around* me, *through* me. He cussed my opinion, the company, and anyone who thought he had any babyface in him. He said, "How stupid can you sons of bitches be? I'm a heel! Goddammit, I was born to be a heel! That's what I want to be!"

I calmly told him, "Hey, be whoever you want to be, but ultimately, the people who buy the tickets are going to decide whether you're a heel. And by the way, some of Hogan's biggest years came from selling T-shirts and gimmicks. That's 'bump-free' money! But hey, you know a lot more about this than I do, so I'm sure you'll make a lot of money selling merchandise as a despised heel."

After that, he changed his tune a little bit, and I could see the wheels turning. But even if he had insisted on remaining a heel, the fans were very slowly turning him babyface.

Austin exemplified what I was trying to do as head of the talent relations department. WCW was featuring past WWF main eventers to great effect, but we were assembling guys who were hungry for success. Who, from bell to bell, could get the job done. And I knew Austin could do it because I had called his WCW matches in the early 1990s. And in that whole time we were together in WCW, we were friendly, but not what I'd call friends. But that was about to change.

"Hey Jim, my year-to-date money isn't what I think it should be," Austin said after our King of the Ring PPV, in which he'd been crowned "King." "I was hoping for more. I'm working hard, getting over . . ."

I told him, "Wait right here. I'll go talk to Vince right now."

Austin had just cut the blistering "Austin 3:16" promo at King of the Ring that I knew Vince loved. Vince and I both knew Steve was going to be pretty special, but Steve was not happy because he felt undervalued, under-appreciated.

I walked into Vince's office and said, "Austin's out there, and he's fucking fuming."

Vince and I went through his deal, which was a fairly standard contract for a mid-card guy with solid skills and a fair amount of experience—which was how the company had viewed Austin when he came in.

It was now clear Austin would be more than Vince had originally thought, and Stone Cold had quickly figured out that he was worth more than his original contract. Vince asked me what it would take to make him happy. I gave him a number that was much healthier than Austin's original deal called for.

Without missing a beat, Vince said, "Do it."

I went back to Austin and said, "OK, let's just tear up your original contract and sign you to a new one. And it won't be the last contract you get."

That was what he wanted to hear and, for Austin, it wasn't just a matter of dollars and cents. He liked knowing that he was appreciated.

"You know, in WCW I injured my arm and they fired me with a FedEx," Steve said.

"I'm not like WCW, Steve."

Austin smiled. It was a very, very rare occurrence. He saw that we cared about his issues and were willing to solve his problem immediately, without any B.S., without any corporate runaround, without scheduling a series of meetings.

He put out his hand for me to shake. "You're alright, man."

And with that handshake we began to understand each other a little better.

Chapter Fifty-Five

THE BLACK HAT

January 1997

Vince took one look at me in the hat and said, "That's a good look. I like that."

I pretty much gave up the fight against becoming "Good Ol' JR" as the Royal Rumble was to be held at the San Antonio Alamodome. It was just too long a fight, in a place that was awash in cowboy hats.

Vince felt that, whether stereotypical or not, the hat would make me look like I sounded—a rural southwesterner.

"I understand the thought process but, just so you know, not everyone in Oklahoma wears a hat."

Vince said, "JR, we're stereotypes, and yours happens to be Oklahoma—rural, ranchers, gunfights—so now that you're wearing the hat, you look like you sound."

And I hated to admit it, but that hat really did fill in a missing piece of my public persona. The only thing negative was I remembered Randy Savage wearing those hats and he always traveled with a hat bag.

I decided there and then that if I was going to have a hat, I was just going to wear mine.

After Vince left, I quietly remembered the first time anybody ever mentioned I should wear a hat: it was Jessie Ventura in 1992, when we were working the "SuperBrawl II" pay-per-view for WCW. He even called me JR in a throwaway remark. Little did he know then how prophetic it would be over the course of time.

I was used to wearing a ballcap a lot, but I never wore a cowboy hat as a kid growing up, or as a young adult or nothing. My dad did. My grandpa did. But I didn't. Maybe I was being defiant, or I didn't want to be a cowboy. I didn't want to be that farmer. I didn't want to wear a hat.

Waiting to go out on PPV, I thought of my father. I was happy I took the time to fly down to Stilwell to see him more. To talk more. We got the chance to make up and understand each other.

Instead of running from what I didn't want to be, I started to embrace more what I did want to be. Hat and all.

Chapter Fifty-Six

SO LONG, DAD

February 1997

I was at home with Jan watching *Raw* when my phone rang. It was a collect call from Stilwell, where my father lived. As I waited for the person on the other end to talk, I saw The Legion of Doom return to WWF on my screen.

"Hello," said the voice on the line. "Is this Jim Ross?"

Hearing such a question over the phone sent a little shiver down my spine. "It is," I said. "Can I help you?"

"This is your father's neighbor calling," said the voice. "I'm afraid he's had a heart attack and they've life flighted him to Saint Francis's in Tulsa."

"What?" Jan could see by my face that something was horribly wrong.

"I'm sorry. I'll call you back when I find out more," said the man on the line.

And then he hung up.

I didn't know what to do. Should I get a flight? Wait by the phone? Call the hospital? Call my mom? I explained to Jan what was happening and we both sat staring at the phone until it rang again thirty minutes later. Same collect call, same voice of an older gentleman on the other end.

"Hello," he said again.

"How is he?" I asked.

"I'm afraid your father didn't make it. I'm sorry."

After those words, I'm sure we said some other things to each other, but I couldn't remember what. Jan took the phone from my hand when the call was over. She could hear what happened. I sat in shock and my gaze found *Raw*, muted, on my TV screen. Jan tried to console me, tell me we'd get through this together, but all I saw was my big, old man. His hands, the dollar for a haircut, the silent fishing by the pool. The last time I saw him, he still looked huge. And healthy. And now he was gone. And I didn't get to say goodbye. I didn't get to say some things I wanted to say. All the strength in the world couldn't get him past his sixty-fourth birthday.

When I got to the funeral home, his wife hadn't decided on what my dad should wear. So he lay on the table covered in a white sheet, but otherwise naked. My father, alone in a room, without any clothes and no one to make sure he was being looked after. The sight of him there stayed with me.

He was a tough bastard.

He was my hero.

My John Wayne.

And now my hero was gone.

Chapter Fifty-Seven

SITTING DOWN
WITH FOLEY

May 1997

Mick Foley was as smart as they came. He was quick-witted, introspective, measured, kind, thoughtful, and sensitive in his own way.

The character he played on TV, however, was none of those things.

I knew Vince didn't know much about Mick. He knew the look, but not the work. He'd heard about the wild stunts, but not of the man doing them. Mick's in-ring work already was solid; some of the stuff that he did was ill-advised, albeit spectacular. I never did enjoy those insane bumps, though. Personally, I always felt like he was destroying himself, as the body's not meant to take that kind of abuse. The ring is hard enough on the human body. I knew from looking at a lot of the old timers who used walkers and canes that taking bumps in a ring over a period of time is destructive enough—much less taking bumps on the concrete floor.

Although Mick had come in and done a great job, we felt it was time to add a little backstory and "humanity" to his character, Mankind. I knew Mick personally. I knew his real-life character. I knew his heart. I knew where all that was. There was an intangible there that I felt could make him even more successful. But the dilemma was how do we show the world what

I knew to be true? How do we invite our audience to know the man under the brown, leather mask?

We take a risk. We try something different. We sit down and we talk.

We'd done all kinds of interviews before; some in the ring, some backstage, some live, some not, but we'd never done an interview where the character and the person playing that character became intertwined as the interview rolled out.

Going in, all we knew was two things. The first was the overarching question we wanted to cover: *How do you go from being a Long Island educator's son to a scared, sadistic lunatic who rips out his own hair before mauling people?* The second was the ending. Everything else was on the fly.

Through the course of the taping, we traced Mick's love of wrestling and his tough road into the business. We talked about his childhood, the reasons he came to be who he was, as clips of a young Foley filled the screen. Knowing where it was heading, we let it get there organically as he talked about feelings of rejection and being an outcast, both in his youth and later in the wrestling business.

It was new ground for us, and I could feel the extra pressure of knowing that Vince was watching from the darkness, just off camera. I vouched for Mick continually when I *wasn't* head of talent. Now that I *was*, Mick and I were literally under the lights, about to find out if Vince was right about Mick's character being my first failure.

Finally, my questioning led to the moment of truth, where I asked him if he could admit he was responsible for his issues: "Don't you think, it's about time in your life, where you looked squarely in the mirror, and accepted personal responsibility for who you are? Don't you believe that you, yourself, have caused/brought on all these problems?" And with that he snapped, yelling at me and laying me out with his paralyzing finishing move, the Mandible Claw. People off camera were screaming and freaking out, as planned. The key to my end of it was to remain largely quiet. I wanted Mankind to be so vicious, and his finishing move to be so dangerous that when he locked on to you, there was nothing you could do.

Not even scream. Not even shout. You could do nothing but just lay there as paralysis set in.

When he finally let go, Foley added a line that showed the humanity beneath the sadist, saying as he staggered away, "Jimmy? Jimmy? Uh, he's gonna need some help!"

By planting the seed of him being human under all that craziness, Foley turned the corner from being a compelling villain to a full-formed character who the fans could understand, or detest, as the storyline called for it.

From my "unconscious" position on the floor I could see that Vince was enthralled by what he saw from Mick. I knew by the mere look on the boss's face that we had broken new ground and that Vince could see the potential of Foley as a weekly TV character.

Mick had positioned Mankind as an obsessed wrestling fan who saw himself as a handsome, grandiose babyface headlining Madison Square Garden—but everything went haywire and he instead became this Mankind character.

Vince's creative wheels began turning almost immediately. "I have a vision for what this guy can be," he said as we left the room.

I think the boss began to see both Mick and me in a different light.

And live on *Raw*, over four episodes, the interview aired. After that, I think the fans started seeing Mick in a different light as well.

Chapter Fifty-Eight

PILLMAN

October 1997

There was a big adjustment because everything else in my life—doctor visits, family matters, everything—had to be scheduled around the show when it was live. And with the competition from WCW, WWF decided it was going to go live more often.

There were very few times when Jan and I could slip away for a long weekend, and trying to book a vacation was a complete no-no. We were in the trenches battling for ratings and available talent. If Vince McMahon's work ethic was insane before, it was otherworldly now that he felt the heat of true competition down his neck. He never felt like WCW were trying to compete with him, he felt they were trying to put him out of business. That meant that no one could take their eye off the ball. No breaks, no rests, and no retreat.

Even when I'd come home late at night, the phone was always in arm's reach, and there was always someone on the other line with an issue.

Some of those issues I got to hear about at home and some on the road.

We were in St. Louis getting ready for that night's "Badd Blood" pay-per-view when we got the news about Brian Pillman's passing. He had been found dead in his hotel room in Minnesota, where he had wrestled the previous night. Vince and I flew to Cincinnati to see his family, as we both wanted to pay our respects. We visited his wake which was a little more convivial than your typical memorial service, with stories and memories of Brian being shared. They had the casket open and it hurt me deeply to see Brian lying there. The part I found the hardest about running the talent department was keeping a distance from the wrestlers. I got too close to some of the guys and, when tragedy struck, it was like losing a family member.

Brian Pillman had been like a little brother to me, a mischievous kid.

Even though I knew relationships in the wrestling business were often fleeting, I felt a kinship to Brian. He could talk to you intelligently about a variety of topics. He was a real renaissance man, the opposite of many people's image of a "dumb ol' rassler." He just had trouble controlling his social urges and, sometimes, the guilt he derived from that could also become an issue. He was often in a great mood until he thought about what he had done or said two nights before—and then he made himself miserable about it. He was often his own burden. And despite his image as a wild man, Brian was not using drugs, in my opinion, for recreational purposes; he was taking the medication to help him heal from that awful accident, but it was medication that still was against company policy.

"When I said you're going to get your heart broken," Vince said on the flight back, "I simply meant don't get too close to the Boys."

Ironically, Linda McMahon had once told me the same thing regarding Vince. "Don't get too close to the flame," she said.

Chapter Fifty-Nine

MONTREAL

November 1997

I was sequestered to Vince's office backstage at the Molson Centre in Montreal, Canada. A security guard walked me to the door on Vince's insistence, and was told not to leave until I physically locked myself in. Outside I could hear disturbing sounds of shouting, arguing, and utter confusion as to what had just happened. I kept running the finish of the match over and over in my head. What did this mean for the title? What did it mean for the company? What did it mean for Bret and Shawn? Their simmering, personal, real-life feud had just peaked live on PPV, and the aftermath was playing out just beyond the door I was told not to open. A lot of us could see that the tension between both men would end up doing neither any favors—but no one saw this coming.

At least I certainly didn't. Although it was a long time brewing in the background.

Shawn Michaels and Bret Hart were two of the best. They came up through the ranks together, and in many ways their paths ran parallel. Both men were amazing performers; both men had the necessary ego that came with that. Both men, in the end, let those same egos guide them into trouble.

293

As their professional conflicts got personal, both men tended to take their issues straight to Vince. Shawn already had a rapport with the boss, so I tried to avoid his issues as much as I could. I knew Shawn was a good-hearted human being, but the person that he had become was not a professional, likable version of himself. His behaviors were a product of feeling the continuous pressure to be the best while mixing in too many medications he was taking to deal with the pain from years of bumps. He was certainly not unique in that regard. Like so many of the guys the physicality took a toll, and handling it with medication often affected the thought processes, leading to sometimes unsound decision making.

Shawn left in early 1997 after vacating the world title. He gave a TV interview in which he said he needed time off because, "I lost my smile." The bottom line was that Shawn needed time off to get help. And like Vince always said, "If we can't solve the problem, we can always eliminate it."

I was dealing with guys on the roster who wanted to know why Michaels had left so abruptly, and I quickly reached the point where I just started telling them that the reason didn't matter. The only issue that mattered was, who was going to step up? WWF business wasn't exactly on fire, and I knew we had other talented guys on the roster; a lot of them hadn't had a chance to get much playing time. My job was to make sure the talent was ready and keep them focused on making the most of every minute they were on TV. It didn't matter if it was a long match, a short interview, or anything else— every minute they were on air was a chance to show Vince why the company should invest in them.

Shawn's departure from the main-event picture also meant the reshuffling of WrestleMania 13. Instead of a title rematch against Shawn, former champ Bret "Hit Man" Hart would now be facing "Stone Cold" Steve Austin, with whom he had been feuding for months, in an "I quit" match.

I knew it would be good, but those guys definitely exceeded expectations, as the match was a work of art. By the end of it, Hart was a villain, while rowdy heel Austin was on the verge of becoming WWF's next great hero.

As with Murdoch-DiBiase in Mid-South, pulling off a double-turn was delicate work—but they did it to perfection. Austin was close to being cheered anyway, and because of Bret's ever-increasing popularity in Canada, some American fans started seeing him as more of an outsider. I love my country, but Americans can be strange ducks sometimes in how they view nationalism. When Bret did an interview somewhere praising Canada, even though he didn't say a bad word about the United States, some American fans took it as, "He's knocking the USA! Well, screw him!"

WrestleMania 13 was the match that made Austin, with Bret Hart basically welcoming Austin into the main-event club.

Bret's on-screen turn led to the formation of The Hart Foundation: Bret Hart, Owen Hart, Jim "The Anvil" Neidhart, Davey Boy Smith, and Brian Pillman.

It was one hell of a unit.

Not only were they a talented crew, but they played up being an anti-American, pro-Canadian faction, which created an interesting dynamic. They'd be villains in the States, heroes in Canada and Europe, with Austin and our other heroes in the opposite role.

That group peaked in July 1997, at the "Canadian Stampede" pay-per-view held in Calgary, Alberta, Canada, where Bret and Owen's dad, Stu Hart, had run the local territory for decades. The show was a homecoming for The Hart Foundation, and it was as emotionally charged a night as I had experienced in wrestling.

The main event was a ten-man tag match, pitting the five-member Hart Foundation against Steve Austin, Ken Shamrock, Goldust, and The Legion of Doom. Austin's team, who would have been huge fan favorites in the states, damn near got booed out of the building. The hometown Hart team got a reaction that got louder and louder as each member was introduced individually. Finally, when Bret Hart came out, the 12,000 fans in attendance gave as loud a cheer as I've ever heard from a wrestling crowd, of any size.

Despite great nights like that one, things were getting ugly between Bret and Shawn backstage. Shawn had returned to duty in June after taking a few months to decompress, but he and Bret had developed friction that was only getting worse. It was sad to watch two former best friends continue to slide into a deep, personal feud with each other.

Soon after, the two even had a locker room scuffle, which led to Shawn storming out of the building in New Haven. The fight was inevitable, I guess. A flood of emotions finally overtook them both. Poor Pat Patterson got caught in the middle, literally. He was in the locker room, talk about wrong place at the wrong time, and they almost suffocated him trying to get at each other. It wasn't a long fight. They fell through a flimsy wall, where Jerry Lawler was using the bathroom.

My main focus had to be on getting everyone else on the roster calmed down, refocused on getting that night's *Raw* done, and getting back to work.

In August 1997, an accident during the SummerSlam pay-per-view put our hottest new star on the shelf and made for a scary moment for me, personally. In a match against Owen Hart, Steve Austin suffered a neck injury when Owen misjudged his placement of Austin on a piledriver and Austin's entire body weight came down on his neck. He lay there, after the match, unable to move, and had to have help getting from the ring.

* * *

I was more worried about my friend than any effect of Austin's absence on the business—but I tried to stay focused as we still had a show to call. Backstage producers did, thankfully, keep us posted on Austin, and before the night was out I was relieved to hear he'd already regained some feeling in his limbs. Although I'm sure he didn't feel this way at the time, Steve was lucky that the injury wasn't crippling as spinal injuries can be.

Weeks later when Steve came out of surgery in San Antonio, he woke up in his hospital room to find me sitting at the foot of his bed. I wanted to be there for him, and I also wanted to represent Vince and the company.

Owen Hart felt awful about it, and didn't know quite how to handle something that was unprecedented for someone as careful and skilled as Owen. He asked me frequently how Steve was doing, but he was hesitant to call because he was embarrassed and felt horrible about it, and just didn't know what to say.

Steve's absence put the spotlight back on Shawn and Bret.

I was aware of Bret's contract talks and that he had an amazing offer from WCW on the table. Scott Hall and Kevin Nash were encouraging him to come, in part because their WCW contracts had clauses known as "most favored nations," which meant that their salaries rose with the hiring of any new signee, making more than their current rates.

WWF couldn't afford the seven-figure annual salary WCW was dangling, so even though I know with certainty that Bret didn't want to leave, the financial security was more than he could ultimately reject. Whatever happened to end the contract negotiations between Bret and WWF, I was made aware that we weren't going to be able to keep him.

At that point, the company's issue became: How to get the WWF's world title off of a guy who was now bound for the competition? That was also the point at which I was no longer involved in the situation. Once Bret's leaving was inevitable, it ceased to be something I could help manage, via talent relations. Figuring out how best to get the title off of Bret was for creative to decide, and I was not part of that process.

For a while, I'd thought Bret would drop the belt at the non-televised event in Detroit. I thought that would have been a great idea to show fans that anything could happen. Then the new champ could do a non-finish with Bret at Survivor Series, and that would be that.

Vince ultimately decided to do it on the pay-per-view so the fans could see the title change, which I can understand.

Going into Survivor Series, Lawler and I had decided between us that the less we knew the better off we'd be, as was our general policy. Before we walked out, Jerry Brisco asked if I knew what we were doing that night. I said, "No, last I heard, it was going to be a DQ, but I don't even know who's getting DQ'd."

He didn't offer any more, which suited me perfectly. I liked to call the matches as I saw them. Too much info on what was about to happen usually killed the "realness" of the call.

What Lawler and I *did* know was that Bret Hart and Shawn Michaels were two of the best in the world, and their pride wouldn't let them give anything less than a stellar match.

"Ready, JR?" Lawler said.

"Always, King," I replied.

I could feel the energy in the building as we sat in our commentary position at ringside. The building was hot, and we both knew we were in for a memorable night.

Shawn and Bret had a good match, with the Canadian, pro-Bret crowd getting more rabid as the contest went on. I glanced up from the monitor embedded in our announce table and noticed Vince was at ringside, along with a couple of the agents. I didn't see them come out, because I was watching the TV feed of the match, not the ring, so that my call matched what the audience at home was seeing. I just presumed Vince was positioning himself to be part of the finish, causing the DQ.

In the ring, Shawn got Bret in Bret's own Sharpshooter finishing move—which also wasn't unusual as heels had used the heroes' own finishers on them for ages.

But then suddenly, without Bret submitting, referee Earl Hebner made a sign that Bret *had* submitted and the bell rang. I looked over to time-keeper Mark Yeaton because I thought he had rung the bell by mistake. I thought, *bad time to make a mistake like that with the boss down at ringside.*

But Vince didn't react. It was in that split second I knew something was up. The match *was* over, and Shawn's music began playing.

I said to the audience at home: "What happened? What happened? Bret Hart submitted to the sharpshooter?"

Shawn was declared the winner and new champion. Bret looked utterly confused, and then utterly furious.

Lawler and I looked at each other like, "What the hell just happened?"

Down through my headsets I was given the call from backstage to get off air. With Shawn's music still playing, I simply said, "Ladies and gentlemen, from Montreal, good night!" before we went to black.

The fans began to throw stuff at the ringside area. Bret was irate. Vince was still there, and he and Bret were eyeballing each other. Bret, from the ring, spat right in McMahon's face. Vince barely reacted at all, except to wipe the spit from his face. Lawler tapped me on the arm and gave me the signal to move. Both he and I made our way backstage as something bad was brewing for real at ringside.

When Lawler and I reached the back, referee Earl Hebner was gone, Shawn was gone, and Jerry Brisco was gone. Lawler looked at me and said, "Did you know that was going to happen?"

"No! No idea," I said.

Vince reappeared backstage and immediately walked toward me. "JR, I want you to go to my office and lock yourself in . . ."

"What?"

"Listen to me. This could get bad. Move. NOW." Vince motioned for a security guard to bring me to his office.

Bret was still in the ring, and The Hart Foundation had joined him. Vince was staying put. I was shown to Vince's office where I began to process a significant amount of information. The noises I began to hear were disturbing, as was the eventual sound of silence. There was shouting, arguing, tension—and then nothing. I wanted to see what was going on but knew Vince wasn't messing around when he told me to stay put.

After a while I heard some familiar voices approaching the door. Jerry Brisco and Shane McMahon helped Vince in through the door. The boss was groggy and there was a noticeable mark on his face. Neither man said anything for a minute or two, until Vince looked up from the ground. His stare belonged to a man whose mind was elsewhere. "I had to give Bret a free shot. I owed him that much," Vince said to no one in particular. He then looked directly at me. "I didn't want you to know."

"I know . . ."

"It was important that you were left out so you could continue to work with the talent after this," Vince continued. "If I had clued you in, you'd never have their trust again."

"I understand." I knew what Vince was trying to do in protecting my position in the company. I also knew that the Boys were mostly going to believe what they wanted to believe.

I cautiously left Vince's office and the first person I saw was Undertaker. His opinion and read on the situation was important, as he was widely seen as the voice of authority among the wrestlers.

"You don't worry," he said before I even opened my mouth. "I got your back."

As I walked out of the building, I tried to address the concerns and apprehensions of the talent. I knew a lot of folks in the Hart camp, his friends and family, believed that because of my role in talent relations, I had to know. Some of the guys believed me, but I also knew others didn't. All I could do was deal with the talent as I had before the incident in the ring: with respect and honesty.

As I got back to the hotel, the fans were catcalling and booing us as we walked in. I spent most of that night fielding calls from concerned wrestlers. Mick Foley was particularly sickened by how WWF treated Bret. But most had decided by the end of the night that this wasn't their hill to die on. Bret was leaving, and getting well paid to do so. Even if the Boys disagreed with what had happened, they knew they had their own families to feed and their own careers to look after. The personal hurt and division in Montreal created a small but noticeable business opportunity.

In TV terms, it created the best heel of that generation: Mr. McMahon.

Chapter Sixty

A LITTLE MORE ATTITUDE

1998–99

From conflict came an opening. Vince, being the ultimate showman, saw the negative response he was getting after Montreal and said, "You don't like me? You don't like the way I operate this company? Well, I'll give you something to truly hate." And he reinvented himself as the top villain in the genre, at age fifty-two.

Vince told me, "You know, JR, there's a difference between Mr. McMahon on TV and Vince McMahon in real life."

"Really?" I said. "And what might that be?"

He struggled to answer. And that was the key. Mr. McMahon was an over-the-top version of Vince, who would come to the surface in real life if someone did something really stupid or ill-advised. Of course, Vince's aggressive nature was nothing that fazed me. I had learned from Bill Watts, who, during phone conferences, would lift out of his chair and attack the speaker phone because he couldn't get his hands on whoever was on the other end.

I had also learned from my dad, who hit a cow with an uppercut—because the cow kicked him. He wasn't looking to abuse the animal, it was completely reactionary. Watts was the same; Vince was the same—reactionary. I chose not to analyze or judge. Seeing alpha males flip that switch was nothing new to me. I could handle it, live with it, and actually thrive around it to reach my paycheck at the end of the month.

Of course, the version of Vince that was catching people's attention on TV was an insanely exaggerated version of who he was, mixed with a natural ability to be a great heel performer. He was so good at it that he had the fans fooled; people really wanted to know how I could work with someone so evil.

And the perfect foil for the character of the overbearing boss was the working man who refused to be anything but true to himself. And that's where "Stone Cold" Steve Austin came in. If Bret Hart was the guy who brought Austin onto that main event mountain, McMahon was the guy who helped Austin build a mansion at the peak. It fit Austin to a "T" for him to be the defiant, anti-establishment guy.

Austin and McMahon, backed up by a cast of hungry, talented, and rejuvenated Superstars, were causing the ratings needle to move back in our direction. It was a needle that I wasn't really paying much attention to. I didn't have time to worry when we were losing the ratings battle, and didn't have time to celebrate when we were scaling back up the mountain again. My focus and obsession was putting together the best roster in the history of the game, and giving everything I had at the announcers table.

I sat ringside to witness Austin win the championship from Shawn Michaels at WrestleMania XIV. Their storyline had spanned months and included boxing legend Mike Tyson as a ringside enforcer and backup referee in Shawn Michaels's corner. When Tyson counted three, the 19,000 fans in Boston's Fleet Center erupted as I passionately called on commentary, "AUSTIN IS THE CHAMPION! STONE COLD! STONE COLD! STONE COLD! THE AUSTIN ERA HAS BEGUN!"

And for all the controversy Shawn Michaels seemed to generate, I saw him give a truly gutsy performance. He was already working through the everyday pain of his high-impact wrestling style when he suffered a severe back injury at the Royal Rumble show, just a couple of months before. Shawn was not a giant, and the volume of huge bumps he took in delivering all those great performances over the years were finally catching up with him. He had to heal and, when that door shut, the Austin door opened.

And Mike Tyson's role in that whole deal was invaluable, too. Tyson first attended a WWF show on air at the '98 Royal Rumble—and the next night his 'Mania role was announced. Tyson was there for the announcement, but Austin came out to the ring and the faceoff between them was a pivotal moment; it blew up around us to become one of the first ESPN *SportsCenter* moments that we ever had.

Tyson was another controversial figure, but he was an absolute pleasure to work with. He'd been a *major* wrestling fan since childhood. He grew up in Brooklyn, New York, and followed his WWF heroes faithfully. He could talk for hours about Bruno Sammartino or Chief Jay Strongbow, and he had a picture-perfect recall of matches and events.

He was always a professional—on time, ready to go, and willing to do whatever he was asked to help the promotion succeed. He truly got it because he had been a longtime fan.

The next night, *Raw* kicked off the Austin-McMahon feud that had been brewing for weeks. A week after that, as the feud intensified, WWF did something it had not done in more than 18 months—*Raw* beat WCW's *Nitro* in the ratings. *Nitro* had made such a big splash that WCW won the ratings battle for 83 straight weeks.

Tuesday morning after the *Raw* that broke that streak, there was some celebrating—but not by me.

After each night's *Raw*, I'd oftentimes go back to my hotel room and watch that night's replay of *Nitro*, and I always thought, *Why are we losing to* this?

I didn't like us getting beaten 83 weeks in a row, but I wasn't going to dwell on it because my thought was, we have a chance to play another game on Monday. With all the duties I was handling, I didn't have time to grieve. I was busy doing payroll for 100-plus members of talent and playing the role of priest, guidance counselor, 12-step sponsor, and school principal, as needed.

I could feel the momentum turn in our favor, and was happy with that.

Right after 'Mania XIV we also debuted Sean Waltman, who made his name previously in WWF as the 1-2-3 Kid, but was now re-introduced as X-Pac, the newest member of DX. That was significant, because it was the first high-profile NWO member to defect to WWF.

While some people were looking to come *back* to WWF, others were looking to work there for the first time.

"Dr. Death" Steve Williams had made it as a major star in Japan but, after a decade of doing most of his wrestling there, Doc was looking to spend more time in the States. Another factor that he, regrettably, was not as forthcoming about was: his body was carrying the effects of years of wrestling his intensely physical style, especially in Japan. Doc still looked like a tank but he was only human, like the rest of us.

Although I didn't know quite know how worn down his body was, I did know he was a 16-year veteran, with a style no one would mistake for easy. Doc reminded me of Vader, where I felt we got him a little too late to really get the most out of him. I was hoping to get one good run out Doc, which would not only help the company, but also get him a nice payday.

And then came the "Brawl For All."

When I got the word from creative, I detested it immediately. I understood that the fans might wonder who would really win in a fight between Wrestler A and Wrestler B, but for us to try it was plain stupid. It immediately created dissension in the locker room as guys took sides with each new matchup, not to mention that it caused injuries that cost the company a lot of money in medical bills and lost revenue and it did not benefit any of the participants. Even the winner ultimately lost out as a result of participating.

Doc was one of the 16 entrants, and with his credentials as a four-time wrestling All-American at the University of Oklahoma, he was one of the favorites to win it all. In a second-round bout with Bart Gunn, he tore his quad during the third round of the fight. The muscle came off the bone and rolled up his leg. I had no idea how Doc was even standing after that, but he wouldn't quit . . . so he got the shit beaten out of him pretty quickly by Bart, a tough man in his own right.

Doc was literally a one-legged man in an ass-kicking contest. He was never the same after that and, because he was seen as "JR's boy," because we were both from Oklahoma, both came up through Mid-South, and we were friends outside of the business, some people began spreading the B.S. that I now somehow had it in for Bart Gunn, which was 100 percent untrue.

It probably didn't help that Doc told people in the locker room that he had already been paid the winner's cash prize.

I began to hear that I was so mad at Bart Gunn for beating Doc that I personally went out and booked Butterbean to fight Gunn at WrestleMania XV. Butterbean was Eric Esch, a super heavyweight boxer who had come from the world of tough man contests, mixed martial arts, K-1, and Pride.

Even though 'Bean had more than a hundred and fifty pounds on Bart, the idea was for both men to battle in one last shoot boxing match for the company. Not only was this *not* my idea, but if I'd been asked I would have objected strongly. Nothing against Butterbean, who was really a nice guy, but I didn't understand why we were taking the only guy who had gotten anything positive from that stupid tournament and risking what little momentum he had.

Butterbean came to me before the fight, the day of 'Mania, and asked me, "Hey, are you guys gonna be mad at me if I knock Bart out in the first round?" He was concerned about it because he was considering getting into wrestling and didn't want to burn a bridge.

"Well, this is supposed to be real, 'Bean, so you do what you gotta do. No one's gonna be mad at you," I said. Privately I was thinking, *Don't under-estimate Bart Gunn. There's a lot of people in that locker room who think Bart's gonna knock the BBQ out of Butterbean.*

Bart was in great shape, had that devastating left hand, had a reach advantage, and had gone through the guys in "Brawl For All" like salt through a widowed woman, as my grandad used to say.

A lot of the guys in the locker room were actually taking bets, and more of them were looking to bet on Bart rather than the experienced Butterbean.

It only took Butterbean 35 seconds to cost a lot of the locker room a decent amount of cash, because he quickly and conclusively knocked out Bart. It wasn't a fluke; there was no lucky punch. As dangerous and powerful as Bart was, he was up against a guy who legitimately beat people up for a living.

Bart was out of the company not long after, as was Doc, so with Brawl For All, we ended up creating zero stars, racking up thousands in medical bills, and even finding a way to make the winner look like a loser.

It broke my heart to have to let Doc go, especially since it strained the friendship we'd built for nearly 20 years—as I knew it would. I understood why he was mad; Doc felt like he had never gotten a real chance in the company. But I also understood the company's perspective. It always sucked to let someone go, but it was worse when it was a friend.

The whole Brawl for All competition was an utter failure, but it was also the actions of a company who was willing to push the envelope to keep the ratings moving in their favor. WWF versus WCW was a very real "war" with very real consequences for the eventual loser. Our locker room looked at it like they were fighting for their livelihoods. As a result, our shows became more brash, the characters more bold, and the storylines more edgy—and far riskier.

Chapter Sixty-One

HELL IN A CELL

June 1998

"Good God almighty! Good God almighty! They've killed him! As God is my witness, he is broken in half!" It was only a few minutes into the match and I genuinely thought my friend was dead, or dying. Mick Foley wanted to top Shawn Michaels's performance in the previous Hell in a Cell match, and the way he choose to do it was by climbing to the top of the cell structure that covered the ring, and goad his opponent, the Undertaker, into following him up there.

Undertaker made his famous entrance and duly joined Mick 20 feet above the arena floor. The weight of both men immediately put the structure itself to the test as their collective 600 pounds tore the wire mesh under their feet as they walked.

I was positioned at the edge of the cell on the floor, and watched in my monitor as both men battled over to the side where Jerry Lawler and I were sitting. Beside us was the Spanish announce team lead by Hugo Savinovich.

On top of the cell, Mick and 'Taker threw punches and went back and forth at the very edge to make the audience think something bad was going to happen.

And then it did.

Undertaker threw Foley from the top of the cell. Mick fell 20 feet, through the Spanish announce team's table at ringside, his 300-plus pound body exploding the table as his body slid limply under the guard rail. From my vantage point, Mick Foley had disappeared under the collapsed table and I had no idea what shape he was in. "Good God almighty! Good God almighty! They've killed him! As God is my witness, he is broken in half!" I shouted. My words were real. My worry for Mick was real. My shock was real.

Lawler, also stunned, was muttering, "Oh my God, Oh my God."

I turned my attention from the audience at home to the people in the back. "Somebody get out here! Really! I mean it!"

As the monitor filled with replays of the fall shot from different angles, I still couldn't believe what I had just seen. All I could muster was, "Look . . . look at that, folks!"

Seconds went by, and Foley was still lying there, and I could feel the anger rising in me. "We need doctors out here. If somebody can get off their butt in the back and get somebody out here!"

But Lawler and I weren't the only ones worried about him. Even though they had recently been feuding on television, Terry Funk left that behind to come check on the man who he'd fought and mentored across the globe.

Lawler was calling for help for the Spanish announce crew, who had been in the path of the plummeting 300-pounder. Jerry noted that Mankind was starting to stir, as medical help finally got to Mick, in the form of a doctor, some officials, and a team of paramedics carrying a stretcher.

Even Vince McMahon set aside his evil on-air persona to see if Mick Foley was OK. Mick didn't appear to be cooperating, and Terry Funk looked almost tearful as he implored Foley to get on the stretcher. I thought Mick's career was over. Maybe even worse. He was alive, he was breathing, but everyone around him felt he was in bad shape. They wheeled him slowly from ringside, with the Undertaker still looking down from on top of the cell.

"Apparently, as quick and unusually as this match started, it has ended," I said.

But Mick didn't get that memo.

The paramedics didn't get too far with "The Hardcore Legend" before he fought his way off the gurney, made it back to the cage where once more, against all logic, he again climbed to the top of the cell!

As big as Mick was, it wasn't easy for him to scale that fence the first time, much less after the damage he had absorbed—but he made it. The fall from the top of the cage onto the ringside table was something Foley and 'Taker had worked out, but the next stunt wasn't in anyone's plans. Undertaker was to choke-slam Foley onto the top of the cage, and Foley would sell it, as Undertaker climbed down and into the ring. Instead, when Foley's body hit the cell, a part of it gave way and it swung open like a steel trapdoor, leaving Foley to fall all the way to the mat, back first. Even worse, the chair he'd tossed on top of the cage earlier was right behind him and ended up smashing him in the face as he landed.

This time, even Undertaker seemed shocked as he looked down at Foley. The doctor, referees, and medics rushed into the cell as Lawler said, "That's it. He's dead."

"The King," known for his sharp humor, wasn't kidding.

Somehow that impact had knocked out one of Mick's teeth, which lodged itself in his left nostril, as a gruesome camera close up would show a few minutes later. The whole performance was scary, and I was doubly convinced the match was over. I was sure Vince was going to come back out and announce that was it and I don't think one fan would have been upset had it ended right then.

I even screamed, "Would somebody stop the damn match! Enough's enough!"

But after being out cold for a minute or so, Mick was apparently looking to finish the match.

The Undertaker climbed down into the ring through the opening Mick's second nasty fall had created. Funk, being the old pro that he was, took a couple of shots from 'Taker to buy Mick a few more seconds of recovery time. Finally they all cleared out, and after a short brawl, Mick pulled out a bag of thumbtacks and dumped them all over the mat.

Of course, the villainous Mankind's plan was foiled, as Undertaker slammed—and then choke-slammed—Mankind onto the thumbtacks before finally ending it with his signature tombstone piledriver.

Everyone took a huge sigh of relief when the bell rang to signal the end.

I was one of Mick's biggest advocates in the company but, as I sat there, I couldn't help but think Mick went way too far in that match. I admired his guts and toughness, but he never needed to get even close to that level of danger.

After he got to the back, Vince thanked him for putting himself out there to make the show, but then added, "Don't ever do anything like that again."

I had a similar conversation with Mick a couple of days later, in my role as head of talent. "You're never going to be around here to make the money that's there for you," I said. "You're too entertaining and too skilled not to figure this shit out. You don't have to be Cactus Jack, splattering yourself on the concrete."

Mick listened to me and Vince. But I had a feeling as I shook his hand there was still that wild look in his eye—that need to give the fans what he thought they wanted from him. His body.

Chapter Sixty-Two

2ND ATTACK

December 1998

"I'm sorry honey, but your mother has passed away," my wife said over the phone. I was in England for the Capitol Carnage show, a British-only pay-per-view.

My mother had dealt with heart issues her entire life, and she had succumbed to a heart attack at sixty-four years of age. I sat in my room, tears in my eyes, remembering how she had become a big wrestling fan who never missed *Raw*. I thought about the work ethic she and Dad had instilled in me growing up.

Vince offered to fly me home as quickly as he could make that happen.

"I'm going to stay," I said. "I'm going to stay and do my job."

"Do you want me to fly Jan here to London so she can be with you?" he asked.

"No, thank you."

Vince and Linda couldn't have been nicer or more supportive, but I wanted to do my work the way I had always done my work, without Jan doting on me. I wanted to grieve in my own way, do my job and get through it. That's the man my mother raised. Someone who would see the job through.

The next night, Lawler and I were calling the first hour of the show when I began to feel some strange sensations. I suddenly had a throbbing headache and the audio coming through my headphones got painfully loud. Every noise felt like it was killing me. My eye wouldn't blink, my tongue went numb, and I began to have trouble enunciating as I lost control of the muscles on the left side of my face.

We were live, and I had to support my cheek with my hand just to keep talking.

I was pretty sure it was another Bell's palsy attack, even though it was a different experience than the first one. This was much more intense. As the night wore on I was hoping it would be Bell's palsy, when the alternative might have been a stroke.

I began to think that maybe I triggered the attack by putting myself under the stress of suppressing my grief; not dealing with my feelings of sadness; instead focusing on preparing for a live broadcast.

Lawler noticed right away that something was wrong, but I wanted to keep going. I wanted to finish the job I'd started. It was important to me as a tribute to my mother and the son she raised.

After the show, I went straight back to the hotel and packed. I knew I had to fly back and see a neurologist. I knew I had to fly back and bury my mother.

When I landed, I was told that Vince got me an appointment to see a highly regarded neurologist in Connecticut. That visit confirmed that it was Bell's palsy and that they still hadn't figured out what caused it—or how to cure it—during the five years between my first attack and this one.

I was prescribed Prednisone and told to stay away from loud noises and certain tones that might trigger the headaches. I was also carrying around artificial tears to moisten my eye when needed. That night I had to tape my left eye shut as I slept.

I wasn't home for long before I felt depression setting in. First it hit me that I was basically all that was left of my family—no brothers or sisters, and my parents and grandparents were all gone. My daughters were attending school in Oklahoma, but my relationships with them were not as good as I'd have liked them to be.

As I made arrangements for my mother, I knew the disconnect with my daughters was 100 percent my fault. I focused so much on my job and all the travel that I thought if I could do over again, that would be the only thing I'd change. As the years went by I moved from Dallas to Atlanta, and then to Connecticut. I was going farther and farther from Oklahoma while they were young women in grade school, high school, and later college. I was sure they knew I loved them, but I wished we could have had a more traditional relationship.

Knowing my mother was now gone left me feeling alone. I loved her, cared for her, listened to her talk about how much she loved watching me on the TV. She was kind and loved me without any conditions. She was only just gone, and I already missed her terribly.

I could feel myself slipping further. I was grieving, ashamed of how I looked, and coming to terms with the distinct possibility that my on-screen career was over.

Appearance was important in wrestling. It always had been. I wasn't sure that WWF wanted a guy who looked like I now looked welcoming a world-wide audience to their product—especially now that half my face was literally sagging. I knew that in wrestling when any promoter saw a weakness his impulse was to remove it immediately. That wasn't just a Vince McMahon thing, it was an every smart booker in wrestling history thing.

The more I thought about it, the more I thought I'd have to shift course and focus on talent relations, or help produce my replacement on-air. Announcing was the thing I loved most, because when they played my "Boomer Sooner" music and I started down that aisle, every problem I had evaporated. It released a joy in me, a way of forgetting everything else except the story in front of me. I couldn't create the feeling a live audience gave me in any other part of my life. But now it seemed like after 24 years of doing it—and through no fault of my own—I would never broadcast again.

Everything else in my life was crumbling.

Except Jan.

She minded me, tried to make me feel better. She watched my physical health tumble and my mental health follow, but she never judged, rushed, or wanted anything from me. She would go by Titan Tower and pick up my memos, payroll information, and everything I needed to work from home.

I knew that the more I didn't have to leave the house, the worse it would be for me in the long run, but I just didn't want to go out. I didn't want people to see me and how I looked. Working from home sounded great, but for me I was letting my home become my personal "comfort zone." I didn't want to go to the office, I didn't go to the grocery store, I didn't want to go out to eat.

I didn't want to do anything but hide.

And then Vince sent me a letter. He had somebody from the office hand deliver it to me. It read:

Dear JR,

It's not the number of times you get knocked down in life that counts. What counts is the number of times you get the fuck back up. So get the fuck back up! Give the Stone Cold hand sign to everyone who wants you to stay down. Use the love, respect, admiration, strength, and will of your friends and family to bolster your spirit, restore your confidence, and help you face the challenges of the future.

You have come a long way, JR. You've earned a great deal of respect and admiration from family, friends, and foes. However, "that was yesterday." I need you, your family needs you, your company needs you to help carry the WWF into the future, black hat and all.

JR you have my utmost respect, appreciation, and love!

Your friend,

Vince.

P.S. There are 5,000 reasons for you to celebrate this Christmas in an envelope on my desk, which will be presented to you on your first day back at the office.

Merry Christmas.

After a few weeks of keeping myself in seclusion, I finally resolved that I could be making myself more useful. I still felt down, I still felt hurt, I still felt brittle, but in January I reported back to work after only a few weeks away.

Vince was waiting with his arms outstretched. "Goddammit, pal, welcome back," he said.

I didn't really want to look him in the eye because of how my face was. I didn't want him to see weakness. I didn't want him looking at me and thinking I couldn't do a job for his company.

"Thank you," I said.

"What for?" he asked.

"Getting me out of the house."

In addition to my existing administrative duties, I started helping to produce the announcing on *Raw* each Monday. I could feel the energy from the crowd through the curtain, but I didn't want to go out there. I was afraid of being mocked. That curtain became my safety net. I could stay on one side of it and kinda make myself forget that I looked the way I did. If I walked the other side the whole world would see. Even the thought of going out there before the people made my stomach turn.

But out I went, and we tried an angle where I was a heel and Dr. Death was going to be my muscle. It didn't click, and it made me feel worse. I wasn't ready, and the people didn't know how to take me being a bad guy. We quickly scrapped it and I hid backstage again.

Michael Cole was my replacement, and even though he was newish and green, I could tell that he was going to be a helluva talent in that position. In my mind, I was finished with the announcers section of my career.

I had no idea that the two biggest stars in the company were already talking to Vince about getting me back out there.

Chapter Sixty-Three

COMING HOME

1999

"Hey, pal, make sure you bring your tux to Philly!" Vince said the week before WrestleMania XV, featuring "Stone Cold" Steve Austin and Rocky Maivia, now a main-evented as "The Rock."

"What for?" I asked. I always wore a coat and tie because I was a senior company official and wanted to look professional. A tux, though, was an unusual request for off-air talent.

"Because I'm going to put you back to work," Vince said.

"Doing what?" I warily asked.

"You're going to call the main event at 'Mania," he said with a smile. "You're ready."

Vince patted me on the shoulder and walked away. I was thrilled to hear that he had the confidence to put me out there with that match, because we all knew what we had with Austin and what we were going to have with Rock, so this main event was huge for the company. But his words also sent a cold chill down my spine.

I quickly found out that Austin and Rock personally requested that I be out there. Both men, and Vince, wanted me to be the soundtrack to the biggest match of their lives. It was a gesture that elevated me and petrified me

316

at the same time. I was still avoiding the world, walking with my head down, not going out unless I had to. I came to work and did my best, but left as soon as I could just in case someone outside the core backstage team saw me. I wanted to call the matches again, and made that known, but ten minutes later I was hunched over with shame. Shame I didn't bring on, but shame nonetheless. I was also conflicted: I was itching to get back out, but petrified that they'd ask me to do just that. I knew I was the same old JR that our audience had come to know, and I knew I wasn't him still, either.

* * *

The night before the show I couldn't sleep. I was worried about everything under the sun: *How would I sound on the show? Would I be able to figure this out? Would I still have my timing? What would the crowd do when they saw me again?*

"I can't do this," I whispered to myself. "I have to quit."

I was like the Tin Man from *The Wizard of Oz*—missing my heart, wishing I could get it back. I shuffled out of bed and sat chain-smoking cigarettes and popping Xanax to help settle myself. Neither worked.

"Are you sure you want to do this?" Jan asked.

"No," I replied.

When we arrived at the Fleet Union Center in Philadelphia, I sat outside for a few minutes planning my getaway. The speech I had conjured up in my mind was pretty convincing. I was sure I could leave and make a pretty good case as to why I'd disappeared. But I walked forward, even though every fiber of me wanted to backpedal.

At every arena, WWF set up various rooms which are designated for various things—including Vince's office, Divas locker room, male locker rooms, and a talent relations room. I spent a lot of time in the talent relations room that day, just trying to stay away from everybody. It took me an hour just to put my tux on, because I kept stopping and thinking, *Maybe I should go tell Vince I can't do this now . . .*

I cried, I lost focus, I got sick. I didn't want to be court-martialed, I just wanted my honorable discharge.

I looked myself in the mirror to straighten my bow-tie and my reflection startled me a little. Not because of *what* I looked like now, but because of *who* I looked like.

My reflection, my hat, my eyes reminded me of my dad.

As I stood there, my head started to fill with thoughts of him and his legacy—the way he had raised his only son. And my mom, how she had been a huge fan of my calls, my passion on-air.

Quitting would be an insult to their memory.

I knew if I turned down this match that I'd be quitting what I loved, for good. Professionally, if I wasn't up for calling the main event at WrestleMania then I'd never be up for calling anything. I thought of Austin and Rock and how they wanted this match to be the best it could be and, in their view, having me out there was the way to do that. This was a match that had been building for a year, and they trusted me with it.

My confidence began to rise slowly and I started thinking, *This is not who you are. This is not how you were raised. This is not the attitude that got you this far. You're not at the Irish-McNeill's Boys' Club in Shreveport; you're not at the TBS studios in Atlanta. You're at Wrestle-fucking-Mania! Grow a pair, get your ass out there, and do what you were born to do.*

I'd finally gotten myself to the point where I'd managed to piss myself off, but it was beginning to work. If this was to be my last time out there, I wanted to go out on the biggest stage of them all, calling the biggest match of them all.

I washed my face and loaded my eyes with Visine, because I didn't want people to know I'd been crying—or think I'd been smoking a joint. I left the safety of my office and walked with purpose. My legs were braver than my mind, but I was going to do this.

"Courage is being scared to death, but saddling up anyway," I thought over and over.

People passed with greetings of "Good luck, JR" and "Welcome back, JR."

Ready or not, it was time to saddle up. Rock and Austin were doing the same, in their own way, as they waited for their cue.

My beloved University of Oklahoma fight song, "Boomer Sooner," began playing through the sound system in the arena to usher me out through the curtain. It was now or never. *Please go easy on me*, I thought as I took a deep breath and cracked open the curtain.

I could feel the energy from the crowd and it immediately raised my confidence a little.

"Don't worry if they boo you," a stage hand said from the darkness.

I stopped immediately. "What? You think they'll boo me?"

"Maybe," he said. "This is the city that booed Santa Claus after all. Have fun out there."

I peeked out through the curtain at the raucous crowd in the arena. "Well, fuck," I whispered to myself as I walked out to face the world again.

As I walked down the aisle, the raucous Philly fans gave me a standing ovation. I tipped my hat to Michael Cole as I walked past him on the way to the announcers table. Folks reached out for me to high-five them and the whole arena was cheering.

They didn't care how I looked. They were just happy to see me. And boy was I happy to see them too.

I sat down at the announce table next to my partner, Jerry Lawler, and put my headphones on, just as he was saying that we couldn't have Wrestle-Mania without good ol' JR.

I said, "Well, King, it . . . I can't describe how it feels!"

The truth was I was afraid to describe how if felt because I didn't want to get emotional on-air. Twenty-five years of learning, making mistakes, meeting my heroes, understanding my deep flaws, being on top of the world, avoiding trouble, being truly down, laughing, moving, driving, paying my dues, leaving the farm, missing my folks, loving my wife, failing my daughters, taking risks, and calling the matches with everything that I had—all led to this. And it just about got too much to hold back.

As I walked into the building that night I thought this was going to be my last match. But as I walked out, happy, relieved, and truly at home, I knew it wasn't.

AFTERWORD BY "STONE COLD" STEVE AUSTIN

I have been a fan of professional wrestling my entire life. As a young boy, the action in the ring, the psychology, and the storylines left an indelible impression on me as I grew up in Edna, Texas. So many memories, so many sights—but also so many sounds.

I grew up hearing great announcers, but it wasn't until I discovered Bill Watts's Mid-South Wrestling that I heard *the* greatest.

Jim Ross's voice was full of energy, enthusiasm, reasoning, under-standing, and passion from day one. When he moved to the NWA, I got to move right there with him. It was an honor to have him call some of my matches. I knew through his unquestioned credibility that Jim could make a bad match better, and a great match into damn near a religious experience.

A few years after Jim left for the Holy Grail of sports entertainment—the WWF—I wound up there, too. JR may have had something to do with that because he always believed in the potential of an athletic and aggressive prospect from Victoria, Texas. Soon thereafter, the "Monday Night Wars" begun and Good Ol' JR was the voice that captured all of the triumph, rage, excitement, and heartbreak of that Attitude Era.

From a personal standpoint, I truly appreciate how Jim was able to seamlessly understand and explain the "Stone Cold" character to the world. Simply put, Jim Ross's work made people better. And he didn't do it just do it for me—he did it for the entire locker room.

I know that, along his journey, JR has suffered many personal setbacks. He was fired a time or two, which I'm sure you've read about in this book. He also comes from a tough background, and I believe it is that tough background that made him into the man he is today.

He is, in my opinion, the greatest announcer to ever call a match. But more than that, he's my friend. He gave me support, advice, guidance, and was always there when I needed someone.

Stay tuned, folks. Business is about to pick up.

ACKNOWLEDGMENTS

JR

My late wife Jan, who was my biggest fan and the most positive voice in my life.

My mom and dad, J. D. and Elizabeth Ann Ross, for allowing me to dream big.

My wonderful daughters Kasi and Amanda for enduring my crazy schedule and, at times, my unhealthy obsession for my work. Thanks for always persevering and for always loving your dad.

Leroy McGuirk and "Cowboy" Bill Watts for providing me my first job opportunity in the pro wrestling business in 1974, and for being compelling mentors to a wide-eyed country boy who loved "rasslin."

Vince McMahon for hiring me in WWE in 1993, and for providing me the opportunity to grow as a professional and as a man. Your work ethic and passion for the genre, along with your vision and leadership, is unsurpassed.

Kevin Dunn, my executive producer at WWE during my tenure there, my fellow Oklahoma Sooners football fanatic, and who was instrumental for helping "bring me home" to WWE in 2017.

Barry Bloom, my manager and trusted friend, who has strategically guided my career to new levels after a not-so-great start to our relationship.

All the men and women in the sports entertainment world, especially all the in-ring talents, who I have worked with for forty-plus years.

My many broadcast partners over the years including Michael Hayes, Bob Caudle, Tony Schiavone, Jim Cornette, Les Thatcher, the great Gordon Solie, Terry Funk, Magnum TA, Missy Hyatt, Bobby Heenan, Gorilla Monsoon, Vince McMahon, Jerry Lawler, Paul Heyman, Taz, Mick Foley, and Josh Barnett.

Scott Williams left us too soon in 2016 while working on this book but whose contributions were invaluable. Simply getting to know Scott when he would come to Norman from Houston to do research on our project was a blessing. I never met a bigger wrestling fan.

Paul O'Brien has been the best writing partner a person could ever want. Paul's talents and sensibilities are God's gift, and my Irish friend heard my voice and captured it magnificently.

To my friends Jacob Ullman, Andrew Simon, Adam Swift, the late Darrell Ewalt, Dennis Brent, Russ Myerson, Wallis Marsh, Barry Werner, and countless others who have befriended me over the years and who still serve as an inspiration as to what being a true friend means.

My friend Bob Stoops, or simply "Bobby" to me, who facilitated many of my most cherished memories during his eighteen-plus-year tenure as the winningest football coach in Oklahoma University history. Thanks for allowing me to ride along on your amazing journey.

Paul O'Brien

To my uncle Jimmy, who taped WWF to VHS for me, who let me come to his home to watch wrestling any time I wanted. I wouldn't have been able to fall in love with wrestling as a kid without your kindness toward me.

To Mick Foley, who answered a tweet that started a magical journey for me and my writing in the wrestling world. I'll always be grateful.

And to JR, thank you for taking a risk on asking a guy who you never met to help write your life story. I've never been so honored, or anxious, in having the voice of wrestling living in my head for eighteen months. Thank you, friend.

INDEX

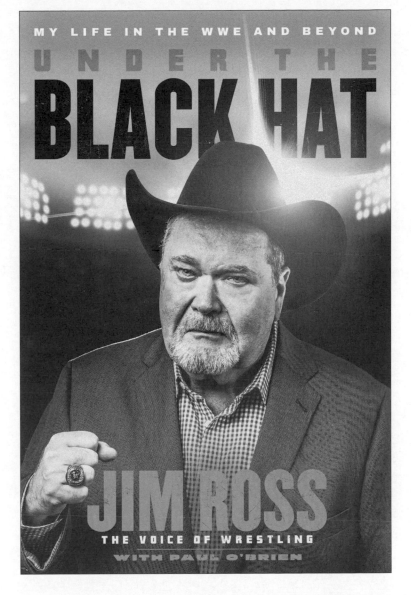

MY LIFE IN THE WWE AND BEYOND

UNDER THE

BLACK HAT

JIM ROSS

THE VOICE OF WRESTLING

WITH PAUL O'BRIEN

$26.99 Hardcover • ISBN 978-1-9821-3052-7